Oxford Socio-Legal Studies

REGULATING THE AIRLINES

OXFORD SOCIO-LEGAL STUDIES

GENERAL EDITORS   Max Atkinson   John C. Boal
Donald R. Harris   Keith Hawkins

Oxford Socio-Legal Studies is a series of books published for the Centre for Socio-Legal Studies, Wolfson College, Oxford (a research unit of the Economic and Social Research Council). The series is concerned generally with the relationship between law and society, and is designed to reflect the increasing interest of lawyers, social scientists and historians in this field.

Already Published (by Macmillan)

J. Maxwell Atkinson and Paul Drew
    ORDER IN COURT: The Organization of Verbal Interaction in Judicial Settings
Ross Cranston
    REGULATING BUSINESS: Law and Consumer Agencies
Robert Dingwall and Philip Lewis (*editors*)
    THE SOCIOLOGY OF THE PROFESSIONS: Lawyers, Doctors and Others
David P. Farrington, Keith Hawkins and Sally M. Lloyd-Bostock (*editors*)
    PSYCHOLOGY, LAW AND LEGAL PROCESSES
Sally M. Lloyd-Bostock (*editor*)
    PSYCHOLOGY IN LEGAL CONTEXTS: Applications and Limitations
Mavis Maclean and Hazel Genn
    METHODOLOGICAL ISSUES IN SOCIAL SURVEYS
Doreen J. McBarnet
    CONVICTION:
    Law, the State and the Construction of Justice
Alan Paterson
    THE LAW LORDS

Already Published (by Oxford University Press)

Genevra Richardson, with Antony Ogus and Paul Burrows
    POLICING POLLUTION: A study of Regulation and Enforcement
P. W. J. Bartrip and S. B. Burman
    THE WOUNDED SOLDIERS OF INDUSTRY Industrial Compensation Policy, 1833–1897
Donald Harris *et al*.
    COMPENSATION AND SUPPORT FOR ILLNESS AND INJURY
Keith Hawkins
    ENVIRONMENT AND ENFORCEMENT: Regulation and the Social Definition of Pollution

REGULATING THE AIRLINES

Administrative Justice and Agency Discretion

ROBERT BALDWIN

CLARENDON PRESS · OXFORD
1985

Oxford University Press, Walton Street, Oxford OX2 6DP

London Glasgow New York Toronto
Delhi Bombay Calcutta Madras Karachi
Kuala Lumpur Singapore Hong Kong Tokyo
Nairobi Dar es Salaam Cape Town
Melbourne Auckland

and associated companies in
Beirut Berlin Ibadan Mexico City Nicosia

Oxford is a trade mark of Oxford University Press

Published in the United States by Oxford University Press, New York

British Library Cataloguing in Publication Data
Baldwin, Robert
Regulating the airlines.— (Oxford socio-legal studies)
1. Civil Aviation Authority
I. Title
354.410087'77   HE9843.A4
ISBN 0-19-827515-3
ISBN 0-19-827516-1 Pbk

Library of Congress Cataloging in Publication Data
Baldwin, Robert,
Regulating the airlines.
(Oxford socio-legal studies)
Includes index.
1. Aeronautics, Commerical—Law and legislation—
Great Britain. 2. Great Britain. Civil Aviation
Authority. 3. Administrative procedure—Great Britain.
I. Title.   II. Series.
KD2732. B34   1984   343.42'097   84–18962
ISBN 0-19-827515-3   344.20397
ISBN 0-19-827516-1 (pbk.)

Printed in Great Britain
at the University Press, Oxford
by David Stanford
Printer to the University

To my Mother and Father

Contents

Preface

This study arises out of a long-standing interest in regulatory agencies, one that began with work on broadcasting licensing in the early seventies but which was soon drawn to the world of aviation regulation. The book is the product of two distinct periods of work. In 1973–6 I undertook, on Social Science Research Council (SSRC) funding, a study of the early years of Civil Aviation Authority regulation and this was the basis of an Edinburgh University Ph.D. thesis. Some years later, whilst a member of staff at the Centre for Socio-Legal Studies, Wolfson College, Oxford, I conducted further research on CAA licensing and sought to place the agency in its wider political and constitutional contexts. Although such an extended period of study created some difficulties in itself, it did allow me to monitor those important changes in regulatory strategy that occurred during the CAA's formative years.

Since the main text was written, there has been a major reconsideration of aviation policy which should be noted. When, in 1983 the Government announced its intentions regarding the privatisation of British Airways (BA), it invited the CAA to review the implications of this for competition policy and for the development of the British airline industry. In its subsequent report ('Airline Competition Policy', CAP 500, CAA July 1984) the CAA advocated, amongst other things, a reduction in the size of BA relative to other UK airlines, additional competition on intercontinental routes, a number of route transfers away from BA, a strengthening of Gatwick services and an experimental period of liberalised entry and price regulation on domestic routes. The Government's responding White Paper ('Airline Competition Policy', Cmnd. 9366, October 1984) soon revealed that BA had won the behind-the-scenes battle to influence policy. Considerations relevant to privatisation had prevailed over the CAA's recommendations for a more evenly-balanced industry. There was to be no forced reduction in the relative size of BA, BA was not to lose its Gatwick services to other operators, it was to keep its regional routes to Europe and, instead of a compulsory transfer of intercontinental routes from BA to British Caledonian, there was to be a more modest and 'reciprocal' redistribution of intercontinental routes. Liberalisation of domestic regulation was one of the few topics on which the Government welcomed the CAA proposals.

In relation to the arguments presented in this volume, such debates over policy emphasise the extent to which regulatory agencies exist in an environment that, periodically at least, becomes highly political. It also points to the difficulties that are encountered in developing specialised policy in such a contentious world. It is now as clear as it ever was that the legitimacy of the regulatory agency depends on its effecting a series of highly delicate balances. For these reasons and others, the progress of the CAA will remain a matter of great interest in the forthcoming years.

GRB   November 1984
                                                                 London

Acknowledgements

In the course of my researches, I have been spared countless hours by staff of the CAA, government departments and the airlines. Those who have been so generous with their time and help are too numerous to list in full but I record my gratitude to them here. Particular mention, nevertheless, must be made of the assistance given to me by Raymond Colegate, Michael Overall, John McInally, Elizabeth Diamond, Jerry Ducker, Tony Fortnam, Vivian Slight, Reg Bench, David Beety and the late Arnold Heard.

In looking at aviation regulation in the USA the staff of the Civil Aeronautics Board and the Office of the Secretary of Transportation were unstinting in their cooperation and I owe particular thanks to Daniel M. Kasper, Dan Kaplan, Douglas V. Leister, Mark S. Kahan, David Kirstein, Vance Fort, Ed Oppler and Judge Elias C. Rodrigues.

My colleagues at the Centre for Socio-Legal Studies, Oxford made considerable contributions to this work from a variety of viewpoints: I was particularly lucky to work at an institution so peculiarly amenable to multi-disciplinary research. Special thanks for their comments on drafts are due to Richard Markovits and Keith Hawkins. Outside the Centre I owe a great debt to my Edinburgh supervisors, Neil MacCormick and Tony Bradley. Since then I have also benefited greatly from the comments and advice of Frank Lyall, Kenneth MacKinnon, Christopher McCrudden and Jeffrey Jowell.

In preparing the manuscript, the administrative and secretarial staff of the Centre have been endlessly patient and I am grateful to John Boal, Noël Blatchford, Rosemary Stallan, Jennifer Dix, Jeanne Bliss and Linda Peterson. My thanks also to the series editors and the Oxford University Press team for their assistance in preparing the manuscript.

My residual debts are to my wife, Felicity Jones, who has supported me in all ways during the time that I have been engaged in this work, and to my parents, to whom the book is dedicated.

Abbreviations Used

ABCs	Advanced Booking Charters
AEA	Association of European Airlines
AOC	Air Operators Certificate
APA	Administrative Procedure Act
APEX	Advanced Purchase Excursion Fare
ARB	Air Registration Board/Airworthiness Requirements Board
ASA	Air Services Agreement
AT&T	Aircraft Transport and Travel Ltd.
ATAC	Air Transport Advisory Council
ATCS	Air Traffic Control Services
ATLA	Air Transport Licensing Authority
ATLB	Air Transport Licensing Board
ATOL	Air Travel Organisers Licensing
AUC	Airline Users Committee/Air Transport Users Committee
BA	British Airways
BAB	British Airways Board
BAF	British Air Ferries Ltd.
BAS	British Air Services Ltd.
B.Cal.	British Caledonian Airways Ltd.
BEA	British European Airways
BIA	British Island Airways Ltd.
BIATA	British Independent Air Transport Association
BMA	British Midland Airways Ltd.
BNOC	British National Oil Corporation
BOAC	British Overseas Airways Corporation
BSAC	British South American Airways Corporation
BTC	British Transport Commission
BUA	British United Airways Ltd.
CAA	Civil Aviation Authority
CAB	Civil Aeronautics Board

CALN	Civil Aviation Licensing Notices
CEB	Central Electricity Board
CRE	Commission for Racial Equality
CSD	Civil Service Department
DGFT	Director General of Fair Trading
DOT	Department of Trade
DOTI	Department of Trade and Industry
ECS	Economics and Statistics Division
EOC	Equal Opportunities Commission
EPC	Economic Policy Committee
EPL	Economic Policy and Licensing
ES	Economics and Statistics
FCC	Federal Communications Commission
HSE	Health and Safety Executive
IAC	Industrial Accident Commission
IATA	International Air Transport Association
IBA	Independent Broadcasting Authority
ICAO	International Civil Aviation Organisation
ICC	Interstate Commerce Commission
ITA	Independent Television Authority
ITs	Inclusive Tours
ITX	Inclusive Tour Excursion Fare
LRCC	Law Reform Commission of Canada
MGD	Machinery of Government Division
NATS	National Air Traffic Services
NEB	National Enterprise Board
NEDO	National Economic Development Office
OIRA	Office of Information and Regulatory Affairs
QUANGO	Quasi Autonomous Non-Governmental Organisation
RPC	Restrictive Practices Court
SACAO	Standing Advisory Commission on Administrative Organisation
SBC	Supplementary Benefits Commission

1
Introduction:
A History of Neglect

This book is the first full-length study by an administrative lawyer of a British agency set up on the lines of the great independent regulatory commissions of America. The importance and utility of these bodies lies in the fact that, unlike courts or tribunals they aim to achieve the best of a number of worlds: they use trial-type[1] methods of adjudication, they develop a special expertise in a particular field and they make policy in politically contentious areas. It is in this very combination of functions, however, that difficulties are encountered and these are the problems central to this volume. How can trial-type procedures be reconciled with the use of an extensive specialist knowledge? Can the 'polycentric' issues involved in economic regulation be decided by these procedures? Can a commission-type of agency render questions 'justiciable' in a way that a tribunal or court could not? What concept of 'administrative justice' is relevant to multi-powered bodies? Can effective policies be developed in the economic sphere by means of trial-type procedures?

These agencies raise not merely legal but governmental questions. How can the broad discretions given to such bodies be controlled by Ministers? In which areas may they be effectively used? How should they be designed or made accountable and what part should they play in government? Such issues have largely gone unanswered in this country but this has not stopped regulatory agencies being used to play an increasing governmental role especially in recent years. They now operate in such fields as broadcasting, aviation and gaming and they multiply whenever governments want to extend intervention in specialist areas or else decide to privatise certain sectors whilst retaining a degree of control. Thus at the time of writing, proposals have already been made for the establishment of new regulatory agencies to cover telecommunications, cable television, dis-crimination against the disabled and data protection.[2] This is a study of the role of such agencies in government, their usefulness and the problems that arise when a particular variety of governmental powers are combined in one body.

Initially, however, more has to be said on what is meant by 'regulatory agencies'. An explanation is due because, although these bodies constitute a well-known and controversial element in American government,[3] they are less familiar here where the expert non-departmental body has been slow to develop and when used has been employed in haphazard fashion.

A more precise idea of our subject can be given by placing regulatory agencies on the map of those entities at the edge of departmental government that are variously entitled quangos,[4] fringe bodies,[5] non-departmental bodies,[6] or public corp-orations.[7] Here there is no shortage of classifications: some look to institutional format or function, others to the motives for using different kinds of body and others combine various factors, perhaps looking also at funding methods or degrees of independ-ence. As a result, no one typology is completely satisfactory. One, however, that has been followed by the Civil Service Department,[8] is that of the Pliatsky report of 1980 which set out the following groups of body:

i.   Nationalized industries, other public corporations and com-panies in which the Government has a major shareholding.
ii. Agricultural marketing boards.
iii. The National Health Service and associated public bodies.
iv. Other non-departmental public bodies, which are of three kinds:

   (a) Bodies with executive, etc. functions, carrying out *inter alia* administrative, executive, regulatory and commercial-type functions.
   (b) Departmental advisory committees and commissions (which generally do not employ staff or incur expendi-ture on their own account.)
   (c) Tribunals and other judicial bodies.[9]

Another customary classification is that set out for public corporations by Professor J.F. Garner in 1966.[10] He divided these into:

i. Those operating commercial undertakings where the profit motive has not been completely removed.
ii. Managerial bodies responsible for administering public services (where the profit motive is virtually absent) and
iii. Regulatory bodies, i.e. those corporations established to undertake particular tasks or implement specified policies, in many cases on behalf of government.

If motives for creating institutions are focussed on, as by Hood and Mackenzie,[11] then we are offered a different spectrum of peripheral bodies, and, in the case of quangos, yet another typology was offered by Holland and Fallon in 1978.[12]

Other commentators have viewed agencies with an eye to both motive and *modus operandi*. David Coombes,[13] organizes thus:

i. The industrial public corporation (including the nationalized industries boards, and the British National Oil Corporation)
ii. Public agencies used for selective public participation in industry (e.g. the Industrial Reorganization Corporation and the National Enterprise Board)
iii. Public agencies with an adjudicative function (e.g. the Restrictive Practices Court, the Monopolies and Mergers Commission, the National Board for Prices and Incomes
iv. Agencies used to devolve executive functions to representatives of employers and unions.[14]

The limited focus offered by such classifications[15] is hardly remedied by confining study to activity that is 'regulatory' since this term is imprecise.[16] Governments regulate private enterprises in many ways, *inter alia* by taxation, licensing, registration, grants, contracts, control of money and by credit restrictions. The word 'regulation' may be narrowed, however, as it is by R.A. Kagan to 'the control of economic activity by means of direct *legal orders*'. He explains:

> Regulation in this sense occurs when businessmen are legally prohibited from practicing a trade without a license or from constructing buildings or processing milk except in accordance with governmentally prescribed health and safety standards. Typically the detailed specification, enforcement and application of these rules is entrusted to specialised regulatory agencies, established to concentrate on control of a particular industry or trade on a particular business practice.[17]

Adapting Kagan's narrow sense of regulation, the concern in this book is with British agencies that share most or all of the following properties: they are non-departmental; act in some sense on behalf of government; make rules that are backed up by force of law; exercise continuing control over an industry, trade or practice; differ from courts or tribunals in employing a substantial number of expert staff and in expending considerable resources;[18] decide issues between parties or enforce a particular body of law. Modern examples of such bodies are the Independent Broadcasting Authority (IBA), the Civil Aviation Authority (CAA), the Director General of Fair Trading (DGFT), the Equal Opportunities Commission (EOC), the Commission for Racial Equality (CRE), the Price Commission and Supplementary Benefits Commission (SBC). Other agencies with operational and promotional as well as regulatory functions, such as the British National Oil Corporation (BNOC) and the National Enterprise Board (NEB) may be fitted into this grouping if some licence is allowed.[19]

To typify the regulatory agency as has been done above is not to ignore the various overlaps that exist within the host of bodies forming a conceptual maze on the edge of government. Clearly some tribunals do regulate,[20] some agencies operate in a quasi-regulatory manner and some bodies (like BNOC) have engaged in both operation and regulation. To pick out 'regulatory' agencies is merely to direct comments at a cluster-concept or model. As we shall see below, a major problem in discussing British agencies flows from the neglect that has left students of the administrative process with a mass of confused bodies that have been created without reference to models.

What should not be underestimated is the significance of the regulatory body in modern government. Although, as can be seen from the classifications cited above, such agencies comprise a small sector in the overall population of non-departmental bodies, they are not merely of growing convenience, they are increasingly contentious vehicles of state control.

For governments there are many good reasons for regulating at arms-length.[21] Agency regulation may, *inter alia*, be preferred to departmental control so as to facilitate the development of a technical expertise, to set up a non-civil-service system of bureaucracy, to hive-off a political 'hot potato' or to make it clear that control is independent of political taint. Where trial-type procedures are employed, and, especially where issues have to be decided between the public and private sectors, then fairness militates strongly in favour of the non-departmental body. The variety of useful purposes served by agencies has been set out in a Canadian study by Frans F. Slatter who notes that there are at least twelve functions that may be performed by an agency in the parliamentary system.[22] These may be listed as: assistant; substantive expert; procedural expert; manager; adviser and investigator; adjudicator; arbitrator; determination maker; rule maker; policy maker; intermediary; political insulator.

As for agencies being contentious, some may welcome them and see their virtue as aiming for the best of a number of worlds: making policy and exerting control on behalf of government whilst enjoying the freedom and continuity of expertise that goes with independence; adjudicating on issues from a position of independence and doing so with a specialist ability and secretarial reinforcement that is unmatched by courts or tribunals. Especially where cultural or technical matters are concerned (where there is a need to take out of politics or where competition between public and private sector activity is involved) the arguments for such control are most clearly made.

From another point of view, the regulatory body may be viewed as the kind of fringe body most fulfilling Otto Newman's description of quangos as 'potent struts in support of the corporate state'.[23] Of the kind of agency with which this book is concerned Newman states:[24]

> . . . the 'most sinister development of all' is the arrival of bodies which combine their 'primary purpose with an entirely separate quasi-judicial function'. Their practices have become the most nefarious. In some instances—i.e. the British Oil Corporation—they act both as a regulatory agency as well as being a trading company in their own right. Elsewhere—e.g. the Central Arbitration Committee—they freely indulge in practices reminiscent of kangaroo courts: lacking even the most basic standards of professional qualification, knowledge and care; pursuing sectarian interest without concern for other considerations; and debasing the majesty of the law into sordid haggling and self-seeking manipulation. More often than not they further perform, without any declaration of interest whatever, as champions in their personal cause. In the stentorian words of Lord Hailsham, 'the amalgamation of a body (the Race Relations Board) devoted to law enforcement with a body (the Community Relations

Commission) devoted to the promotion of good conduct' approaches a state of affairs where 'one ought as well amalgamate the functions of the Commissioner of the Metropolitan Police or the Director of Public Prosecutions with the Archbishop of Canterbury (*Official Report*, House of Lords, 20.7.76, col. 745).

Whatever one's views on the state role of regulatory agencies, it is clear that an understanding of their operation is more than ever necessary in any analysis of government. To this end this book looks in detail at developments in one sphere of regulation but places that study in a wider governmental context.

Civil aviation licensing has been chosen for examination for three main reasons. It is in this sphere that we can see most clearly a progression in techniques of regulation, from ministerial action, through traditional 'quasi-judicial' control to the creation of an American-styled multi-functional regulatory agency in the Civil Aviation Authority (CAA). A second reason for interest is the particular manner in which the CAA was tied into government. When the CAA was set up in 1971 it was thought that a new way had been found both to reconcile disparate functions and to impose overall political control over an 'independent' agency. The device adopted was that of written 'policy guidance' issued by the Government and binding on the CAA. This manner of separating day-to-day policy making and management from political control led some parliamentarians to refer to the CAA as a 'constitutional innovation'.[25] Less than nine years later however, the policy guidance system was scrapped. Here we see how the guidance system worked in practice, why it was deemed to have failed and what lessons may be learned from this experiment. Having made that assessment, we can consider whether the policy guidance system might prove useful to other agencies in other areas.

A final reason for looking at the CAA is that in this field students of the administrative process find discretionary powers being exercised under extreme circumstances. Air transport licensing decisions are subject to political guidance and review; they are made on the basis of a massive stock of specialist information and yet they rely heavily on public hearings and trial-type procedures. Anyone concerned with discretionary decision-making is therefore obliged to investigate the techniques used in attempting to apply those processes to the difficult sphere of regulatory activity.

Before looking at the evolution of a particular form of agency within British politics, it is necessary to examine the use made of regulatory agencies in the century or so preceeding the creation of the CAA. This will show how the CAA, instead of merely following traditional lines, did indeed emerge as a 'constitutional innovation'.

In the United States there has been continuous resort to the multi-powered agency ever since the Interstate Commerce Commission (ICC) was set up in 1887. The British position contrasts sharply. By the time the ICC was created British opinion had long been moving against the idea of government by independent body. The flow of governmental functions away from *ad hoc* boards towards government departments in the period from 1832 to the end of the 19th century has been well documented.[26] Following the shift of power from local authorities to central departments[27] came mounting criticism of the board system.

Though of respectable tradition in both English local and central government,[28] doubts as to the accountability of boards soon came to a head after creation of the Poor Law Commissioners in 1834:

> ... total separation from Parliament had the opposite effect to that intended. So far from making the commission strong and fearless, it made it weak, confused and extraordinarily subject to political pressures. The commissioners lived in dread of unpopularity and inquisitions.[29]

By 1847 the Commission had been abolished in favour of ministerial control. The Railway Commission and the General Board of Health were similarly replaced in 1851 and 1854. By 1889 the same procedure had been followed in relation to emigration, patents and lands.[30] Even when, as between 1845 and 1855, it was common for Parliament to demand the inclusion of MPs or Ministers as members of boards, the decline of the latter continued; there was, after all, no guarantee that whoever was accountable was in actual control of board policy.[31]

F.M.G. Willson recounts how in the later part of the 19th and early part of the 20th century there remained only six boards with more than 'nominal independence of Ministers': 'The later Victorian era was the Golden Age of ministerial administration'.[32] In this period any regulatory function that was not given to a ministerial department tended to be allocated not to an independent agency but to a judicial authority or to Parliament itself. The development of railway regulation exemplified the British approach. In 1840 the Railways Regulation Act gave powers of reviewing the proposals of private railway companies to the new Railway Department of the Board of Trade rather than to an agency. Concerned principally with safety issues, this system of regulation by inspectorate left effective control to the parliamentary committees that scrutinised Private Bills. In 1845 the Department was renamed the Railway Board but changes in power and independence did not match those in nomenclature. Lacking governmental support, the Board was dissolved after three years to leave a system based on direct parliamentary control.[33] In the following year, the Commissioners of Railways were set up as a new department independent of the Board of Trade. Provision was made for MPs to sit as commissioners but they waited in vain for Parliament to vote them effective powers of scrutiny over railway schemes. The Commissioners were abolished in 1851.

The next device to be tried was the tribunal-like Railway Commission of 1873 which took over from the Court of Common Pleas the task of resolving disputes on such matters as rates and preferences. This weak body had little to do with wider issues of railway management. Fifteen years later, it was made permanent and renamed the Railway and Canal Commission but real control over railways policy still remained with the parliamentary committees. After the first war, nationalisation was proposed but was rejected in favour of the Railway Act 1921 and supervision of private owners by the Railway Rates Tribunal. It was 1947 before public ownership was introduced.

In the case of other utilities such as gas, water supplies and tramways, a similar pattern of regulation was followed with direct parliamentary control and Board of Trade officials exercising powers to inspect and to set standards. With electricity there was a minor variation. Though for a period subject to Board of Trade licensing (Electricity Lighting Act 1882), control passed after the war to Electricity Commissioners (Electricity Supply Act 1919) who were given both planning and adjudicatory functions. They exemplified an early governmental willingness to hive-off a broader-based power to regulate private enterprises but they lacked the resources to restructure the industry radically and their regulatory functions were rapidly superseded when the Central Electricity Board (CEB) was set up in 1926. Nationalisation took place in 1948.

Court-like bodies such as the Railways Commission, proved so common that by 1933 M.E. Dimock was to argue:

> The regulation of British public utilities appears to be impaired by placing so much reliance upon the judicial method and the resulting failure to develop the administrative commission.[34]

Of the practice of combining control by departmental inspectorate with the scrutiny of Private Bills by select committee, W.A. Robson said:

> The outstanding fact in the history of utilities in Great Britain is the dominant part played by Parliament in their establishment.[35]

What was lacking in the later 19th and early 20th centuries, therefore, was the development, as in the United States, of a powerful form of agency that would exercise widely-based expertise, employ a specialist secretariat and regulate in the positive sense of imposing a planned structure on the industries concerned. The decline of boards left regulation to government departments, tribunals and inspectorates: structural issues were increasingly left in the hands of regulatees, and the regulators, instead of instituting action, merely responded to the proposals of competing private interests.[36] Parliament was too distrustful of independence to grant the legal or financial powers that would have made positive regulation feasible.

At this stage it should be noted that to point to neglect of the regulatory agency in Britain is not to deny the prominence of the operating public corporation, which Robson called:

> . . . the most important invention of the twentieth century in the sphere of government institutions'.[37]

Especially after the Liberal victory of 1906, the operating agency flourished: the Port of London Authority was set up in 1908 to be followed by the Road Board (1909), and the Insurance Commission (1911). In spite of the Haldane Committee's Report on the Machinery of Government,[38] which regarded the public corporation with disfavour because of its lack of ministerial accountability, the public service board continued to emerge, as exemplified by the Forestry Commission (1919), the BBC (1926), the CEB (1926), as an alternative to the central department or local authority. With the support of champions such as Herbert Morrison,[39] public corporations such as the London Passenger Transport Board, developed in the 1930s and were accompanied by the quasi-regulatory marketing boards for hops, pigs, milk, bacon, potatoes etc. Further support for 'hiving-off' came from the Fulton Committee on the Civil Service in 1967 and was put to effect principally with the creation of the Post Office as a public corporation in 1969.[40]

It is one thing to hive-off operational functions, another to take regulatory activity out of government. Fulton appeared to be thinking principally of operational or managerial functions in speaking of delegating to autonomous public boards so as to introduce:

> ... accountable management ... for many executive activities, especially in the provision of services to the community.[41]

Regulation, in distinction, often involves contention of a highly visible kind. Decisions have to be made between competing interests and 'political' policy formulated. Loud calls are to be expected demanding due process of a legalistic nature. In accordance with Diceyan resistance[42] to untrammelled discretionary authority as opposed to regular law, regulatory functions have proved more liable than operational ones to classification as one of two things: either 'political' (the province of ministers) or 'judicial' (and so for courts); hence, once again, the failure to develop a commission model that would combine political discretion with both expertise and judicial or adjudicatory functions. The options of nationalization and management by public corporation further eased the pressures to develop agencies. Robson again:

> We should expect the regulatory commission to decline in countries which have moved from regulated profit-seeking enterprise to public ownership and administration and this fact corresponds with experience, notably in Britain.[43]

In spite of factors unsympathetic to the independent regulatory agency, the device (at least in muted form) has not, however, been wholly avoidable. Following the brief flurry of the Electricity Commissioners in the early 1920s, road transport emerged as a problem area. By 1930 it was considered that unrestricted road passenger service competition was dangerous and against the public interest.[44] The 1930 Road Traffic Act created the Traffic Commissioners to license public service vehicles subject to ministerial appeals and policy controls. The Act set down factors to be considered in relation to routes, fares, times, personnel and vehicles and a public hearings system was operated. Even here, however, there was no multi-powered body, the commissioners did not organize or structure the industry by developing comprehensive policies; their role was that of a specialist tribunal rather than of a fully fledged regulatory agency and overall control was left in the hands of the Minister, aided after 1947 by the British Transport Commission.[45]

Road goods haulage presented a similar picture initially. The Road and Rail Traffic Act 1933 sought to balance road and rail competition by licensing road services and allowing the railways to negotiate fares. The Chairman of the Traffic Commissioners licensed goods vehicles subject to an appeal, not to the Minister this time, but to the Road and Rail Traffic Appeal Tribunal (the Transport Tribunal after 1947). Once again a system emerged that was heavily reliant on judicial methods rather than combined powers and from the appeal tribunal a case law had emerged in a form:

... much more complex and legal in flavour than was perhaps intended by its originators.[46]

The Geddes Committee recommended the abolition of licensing for all purposes other than safety regulation, conclusions contrasting with the Thesiger committee's belief that 'passenger services licensing had handsomely succeeded in achieving its objectives'.[47]

In another field, that of fisheries, regulating agencies continued in the form of marketing boards. The Herring Industry Board (1935) and the White Fish Commission (1938) were empowered to make reorganization schemes, prescribe standards, undertake research, give grants and act for the consumer. The White Fish Authority (1951) was given extensive powers to regulate by licensing, make conditions and hold inquiries—though in practice it preferred to operate informally by negotiation rather than by formal methods.[48]

After the war further marketing-type boards were set up, exemplified by the Raw Cotton Commission (1948) the Crofters Commission (1955) and the Sugar Board (1956). The Iron and

Steel Board operated from 1946–51 and resumed functions on denationalization in 1953.

Civil aviation, as we shall see, illustrated a twentieth century progression towards independent licensing agency.[49] In the 1920s subsidization was the main tool of governmental control, but after the Second War, regulation was conducted via a ministerial/advisory board system, by a tribunal-like body (the Air Transport Licensing Board (1960)) and then by a regulatory agency (the CAA) in 1971.

By the time the ATLB had been created, another agency had operated for six years. The 1954 Television Act had set up the Independent Television Authority (ITA) with powers to license programme, making companies in the public interest. In broadcasting the need for independence was clearly argued on libertarian grounds. The ITA was empowered to adopt a system of licensing hearings but did not use these publicly, believing that procedures behind closed doors allowed more efficient protection of the public interest. The Authority, like the Traffic Commissioners and ATLB offered a peculiar combination of powers exercised by an independent and specialist agency.[50]

In the later 1960s a series of agencies, some regulatory, some managerial, increased the number of governmental functions conducted outside departments. Notable examples were: the Highlands and Islands Development Board (1965); Race Relations Board (1965); Monopolies Commission (1965); National Board for Prices and Incomes (1966); Industrial Reorganization Corporation (1966);[50] Supplementary Benefits Commission (1966); Land Commission (1967); Gaming Board (1968); Community Relations Commission (1968) and the Post Office (1969).

The 1970s continued the trend with further resort to agency regulation based on perceived needs to 'take out of politics' for reasons of fairness, sensitivity, continuity or efficiency.[52] It was as part of such a movement in favour of arms-length government that the CAA was set up. This agency was innovatory in so far as more than its predecessors it resembled the United States commissions in its tripartite combination of judicial, policy-making and administrative powers. It was new also in being subject to written ministerial policy guidance. Such a system of governmental control had not been instituted by statute before. The nearest equivalent was that provision common in the nationalization Acts of 1945–50 empowering Ministers, after consultation, to give Boards 'directions of a general character' as to the exercise of their functions.[53] Even in the case of nationalized industries however, such powers had been employed only rarely due to doubts concerning the legality of any potential direction.[54]

In these two respects, then, the CAA, when set up, constituted a major innovation in government at arms-length. In order to understand how such a development occurred the major part of the volume describes how it was that civil aviation regulation progressed through its various stages to end up in the hands of a multi-powered agency and why it was decided after only nine years that the revolutionary system of policy guidance had failed. The final chapters examine the strengths, weaknesses and potential of the multi-powered agency in the British political system as well as the utility of control by written policy guidance and the role of trial-type procedures in regulation.

2
Civil Aviation Regulation to 1960

Few areas of economic activity have been subjected to as many different regulatory regimes as the British civil aviation industry. In only fifty years, government control has operated via subsidies, ministerial permissions, licensing tribunal and specialist agency. It is surprising, however, how slowly regulation first came upon the industry. It was some time after the first air service from Blackpool to Southport in 1910 and the First War boom in aviation that the Government showed initial concern by setting up a Civil Air Transport Committee under Lord Northcliffe in 1917. Two reports that emerged a year later, suggested, *inter alia,* that the best way to develop commercial aviation, especially on imperial routes, was to provide state assistance for private enterprise through control powers vested in the Air Ministry[1]—this course was deemed more conductive to enterprise than either state operation or the constitution of a chartered company combining state and private capital.[2] Justification for state subsidization was based, not merely on the economic requirements of private investors, but on defence implications also. As Sir Frederick Handley Page, Chairman of the Handley Page airline, wrote in a letter to *The Times:*

> Instead of spending large sums for the upkeep of an air force adequate to the defence of these shores . . . it would be possible by subsidising aircraft transport companies to obtain a lien on their use in war.[3]

Peacetime saw the passing of the Air Navigation Act 1919 which extended the powers of the Secretary of State for Air to cover the licensing of air transport operations. A Department of Civil Aviation was created in the Air Ministry and began to compile a set of air navigation regulations. Still there was no system of subsidization but by 1919 two companies, Aircraft

Transport and Travel (AT&T) and Handley Page, were building up scheduled air services to the continent. These operations had to compete with fluctuating traffic and the advent of new competitors—not least of which were the French subsidized operators. Heavy financial losses took their toll and by the end of February 1921 all British services had been suspended. *The Times* bemoaned the government's meagre help for operators and the demise of 'the adventurers who have gallantly tried to make air routes pay'.[4]

The government was forced to come to the rescue and in March 1921, a temporary subsidy scheme was introduced, to be followed within the year by a permanent system. By use of its powers of subsidy, the Air Ministry was able to place three operators on the London to Paris service and to control individual airlines on particular routes. By 1924, four companies were operating regular services from London to Paris, Cologne (via Brussels), Berlin (via Amsterdam) and the Channel Islands. It was still difficult to break even, however: the traffic was light, competition was fierce and costs high. A committee under Lord Hambling was commissioned to look at the subsides system in 1923–24[5] and recommended that, instead of subsidizing a number of small companies, civil aviation could be put on a firm footing only by the creation of a large private operator that would be backed by the state. After long negotiations between the airlines and the Air Ministry, the four major companies—AT&T, Handley Page, Daimler Airways and British Marine Air Navigation—agreed to combine as Imperial Airways under Sir Eric Geddes. Imperial was established with capital of £1 million as the government's 'chosen instrument' for developing aviation and, although a private company, it enjoyed a monopoly of subsidies that allowed it to develop a system of scheduled services on international routes.[6]

By the mid-1930s the Air Ministry had started a radio network for air traffic control and four-engined aircraft could carry nearly forty passengers at over 100 mph, but the financial position was bleak. Imperial Airways, encouraged by the Empire Air Mail Scheme, were concentrating on routes to the Empire but developments elsewhere were held back. In 1935 an interdepartmental committee under Sir Warren Fisher looked into the possibilities for improving European services and decided that instead of supporting only one operator the state would have to sustain two, each with a defined sphere of interest. Taking advantage of this view, a number of unsubsidized airlines merged in November 1935 to form British Airways, which was endorsed as the government's second 'chosen instrument' with a remit covering European routes and the development of West Africa and South America.[7]

If times were hard on international routes, they were worse domestically: internal air transport had to compete with road and rail services over short distances and by the mid-1930s around twenty operators struggled to keep some 76 routes open. Companies were aided *ad hoc* by subsidies or air mail contracts and their numbers fluctuated from nineteen in 1935 to sixteen in 1936: they were small, ill-equipped and many operated seasonally. It was in these straitened circumstances that the first major review of domestic air transport took place in 1936 when the Maybury Committee[8] advised the government on measures that could be taken to promote air services on a national basis. This body described operations as: 'a kaleidoscope of different and competing companies, some of them very short lived and most, if not all of them, losing money.'[9] Reporting only six years after the Royal Commission on Transport[10] had responded to fierce competition on the roads by laying the foundations of the Road Traffic Act 1930 with its system of licensing by the Traffic Commissioners, Maybury advocated further mergers the of principal companies in aviation, greater co-ordination with surface transport, the elimination of cut-throat competition by restricting new services and 'provisional regulation' of selected routes so as to maximise the chances of services becoming self-supporting.[11] Noting that the Air Navigation Act 1936 had provided for the licensing of air transport services,[12] the committee advocated the licensing of all regular operations 'with a view to securing the most effective service to the public'.[13] A licensing authority, it was said, should be set up for this purpose, to allocate to operators exclusive five years licences renewable on satisfactory performance. To improve safety controls it was urged that a comprehensive air traffic control system be managed by the Government and that pilots should be licensed.

This report emerged in 1937 but no action was taken on its proposals before a Commons debate on civil aviation brought matters to a head in November of that year. Discussion concentrated on international services, and Imperial Airways was criticised severely for its lack of efficiency and enterprise. The government reacted by setting up another committee, this time under Lord Cadman, to look at these charges and to examine the general state of British civil aviation.

Cadman reported in March 1938 and promptly urged action on the Maybury recommendations.[14] On its own account the committee advocated the strengthening of departmental control over civil aviation by the appointment of an additional Under-Secretary of State at the Air Ministry whose sole responsibility would be civil aviation.[15] This, it was hoped, would aid more vigorous policymaking and planning by the Government.[16] Imperial Airways, was rebuked both for its failure to co-operate with the Air Ministry and for its staff relations.[17] In addition, its managing director was said to have 'taken too commercial and narrow a view of his responsibilities, given the degree of subsidization enjoyed.[18] The suggested solution was direct control by a newly appointed full-time chairman who was urged to secure closer coordination between Imperial and the new British Airways.[19] Cadman advocated developing services rapidly with a small number of well-funded and substantial organizations,[20] using Imperial and British Airways to concentrate on Empire and European routes respectively.

In response to the recommendations made by these two committees, the government acted on the domestic and international fronts. In November 1938 an Air Transport Licensing Authority (ATLA) was set up and a system of subsidy and licensing by formal hearing was created.[21] All services in the UK to be operated from November 1938 were to be licensed by the ATLA and the Air Navigation (Financial Provisions) Act 1938 provided subsidies of up to £100,000 per annum for operators of licensed services. What effect such a scheme might have had on the eleven companies initially eligible under it we do not know since any opportunities to effect changes were cut short by the war and revocation of the licensing scheme.[22] Some have expressed doubts *ex post facto,* Dyos and Aldcroft have commented that it was 'extraordinary' that the Government could have hoped to keep nearly a dozen operators afloat domestically when so much difficulty had been experienced with the subsidized monopoly enjoyed by Imperial Airways.[23]

Internationally, the government acted on Cadman by doubling its subsidy limit to £3 million, by changing staffing at the Air

Ministry and by developing a medium sized all-metal airliner for British Airways' use. Another Cadman recommendation was put into effect in June 1938 when Sir John Reith of the BBC accepted the chairmanship of Imperial Airways and worked immediately for the amalgamation of Imperial and British Airways.[24] His endeavours resulted, in 1939, in the birth under his chairmanship of a new public body, the British Overseas Airways Corporation (BOAC).[25] The Conservative Government hoped[26] that the creation of a monopolistic corporation, funded, like the BBC, by public money rather than by shareholders, would encourage provision of those services that Cadman had shown private companies to be reluctant to offer. Some degree of governmental control over BOAC was given by reserving to the Secretary of State for Air a set of discretionary powers closely resembling those later to be found in most nationalization schemes of the 1940s.[27]

During the Second War, BOAC was placed at the disposal of the Secretary of State for Air and operated alongside RAF Transport command under direction of the Air Ministry.[28] Civil and Military operations were only separated after the future of civil air transport had been discussed by a committee under Lord Beaverbrook, after a Minister of Civil Aviation had been appointed in October 1944 and a new Ministry had been established early in 1945.[29]

A major reason for dividing civil and military affairs was the need to send a strong deputation to the Chicago Conference of November 1944 at which the representatives of fifty-four nations met to discuss the control of post-war civil air transport. Since the domestic regulatory authorities of each nation had (and still have) to operate within a system of international controls on traffic rights (inter-governmentally agreed permissions to fly), the Chicago and subsequent Bermuda agreements were of crucial importance. The United Kingdom team went to Chicago favouring the control of routes and capacities by an international authority but the United States advocated an unrestricted market and, in the end, delegates failed to agree to a multilateral exchange of traffic rights. The Chicago Convention was signed, however, and set up the necessary machinery for post-war regulation of international aviation and air navigation standards.[30] It also established the International Civil Aviation Organization

(ICAO), a body later to become part of the United Nations and the central planning organization for the international industry.

In Britain, the Coalition Government reviewed the future of civil aviation in 1945. Conservative members followed Lord Swinton, the first Minister of Civil Aviation, in proposing both to reintroduce a large element of private ownership into British international aviation and to retain this in domestic services.[31] This was to be done by allowing shipping firms to take shares in a new corporation based on BOAC and by creating a railway-financed corporation to operate domestic and European routes. Subsidies would be controlled and reduced and regulation used to preserve a balance between capacity offered and traffic available. Reliance on monopolistic corporations rather than competition was deemed necessary for the controlled development of routes.

As a sweetener, the independent operators were offered the chance to take a 5% holding in BOAC but they objected to being 'dragged into involvement in a monopoly without consultation'. They considered the abolition of the Air Transport Licensing Authority to have been unjustifiable and argued that it should be re-established as a semi-judicial body independent of the Government and free from political interference. Regulated competition, they said, was necessary to provide a yardstick for efficiency.[32]

Before these proposals could be dealt with, however, a new Labour Government of July 1945 was involved in further attempts to secure an agreement on international traffic rights. In February 1946 the United Kingdom and the United States signed the Bermuda agreement in which it was agreed: (1) routes would be operated by airlines designated under the agreement by both countries; these would be negotiated and specified; (2) on routes joining the two countries directly there would be no restriction on frequency of service or on capacity offered; (3) traffic on intermediate sectors would be allowed if reasonably related to end-to-end traffic; (4) an *ex post facto* review of capacity might be requested; (5) fares would be reached in the first instance by airlines through the International Air Transport Association (IATA) but these would be approved, and so regulated, by Governments.

The Bermuda Agreement served as a model for most subsequent bilateral air agreements and established those systems of

traffic rights negotiation, airline designation and fares approval
that still prevail. Having achieved this advance, the Government
returned to matters of domestic organization and abandoned the
'Swinton Plan'. Introducing the new Civil Aviation Bill in May
1946, Mr Herbert Morrison argued that unregulated competition had been tried and had failed: that regulated private
enterprise would founder in red tape and that, accordingly,
there remained no alternative to nationalization by use of
Corporations.[33] Subsequent legislation set up two new air corporations: British European Airways (BEA) and the British
South American Airways Corporation (BSAC). BOAC was
modified and all three corporations placed under ministerial
powers of direction. Furthermore, all scheduled services involving at least one location in the UK were reserved for the public
sector.[34] Morrison argued that the public enterprise system
would allow parliamentary control of general policy whilst leaving day to day administration to the Corporations. It would, by
freeing them from the shackles of detailed control, allow them to
act in a more enterprising and socially responsive fashion than a
body like Imperial Airways could.[35]

Although the 1946 Act put into effect the Labour Government's preference for nationalization as opposed to control by
licensing, a small step was taken in the direction of formal
regulation. To aid the Minister, the Act provided for the setting
up of an Air Transport Advisory Council (ATAC).[36] Members
of ATAC were appointed by the minister who also supplied staff
and premises. The Council's function was to consider representations from anyone concerning the adequacy or cost of facilities offered by the Corporations. Its reports went annually to
the Minister who laid these before Parliament.

Such a weak body did not impress the Conservatives. They
still wanted a mixed, public and private industry regulated
independently of government. It is notable, however, that over a
decade after the start of the United States' New Deal, the Conservative party did not want an expert regulator on the lines of
the American commissions, they sought a court-like licensing
body. Their spokesman, Mr Lennox-Boyd said of the ATAC: 'It
is the policy of the opposition that the tribunal should not be
advisory but judicial with full legal powers and sitting under a
legal chairman. It should sit in public and all should have access
to it.'[37]

The ATAC was set up by Order in Council[38] in 1947, with Lord Terrington as its first Chairman. Though envisaged as a mere consumer body, it soon assumed larger functions. In its first year it considered only 15 complaints from passengers and none was considered to be of sufficient general interest to require a public hearing.[39] At the same time it began to advise on applications from private charter operators for permission to operate scheduled services. It did so at the Minister's request after he had announced in the House of Lords, on 26 January 1949, that, until BEA was in a position to satisfy all demands for scheduled air services, charter companies should be allowed to operate certain services as corporation 'associates'.[40]

Relationships between the government and ATAC were placed on a more formal basis in 1949 when the Minister issued a directive 'giving guidance in general terms' about how the council should treat applications for associate agreements.[41] Published in the ATAC annual report, the guidance contained an undertaking by the Minister to give written reasons where he did not accept a recommendation of the council. In this manner the ATAC was given a limited role as a licensing body. The guidance made it clear, however, that the associate agreement was an interim measure and that, in normal circumstances, scheduled services should be operated by BEA. As far as control of operations was concerned, the ATAC was empowered to lay down maximum fares. The agreements were not normally to exceed 2 years duration and the Minister reserved the right to terminate these without notice or compensation.

At this stage in an account of developing civil aviation regulation the position should be viewed from a distance. By 1949 licensing systems for road goods and passenger transport had been in operation for nearly twenty years. In aviation a different route had been taken and a makeshift regime had resulted. Instead of controlling routes and prices by licensing with an expert, a judicial or an executive body, nationalization had been relied on in combination with a system of informal licensing that was run by a body ill-equipped to perform this function.

The peculiarity of the ATAC's status evidently did little to affect the acceptability of its decisions to Ministers. This was perhaps due to the ATAC's lack of authority and its consequent adherence to ministerial policy lines. In 1949 the ATAC recommended approval of agreements in 55 cases and in respect of only two applications was its advice rejected. By 1950 the council had devoted itself almost entirely to such advice and gained a similarly high percentage of acceptance (55 cases out of 59). As a vote of confidence, the Minister, in issuing new directions to the ATAC on 26 September 1950, raised the maximum period of airline agreements from two to five years.

A step in the direction of more independent licensing came following the Conservatives' return to power under Churchill in October 1951. Responding to this political change, the ATAC used its fourth annual report to argue for more liberal licensing policies. It noted that in the previous year less than half the applications received from operators had resulted in approved agreements (44 out of 111) and argued that operators had been hindered in attempts to create networks of routes by a condition in the Minister's directive that proposed services should not compete with either BEA's present services or with those planned for the future. Furthermore, the ATAC said, independents were finding it difficult to operate economically when only allowed on seasonal routes.

The new Minister of Transport and Civil Aviation, Mr Lennox-Boyd, informed the ATAC Chairman on 9 November 1951 that he would review general policy with a view to extending the opportunities for private companies to participate on scheduled operations and thereby to improve networks. The case for the independent operators was given further momentum early in 1952 when Cambrian Airways wrote to the ATAC complaining that BEA was proposing to commence a Liverpool to Channel Island operation in competition with their existing service. The Council found that the Corporation's freedom to commence operations on a route at any time posed an important issue of security for the independent airlines and it expressed concern to the Minister. Mr Lennox-Boyd asked BEA to delete the increased services and requested that the Corporation should consult the Ministry at the planning stage of any new service.

The Conservative government's preference for regulation as opposed to nationalization further militated in favour of the ATAC's growth as an independent force. On 27 May 1952 the Minister told the House of Commons that opportunities to develop new overseas scheduled services would be offered to the Corporations and independent companies alike. Applications for these, he said, were to be made to the ATAC. He hoped that independents would develop 'all freight' markets and saw opportunities for special services to the Empire at cheap rates where these did not compete with the Corporations. There was a further act of faith in the ATAC: associate agreements would be granted for seven year periods.

Conservative policies on regulation were thus being put into operation by machinery designed to supplement Labour nationalization plans. Involved in this process was the erosion of BEA's privileged position. On 16 July 1952 the Minister told the Commons that the Corporations would no longer be protected against competition on their *planned* routes but only over their *existing* routes.[42] He added that in future the Corporations, whilst protected in their first and tourist class activities, should have to apply to the ATAC for extension of their services outside this field. Outside the protected area they would compete on equal terms with independents.

Such liberalization was eventually to increase the role of the ATAC but, in one of the first ministerial statements of resistance to the growing power and independence of the Council, the Minister said that private operators' proposals should be put to him and that decisions on these 'ought properly to fall on the Minister and not on the ATAC'.[43]

In spite of such statements, further progress towards a licensing system resembling that of the Traffic Commissioners followed the publication, in July 1952, of new terms of reference for the ATAC.[44] These gave protection only to BOAC and BEA's existing services; they also indicated that competition would be allowed provided that 'material' diversion from present services was avoided. The ATAC responded in a manner that was predictable in the light of previous systems of British regulation; it adopted increasingly judicialized procedures. It asked for more detailed information from those companies applying for scheduled services. It also decided that it would hold public hearings in order to receive evidence when several parties contested a case.[45]

Structurally the ATAC now fell between a number of stools. It was neither court-like nor departmental, it was neither expert nor independent. It sought, nevertheless, to develop its own stock of knowledge by holding meetings with the corporations, air advisory councils, airport boards and the British Independent Air Transport Association (BIATA) to discuss developments in the industry. When it came to applying this knowledge, however, it freely admitted that in looking at applications its small staff was 'greatly assisted by the Ministry of Civil Aviation'.[46]

Thus closely locked into government, it was not surprising that in 1953, by which time the council had become a full-time licensing authority and had abandoned all consumer functions, the Minister dissented from not one of its recommendations. It began to hold more formal public hearings, conducting forty-one of these in 1954. Competition was increasingly allowed and applications were refused only on limited grounds such as the entry of a superior application, diversion from established or protected routes, lack of experience, resources or ground facilities or because of failure to obtain foreign traffic rights permission.

It is clear from the policy statements made by the ATAC in the mid-1950s that any regulation attempted was of a wholly reactive kind. The ATAC did not assume or develop a level of expertise that allowed it to rule confidently on, say, a route's viability. It had, as a result to be prepared to take risks. In its sixth annual report it stated:

> . . . in several instances where the economic prospects of a proposed service appeared uncertain, but where no other operator was likely to be affected, the Council once again took the view that the public interest would be served by allowing the applicant to develop his service.

Such an approach was to contrast with the more positive (and paternalistic) approach of the ATAC's more powerful successors.

There was to come a point when a small body could no longer regulate an expanding industry. By 1958, the ATAC was considering over 600 applications a year (together with a handful of complaints under its consumer function). At this time inclusive tour applications were multiplying. Both their number and the airlines' practice of failing to operate tours for which licences had been granted, increased uncertainty and aggravated processing difficulties. On 5 June 1958, the Minister, who at the time decided circular tours applications, handed this additional function over to the ATAC. Another burden was thrust upon a body whose constitution had been directed towards advising on complaints rather than full-scale licensing.

Since the ATAC lacked the resources with which to review the quality of appliactions in depth, it was open to accusations that operators could abuse the licensing system. Thus on May 6 1958, Mr Ian Mikardo, who chaired the union side of the National Joint Council for Civil Air Transport, complained that independent operators were making 'dog-in-the-manger' applications to the ATAC for licences that they were in no position to operate and that this was depriving the corporations of opportunities on these routes.[47]

During 1958 there had commenced a movement towards regulatory reform. The ATAC faced more and more work as pressure increased to allow private operators to compete more easily with the corporations.[48] At the annual dinner of the British Independent Air Transport Association (BIATA) on 12 November 1958, the Minister for Transport and Civil Aviation, Mr Harold Watkinson stated that he favoured the creation of a new statutory licensing authority for civil aviation—not anything as elaborate as the US Civil Aeronautics Board, but a body that would 'fairly and efficiently hold the balance' between competing interests. He referred to a letter written to him sometime earlier by Captain T.M. Morton (Chairman of BIATA) suggesting a licensing system. This proposal had been studied by both his department and BIATA and Mr Watkinson commented that he had 'a feeling that things were becoming too complicated to be handled by the ATAC and his department'. To meet foreign competition, he said, British operators, both public and private, had to be encouraged.[49] Early parliamentary mention of a new licensing body was made in January 1959, when Mr Watkinson[50] advocated discussion of 'the proposition that we should have a more locally based licensing authority for the air.[51]

Those whose principal concern was to protect BEA and BOAC from the predations of private operators under licence from an independent body soon had to contend with a weakening of their case: the Select Committee on Nationalized Industries reported on the Air Corporations in May 1959,[52] and found that in most respects the Coporations had not been unduly affected by the activities of the independent companies.

Five months later, the Queen's Speech announced that a Bill would be introduced 'for improving the arrangements for licensing air services and airline operators and to ensure the

maintenance of high standard of safety'. Mr Gaitskell promised
that the Opposition would strongly resist any moves to favour
independent airlines at the expense of the Corporations.[53]

Why was the need felt for a new licensing board? Firstly, as
already noted, the ATAC had been set up as a consumer council.
It had become an advisory body and then a de facto licensing
authority: its constitution was therefore unsuited to the task of
full-time licensing. Secondly, the fiction of the 'associate agreement', used to circumvent section 24 of the Air Corporations Act
1949, required revision: it appeared absurd to the Corporations Act
who opposed a large percentage of applications.[54] Thirdly, the
ATAC system was geared to control only services classified as
'scheduled' under section 24(2) of the 1949 Act. A number of
'closed group' (charter) operations offering near-scheduled services had mushroomed. These escaped both economic controls
and safety regulations and were undermining regulated services.
A new licensing system was required to extend economic and
safety regulations to cover both types of operation. Fourthly,
(and politically most significantly) private operators sought
relief from the burdens imposed by associate agreements. They
desired a system wherein applicants, public or private, could
compete for licences equally before a non-departmental board.
Conservative ideology further endorsed demands for a specialist,
'quasi-judicial' body.[55] This was a method of regulation that
would free the forces of enterprise in a way impossible in a
system using public corporations as control mechanisms: judiciality would produce a system in which Ministers (even possess-
ing appeal powers) would be reluctant to interfere for the sake of
protecting the public sector. A system based on legal rationality
would, it was supposed, deal with cases on their true merits and
offer the consumer the best air services possible: the time was
right to end a system of regulation that had grown up in an *ad hoc*
fashion and devise one that was predictable yet conducive to a
liberal style of control.

3
A Hopeless Compromise?
The Air Transport Licensing Board is Created

The ATLB was an agency formed in the traditional mould out of which the CAA was to break. In seeing this it helps to distinguish between two models of adjudicating body: the judicialized *tribunal* and the administrative *commission* (or in Abel-Smith and Stevens' terms, between the 'court—substitute' and the 'policy—oriented' tribunal).[1] Here the 'tribunal' is typically a body that is neither departmental nor a court of law but exercises primarily adjudicatory functions akin to those of the courts.[2] The 'commission' also adjudicates independently but is specially equipped (in terms of expertise, staffing or other resources) to develop policy in a particular area.

In the case of the ATLB we see how a body more closely resembling the tribunal than the powerful commission failed to operate effectively within the British system of ministerial government.[3] This is done by focussing on three issues of central concern here: the ATLB's relationship to government, its employment of trial-type procedures in policymaking and the use it made of its regulatory discretion. A preliminary question, however, is how the ATLB came to be set up as a particular legal package.

When the Conservative Government introduced a Bill to set up the ATLB in 1960 its purpose was, in accordance with statements made in the final years of the ATAC, to create a licensing process that would deal with private and public operators on the same basis. In the aftermath of a charter plane crash at Southall in 1958 with the loss of seven lives, emphasis was also placed on improved regulation of air safety. At that time scheduled services, requiring ministerial approval, had to comply with the demands of the Ministry's Director of Aviation Safety, but charter operations (which did not need approval) by-passed this procedure. The Bill provided that *all* commercial operators should require an 'Air Operators Certificate' (AOC) to be issued by the Director of Aviation Safety.

On economic regulation Mr Duncan Sandys, who introduced the Civil Aviation (Licensing) Bill in the Commons, dealt with the ATLB in a manner that seems in retrospect to have involved a naïve belief; namely, that it was possible to create a judicial body and thereby secure its independence and legitimacy no matter what environment it was placed in. He promised that, apart from the Corporations' scheduled service monopoly, operators would be free to apply for route licences to the Board, which would be 'as independent as it is possible to make it'.[4] He promised that ministerial powers of supervision would be minimized: the only important ones retained would be the veto of applications affecting foreign relations or traffic rights, the power to approve international fares agreed on by IATA and that of deciding appeals. Of the latter he said that he had considered setting up an independent appeals machinery (which would have accorded with the recommendations of the Franks Committee)[5] but he had felt that MPs would not have wished such matters to be decided by anyone except a Minister accountable to the Commons.[6] The retention of this major power, though unusual, had a clear precedent. Lord Mills, introducing the second reading of the Bill in the House of Lords, stated that the procedure was based largely on the experience of the 'highly successful' system of licensing bus transport introduced in the Road Traffic Act 1930.[7]

Mr Sandys clearly saw the developed ATLB as being able to use its trial-type procedures to make policy. It would have a wide discretion to do this free from governmental control:

> The future pattern of British aviation will emerge progressively from the decisions of the Board and from the results of appeals to the Minister. A kind of case law will gradually be built up. Since I have no intention of trying to settle this in advance I cannot tell the House just how it will all work out. I can, however, give some indication of the general trends which I hope to see develop as a result of this Bill.[8]

It was clear from the Labour Opposition's reaction that they believed Mr Sandys when he said that he did not know how things would work out. They did not oppose the Board but voted against the Bill on the grounds that it was so vague that no one knew what the consequences would be and from a fear that the Corporations would be damaged.[9] Mr Strauss was worried that the Board was too free to make its own policy. He said that since the items to be considered by the Board in licensing were stated in general terms, 'no one can know what its principles or policies are likely to be'.[10]

On this point the debate went to the heart of the issue and raised the question that was to be asked a decade later when the CAA was set up: how could Ministers control bodies that were either expert or judicial? In the case of the ATLB, conservative models of judiciality blinkered the government's approach to the problem. The Opposition advocated publication of Ministerial statements and the laying down of 'firm principles' which would bind the Board.[11] The Parliamentary Secretary, Mr Rippon, however, emphasised that the ATLB's use of trial-type procedures would bring the bases for appeals out into the open. This, he said, would limit interference. In support of ministerial appeals he also noted that the Thesiger Committee on the Licensing of Road Passenger Services had recommended in 1953 against any change in such an appeals procedure.[12]

In Committee a central issue once more was the balance of power between Board and Minister. In some respects, the Board's position was strengthened: a Government amendment provided that it should initiate proposals for setting international fare levels but that these should be subjected to ministerial approval. ATLB independence was also increased by the Government's agreeing to strike out a provision giving the Board a general duty to consider observations by the Minister. Mr Sandys had, at an earlier date, stated that, since issues of public policy would arise, it would be for the convenience of all concerned were the Minister 'from time to time to send his general observations to the Board on broad questions of policy'.[13] He accepted, however, that there was a danger that a power to observe would corrupt into an instrument of direction[14] and he seems to have been satisfied that the Minister had already been given substantial controls via such powers as that to decide appeals.

Ministerial control was so well provided for that the trade magazine *Flight* (26 February 1960) said that the ATLB would not be the powerful autonomous body that was needed but was 'in danger of being a mere puppet of the Minister. . .' Particular criticism was made of the Minister's power to direct the ATLB to refuse a licence on the grounds that it involved inexpedient traffic rights negotiations. It was argued that this factor was too fundamental to regulation to be withheld from the Board's control.

Procedurally, the Bill made no provision for public hearings, though Ministers had promised that these would occur. *Flight*, on this count, feared that the ATLB might be a 'secret court' like the ATAC 'whose every sitting has been banned to the public and the Press'.[15]

Functions, Powers and Duties

It is important in looking at the creation of the ATLB to see that, whatever any assumptions about its 'judicial' independence, its real position was not so simple. In fact, the Board was set up to carry out functions closely related to those being undertaken by a central government department, the Board of Trade. The ATLB's main function was to issue route licences but possession of a licence did not always mean that operators could start flying. On international routes they also had to obtain traffic rights permission. Traffic rights were, in the absence of 'freedom of the air', negotiated inter-governmentally by treaty and were obtained for the operator by the government rather than any licensing agency.[16]

The airline had also to satisfy certain standards. The Air Registration Board (ARB) and the Director of Aviation Safety of the ministry were responsible for technical safety and the latter issued Air Operators Certificates (AOC's) which certified technical fitness to operate.[17] Although the ATLB had a duty under section 2(2) of the 1960 Act to consider a wide range of factors when licensing, section 2(4) stated that it should not consider matters in respect of which AOC's were required.

The 1960 Act made the Board responsible for setting domestic tariffs and consumer representations[18] but, as noted, international fares were ministerially approved. The government department, in addition, set fares on colonial routes, laid down licensing procedures,[19] conducted accident investigations, enforced licensing conditions, licensed personnel (crew and pilots) and, jointly with the Ministry of Defence, provided Air Traffic Control services.

As far as statutory policy control over the ATLB was concerned, the Board was given a general duty to further the development of British civil aviation (section 1(1)) and, in licensing, was under a duty to consider a series of items (such as financial resources and the need and demand for a service) set down in section 2(2) of the Act. This guidance was less specific than the Minister's terms of reference to the ATAC had been, but the listing of criteria was similar to the vague objectives given to the US Civil Aeronautics Board (CAB) in the 1958 Federal Aviation Act (sections 102 and 401).

Any government, therefore, that sought to control aviation licensing policy was liable to rely on influence derivable from the three principal powers left to the Minister: the decision of appeals (section 5(1)); the negotiation of international traffic rights and the approval of international tariff levels (section 2(5)). Consideration of the ATLB's style of regulation and its governmental role must look to these ministerial powers of control. This would not necessarily be the case with any agency (other factors might prove more important) but with the ATLB the exercise of these powers was crucial in shaping regulatory policy.

4
The ATLB and Governmental Control

The ATLB was established at Therese House, Glasshouse Yard EC1, and operated with a small secretariat of under thirty persons.[1] Board members were ministerially appointed and, for the most part, lacking aviation experience. Staff were civil servants and, like premises and equipment, were supplied by the Ministry.[2] Contention might have been predicted given the establishment of a body that was dependent on the ministry for resources, whose functions were closely intermeshed with those of the Board of Trade, and yet which saw itself as a rigorously independent body.

General Attitudes

The ATLB's governmental role and the Minister's use of his various control powers should be seen in the light of the ATLB's approach to control, the two main features of which were its rejection of informal ministerial guidance and its adoption of a court-like posture. Of the latter, there can be little doubt. Although, of the ATLB's three chairmen (Lord Terrington (to 1961), Professor Sir Daniel Jack (1961–70) and Mr James Lawrie (1971–72)) only its first was a lawyer,[3] the ATLB did adopt a 'judicial' stance from the start. As it came under greater pressure in its early and middle years it increasingly shielded behind its judiciality.[4] Senior staff of the ATLB came more and more to resent interference from the Department of Trade and relations were further strained by personality clashes and the aggression with which the Board fought for a high level of autonomy.[5] The members and staff of the ATLB indeed, had little contact with the Department and little influence, on or knowledge of the processes by which ministerial policies were developed.

Concomitant with such an attitude was the ATLB's insistence

that relationships with the Minister be kept on a formal plane. It staged its declaration of independence in what became known as the European case of 1961.[6] At that hearing BEA opposed the licensing of independent operators in competition with them, stating that traffic rights agreements would be prejudiced. The Board replied that, since the Minister had powers under section 2(3) of the 1960 Act to direct it to refuse an application because of the inexpediency of negotiating traffic rights, then, if no such direction was issued, the Board was not at liberty to invest itself with his function by refusing an application solely on those grounds. Accordingly, the Board refused to consider ministerial advice on such matters except in the shape of formal directions. It affirmed this stance in its second Annual Report:

> We must interpret the Act as it stands and not by reference to statements by Ministers. . . . We shall continue to rely upon our own interpretation of the Act unless we are overruled by a court of law.[7]

Since the Minister was reluctant to direct the Board formally and the Board believed that it should disregard any advice given, the result was a 'nonsensical' duplication of policy in the international field.[8] One solution to this impasse might have been provided by some form of semi-formal policy guidance: the ATLB, however, had no duty to follow Ministerial advice on policy. Indeed, the most open challenge to its independence occurred when such guidance was offered. In October 1964, soon after a Labour Government had been formed, the new Minister of Aviation, Mr Roy Jenkins, was pressed to give the ATLB a statement of policy guidance. The ATLB itself had commented annually on this topic saying in its 1963–64 report that the absence of a statement of general policy was continually criticised by operators, that the development of aviation called for large and long-term investment and that:

> . . . such investment may be inhibited, or, if made, in part wasted, if the operator is unable to form a reasoned judgement of the licences he and his competitors are likely to secure.[9]

What was required, said the Board, was 'something in the nature of an organizational plan for the future development of British civil air transport'.[10]

The Minister responded, not by amending the 1960 Act, but

by making a statement on civil aviation policy in the House of Commons on 17 February 1965 so as to: '. . . lay down some guidelines to the Government's ideas of the objectives of licensing policy'.[11] In doing so, he echoed practice in the ATAC era and anticipated to some extent the CAA's later policy guidance system. The guidelines themselves dealt with three main issues, coming out against the restriction of inclusive tour charters, against competition between British operators on inter national routes, and against increasing the competition for BEA offered by private operators on domestic routes. On enforcing his international policy, a warning was given: the Minister would not re-open negotiations for traffic rights where acceptable terms had not been reached, and he would use his section 2(3) powers to direct the ATLB to refuse applications where it appeared to him that foreign rights could not be obtained without detriment to an established service. So as to avoid prejudging issues he stressed that the guidelines were subject to exception and were without prejudice to the ATLB's giving full attention to evidence and argument in particular cases.[12]

In spite of such a qualification, the statement and its restrictions constituted a challenge to the pro-competitive policies of the ATLB. The pronouncement had no statutory basis, was not legally binding on, and yet was clearly intended to guide the ATLB. In response, the Board fell back on its court-like stance, it did not negotiate with the Minister on policy issues but used its fifth report to assert of the Jenkins statement:

> . . . it has been widely interpreted as supplying the guidance whose absence we earlier remarked, and indeed as undermining the purpose of our existence. We do not take this view.[13]

The ATLB asserted that its legal framework was unchanged. It still had a duty to decide on the merits according to the Act and did not find it 'necessary or appropriate'[14] to agree or disagree with views expressed on behalf of the Government.

When the statement was debated in the House of Commons on 1 March 1965,[15] members had very different ideas concerning its standing. Mr Stonehouse, the Parliamentary Secretary to the Minister of Aviation, argued that Mr Sandys' promised 'case law' had not emerged from ATLB decisions and that the guidance had come none too soon ('The industry has staggered from one *ad hoc* decision to another'[16]). Conservatives, on the other

hand, were loyal to the idea of an independent tribunal. Mr
Maude stated that a case law that was proof against political
decision-making was indeed emerging from ATLB decisions[17]
and Mr Heath added that the statement was an invitation to
appeal, flouting the intentions expressed by Parliament in setting
up the ATLB.[18]

What became clear soon after the Jenkins statement was
issued was that relations between the ATLB and the department
were both distant and cool. Sir Daniel Jack told the Select
Committee on Nationalized Industries in 1967 that the statement had been given to the ATLB without consultation at 4pm
on the day before its submission to Cabinet and that ATLB
members had not been allowed to take the document away. His
robustly independent attitude was displayed when he was asked
whether it was not important for the Board to know the way the
Minister's mind was working. He flatly denied that this was
necessary.[19]

Amongst the airlines there was confusion concerning the effect
of the statement on the ATLB. BEA welcomed the 'clarification'
of policy,[20] and abandoned appeals that had been lodged against
a number of inclusive tour licences. British Eagle International
took seriously the diminished prospect of increased frequencies
and, three days after the statement, withdrew from their trunk
routes (including the important London to Glasgow service). On
11 May 1965, BUA applied to the ATLB for the revocation of
British Eagle's licence and for Gatwick services to replace them.
British Eagle replied that their withdrawal had been temporary
and induced by the Minister's unfavourable remarks. The
ATLB granted BUA licences to Glasgow, Edinburgh and Belfast
and revoked those of British Eagle. British Eagle appealed to the
Minister and were reinstated on the Glasgow route to give an
extra competitor on the major UK route only months after the
policy statement had proclaimed an end to further competition.
The tide of confusion was at its height.

Did the statement affect the independence of further ATLB
decisions? The Board of Trade witnesses before the 1967 Select
Committee said that, although the ATLB had 'thumbed its nose'
at Mr Jenkins, what it had done since then had been 'remarkably
consonant with his policy'.[21] When the ATLB chairman was
asked whether compliance of ATLB policy with the Minister's
statement had been mere coincidence, he declined to use the

word 'policy' but referred to 'our examination of individual cases' and stated that, though these had been in line with the statement, this was indeed 'pure coincidence'.[22] He said that few applications had brought the policy statement into question.[23] At that time the Board had but recently reasserted in its 1966 Report that it was not obliged to bear in mind what appeared to be, from public statements, the Board of Trade's attitude generally or in particular cases.[24] Priding itself on its hearing all cases on their merits, the ATLB had in addition welcomed a set of ministerial appeal decisions[25] upholding its own rulings in spite of their allowing increased domestic competition. The Board had claimed that this showed the Minister's own willingness to consider cases on their merits rather than in strict conformity with the 1965 guidelines and had urged that such an attitude should continue.[26]

A more pragmatic attitude on the part of the ATLB did not come about until late in the Board's life. It was only then acknowledged that rigorous independence might be extravagant. In relation to the necessity for Board of Trade approval of international tariffs it was admitted in 1968 that:

> No advantage, only confusion, would result if we were to prescribe over a wide field tariffs that we had reason to think would be unacceptable to the Board of Trade.[27]

Again in 1972 the ATLB demonstrated that it had amended its attitude at the eleventh hour. In giving British Caledonian Airways (B.Cal) routes from London to New York and Los Angeles, in January 1972, the Board stated that since Government policy had been reformulated following the report of the Edwards Committee[28] it had tried to adopt a sensible line: it was prepared, for example, to take account of Government policy, as made known to it, so far as to do so was consistent with its statutory duties.[29]

At least, then, in matters of tariffs and competition policy the ATLB, in its later years, was forced to pay more attention to the views of the Government. (At this time in any case, the more liberal policies of the Government harmonized to a greater extent with those of the Board.) What the ATLB at no time acknowledged was the right of the Minister to lay down informal policy to a 'judicial' body. Its general attitude towards ministerial control might be summarized as one of sustained resistance followed by a limited acceptance of the need to co-ordinate on a few topics.

Against this background, we may look in more detail at the way in which ministers used their powers to influence ATLB policy and the effects of such attempts on ATLB strategy. Three major powers of ministerial control were used: those to negotiate traffic rights; to approve tariffs and to decide appeal decisions.

Traffic Rights

In order to fly an international route, an operator requires, as has been noted, both a route licence and traffic rights permission. Thus, for example, an independent operator licensed to operate a London to Paris scheduled service requires designation as a British carrier on the route as laid down by the UK/French bilateral Air Services Agreement (ASA). Since such an agreement might have provided for the sharing of capacity on a route or set up a 'pooling' arrangement between operators of each country, the implications of allowing another operator on the route might be considerable and might demand re-negotiation of the ASA.

During the period of Labour office from 1964–70, the Government's greatest concern was that, where the UK share of a market was limited by treaty, the introduction of a second, usually independent, operator on a route would be at the expense of the existing operator (usually the public corporation). Such a concern might have been expected to conflict with the aims of an agency pursuing a competitive licensing policy.

The problem for the ATLB was whether, in route licensing, it should take traffic rights difficulties into account or ignore them altogether. We have seen that in the European case of 1961 and its Second Report the ATLB indicated that it would not in general consider traffic rights matters, nor would the ATLB consult the Board of Trade or receive directions on traffic rights save formal directions under section 2(3) of the Act.[30] There were no regular contacts with Board of Trade officials and procedures for licensing and gaining traffic rights existed at different levels. Sir Daniel Jack told the 1967 Select Committee that only if the ATLB granted a licence would the Board of Trade have to consider obtaining the foreign traffic rights:[31] the Board thus concentrated only on the first level of a decision that, of necessity, involved two layers. Typical of the problems caused by this narrowness was BUA's application on 21 April 1970 to add the Seychelles as a stop on their Nairobi route.[32] The ATLB allowed this, apparently unmoved by BOAC's argument that East African Airways would 'certainly demand equivalent rights' and that this would affect them adversely. Similarly, BOAC, in opposing the granting of a licence to Caledonian-BUA for the London to New York route[33] in 1972, argued that this would disrupt the UK/USA Air Services Agreement, but the ATLB found that such submissions were not such as to govern a licensing decision by them.[34] There was, of course, a limit to such Nelsonian tactics: the position differed when the Board saw a danger that failure by an operator would affect Britain's standing under the treaty. Thus, the ATLB refused Caledonian Airways (Prestwick) Ltd. North Atlantic licences in 1968[35] because they feared the possible effects of failure on the ASA.

Since a licence (if obtained) offered no guarantee of traffic rights, this made it doubly difficult for airlines and for the ATLB to plan networks of international routes or to forecast future operations. Time and money were wasted on many occasions when independent companies were licensed to operate routes but failed to secure traffic rights. Even BEA complained[36] that few of the routes allocated to independents in the European case of 1961 had been operated. In a Supply Committee debate on 13 May 1963, Mr Frederick Lee listed routes licensed to BUA but lacking governmental approval: these included London to Paris, Milan, Madeira, Athens, Basle, and Dublin.[37] He further described how the ATLB would use failure to secure traffic rights as a pretext for withholding a licence and quoted a statement published by the ATLB on 8 January 1963 concerning BEA's application for a London to Corfu route. This case represented a low point in co-ordination between the ATLB and the Department. The ATLB said:

> We are, therefore, on the evidence at present before us, disposed to grant this application on traffic grounds. . . . However, we have noted that BUA have not yet secured traffic rights for their London to Athens service and we regard the securing of these rights as of more importance to the development of British civil aviation than the securing of corresponding rights for the BEA Corfu service; and we do not wish any attempts to obtain the latter to prejudice the former. We have, therefore, adjourned the

hearing of the current application until the situation regarding the BUA traffic rights is resolved.

The tension between Board and Ministry was clear. A situation had arisen in which the ATLB and Ministry had failed to combine their knowledge; where, on the one hand, the ATLB was using licensing powers in an attempt to influence traffic rights negotiations and, on the other, the Minister (see Mr Jenkins' 1965 statement) was using traffic rights powers to control competition. Together they failed for the major period of ATLB regulation, to control competition on international routes in a coherent fashion.

Further interference with ATLB licensing, but this time on a more formal basis, was contained in the Minister's section 2(3) power to issue directions to the Board instructing it to refuse an application on the grounds that, in his opinion, the service proposed would involve negotiating traffic rights with a foreign country 'which it would be inexpedient for the time being to seek'. This again opened the door to a disparity of policies. In practice, however, the power was rarely used. In the years 1963 to 1967 the Minister directed refusal on 22 routes on 10 occasions.[38] Such directions nevertheless, could involve important routes. A series of orders on 4 December 1967 stopped the licensing of BUA, British Eagle International, Caledonian Airways Ltd. and Transglobe Airways on North Atlantic routes.[38] The sparing use of this power to direct was perhaps an indication that in many cases the less formal method of merely failing to secure traffic rights proved more convenient.

International Tariffs and ATLB Policy

Whereas the ATLB was its own master in respect of domestic air fares, the 1960 Act demanded that ministerial approval be given in the case of international tariffs. Fare levels were generally agreed to in International Air Transport Association (IATA) resolutions which were then adopted by regulatory bodies and approved by the various governments.

A review of policy on one major issue, the minimum price regulation of inclusive tours, provides sufficient indication of the level of co-ordination achieved between the ATLB and the Ministry in the sphere of tariffs. The key to policy here was 'Provision 1'—the IATA resolution that no member airline should charge a price for an inclusive tour lower than the corresponding return scheduled flight fare. The ATLB applied this rule to inclusive tour licences from 1961 onwards although many independent operators considered that its application was unduly restrictive and created pricing anomalies.

In 1966, the British Independent Air Transport Association (BIATA) made a representation to the ATLB under section 4 of the 1960 Act[40] advocating relaxation of 'Provision 1' and urging longer-term licenses for inclusive tours. The ATLB, in a move to allow discussion, published the representation and invited evidence on the matter. The Minister received the Board's subsequent report and ordered it and his own views to be published.[42] The ATLB had favoured retention of 'Provision 1' but stated that this might frustrate operators in the cases of winter holidays and holidays at remote European destinations. It urged the Minister to press British IATA members to secure a revision of the IATA fares structure to eliminate these difficulties and invited him to favour applications for sub- 'Provision 1' fares on long distance tours.

The Minister agreed to the general application of 'Provision 1' but saw difficulties in departing from it for long distance European tours.

Price control, he said, would be difficult without a well understood rule and, since 'Provision 1' was the only such rule, it should not be departed from. He added that the ATLB should be aware of his 'general approach'. Like the Jenkins' statement a year earlier, here was a pronouncement that purported to guide the ATLB. Again the Board resisted. As will be seen below in discussion of further policy developments on 'Provision 1' (see Chapter 5), what happened was that separate policies emerged. Sometimes appeals were used to permit low fares, on other occasions they were used to bridle the ATLB's excessive liberalism. Co-ordination of policy was so lacking that the ATLB itself was to declare rational price control to be 'non-existent' in 1969.

The real problem was a split in policymaking without respect for spheres of interest or for expertise. Thus a witness for the Board of Trade told the 1967 Select Committee that the ATLB had 'precious little expertise' in the economics of aircraft operators, and no more than the Board of Trade:[44] by that time the ATLB had long faced a choice; either to accept a role as the department's messenger or else, to, fight for independence knowing that its policies would be undermined. Having chosen the latter course until 1968–69 it decided, as we have noted, to take a more pragmatic attitude in the autumn of its life.

Appeals to the Minister

If there was a single reason why the ATLB system of licensing was eventually perceived to have failed it was the manner in which appeals were decided.[45] This power allowed Ministers to review not only politically significant decisions but also issues of Board judgement. It is here that we see most clearly a confusion of governmental approaches with a non-expert member of the executive reviewing an expert but tribunalistic body on the basis of policy. As we shall see, matters were made worse by the particular machinery set up for deciding aviation appeals.

In the ATLB era appeals were frequent and major issues were always conducted via a Commissioner who would report back to the Minister for final decisions. The role of the Commissioners was considerable. They heard arguments relating to individual cases and were not primarily concerned with long-term policy. Though usually inexpert in aviation matters, they were in a position to review decisions within the ATLB's sphere of expertise. On the basis that policy, not legality, was at issue on appeal, the regulations imposed no limitations on either grounds of appeal or on evidence admissible.

In looking at appeals a mere numerical analysis tells us little. Typically they related to the more important (and contentious) routes; their significance in policy terms was thus far greater than the figures suggest. There is a further difficulty in looking at numbers alone: ATLB Annual Reports from 1962–71 give the total of appeals as 285 of which 220 upheld the Board and 65 ordered revocation, variation or rehearing. These figures, however, relate to routes affected rather than issues decided on appeal (each of which might affect a number of routes). In the period 1962–71 about 100 *issues* were appealed. In sixty per cent of such cases the Board was upheld, thirty per cent involved a successful appeal (i.e. grant, modification or revocation of a licence) and ten per cent were referred back to the ATLB for rehearing.

From start to finish the ATLB's decisions were regularly over-turned, no 'safe area' was created inside which its decisions would be respected: opportunities to state policies openly were missed and the process of appeal via Commissioner added confusion to the system. Although reversal cannot be assumed to be a bad thing in itself, the overturning of ATLB decisions reached questionable proportions in the 1960s. From the very start there was discord on broad policy. The ATLB's first major decision was the North Atlantic case (A1000) of 1976 in which Cunard Eagle had applied for licences for the New York[46] route and BOAC had objected on all grounds set out in section 2(2) of the 1960 Act. The Corporation sought to protect its investment in a future fleet from 'material diversion' of traffic but the ATLB licensed Eagle in spite of finding that material diversion would occur. The Board denied that this was wasteful, saying that 'freezing' the route in its existing state was a result which it could not believe 'to have been intended when the 1960 Act was passed'.[47] The Commissioner and Minister both disagreed; such diversion, they said, was indeed wasteful.

A split in first instance and appeal-stage policies had rapidly emerged and, nine years later, the ATLB was still being overturned on major policy matters. Typical was the 'test case' appeal on 'Provision 1' of 29 April 1969,[48] which involved the ATLB's refusal of low fares on over 140 routes. The Board had taken a major stand in an effort to retain 'Provision 1' minimum price control over inclusive tours but was only to see the subsequent appeals allowed and the sanctioning of a huge number of tours priced below 'Provision 1'.

Perhaps even more damaging to the ATLB than a divergence of policies was being overruled on matters peculiarly within its area of expertise. This happened with unnerving frequency. An example was the ATLB's refusal in 1962 of Starways Ltd's applications[49] for three domestic scheduled services on the grounds of sufficiency of existing service and lack of demand. The Commissioner, Sir Arthur Hutchinson, having asked the Board to amplify its reasons (under regulation 14(12)), considered that the Board had attached excessive weight to Cambrian Airways' objection of 'material diversion'[50] and recommended allowing the appeals on two routes. This was in spite of the ATLB's attributing 'decisive weight'[51] to the Cambrian objection. Even on a simple matter of judgement the ATLB's status had afforded little protection for its views.[52] There were many similar cases[53] including one in which the ATLB was overruled on a routine manner and for different reasons by both the Commissioner and Minister.

Worse was to come: later in its life the ATLB was overruled on a matter central to its sphere of expertise, its domestic pricing policy. On 25 March 1971 seven airlines applied for increases in tariffs to cover rising costs (application T171). The ATLB decided that an attempt to halt the spiral of inflating prices should have priority over airline needs and accepted that, though a case had been made which would, in normal circumstances have justified the increases, it should refuse all the applications. On appeal, it was argued that the Board's task was to further the development of British civil aviation, not to regulate the entire economy. Sir Dennis Proctor recommended allowing the appeals, and expressed concern that the ATLB might have travelled beyond its terms of reference in the reasons it gave for its decision. The Secretary of State agreed and ordered the ATLB to vary the Domestic Air Tariff accordingly.

The deepest cut felt by the ATLB perhaps came when a Commissioner was to back an airline's judgement against that of the Board. This happened when, on 8 January 1969, British Eagle appealed against tourist tariffs granted to them by the ATLB on two trunk routes.[54] Eagle wanted lower fares than those given by the ATLB in order to compete with rail services. The objectors, Cambrian, argued on appeal that the ATLB fares should be upheld as the Board were as adept as Eagle in assessing the effect of fares.

Sir Ralph Hone said that, with their special knowledge and experience on the routes, the judgment of the appellants, Eagle, was to be preferred to that of the ATLB.[55] He recommended allowing the appeals and either ignored the ATLB's fares policies or defied them. Further embarrassment was only saved by the Minister's ordering a re-hearing of the case.

Even the ATLB's attempts to lay down guidance as to its policies were neutralised on appeal. The principal instance of such an effort involved the 'party organisers' concession whereby one person in twenty would be allowed free carriage on a tour if that person was to take an active part in arranging and escorting the tour. At first the ATLB had refused such concessions in 1964 as beyond the IATA definition of 'tour conductor' and detrimental to 'Provision 1' control. In January 1965, however, the Minister, on appeal, allowed such offers 'without prejudice' to further ATLB consideration. Later that year, in a decision on the Beauvais route, the Board stated that the concession was valuable on tours up to four days long but that the case for a concession was progressively weaker the longer the tour. In a 'test case' of 9 March 1966, however, the concession was granted on a six day tour and its application to six day tours was not challenged in 1967, 1968 or 1969 by either BEA or the ATLB.

In May 1970 the ATLB published a declaration of policy[56] saying that it was not disposed to grant the concessions on holidays involving over three nights' acommodation. In a March 1971 appeal,[57] however, Mr D Henry for Court Line argued that no reason had been given for this change of policy and that it breached a principle that for years had been treated as binding. He said:

> ... the ATLB is required to give reasons for its decisions, in this matter the ATLB had announced a policy in licensing notices, giving no reasons whatever.[58]

He argued that the ATLB 'had not in fact considered the applications on their merits'.[59]

Sir John Lang, the Commissioner, accepted that the Board should have given reasons for a modification of policy and said that this would have accorded with the spirit of the Regulations.[60] He was satisfied that the concession would contribute to traffic and, in a recommendation that was followed by the Secretary of State, advocated allowing the appeal. The ATLB's attempt to structure[61] its discretion had failed and the exercise was not to be repeated in its lifetime.

Nor did the Minister, in overruling the ATLB, always take his own opportunity to define a standard or lay down a ruling of principle. In July 1962 the Minister decided an appeal by the British Transport Commission (BTC) against the Board's decision to allow BEA to operate cheap night flights on trunk routes.[62] BTC objected that these would undercut, and so divert from, second class rail fares. The ATLB declined to make a ruling on a central issue in this case: whether they had a duty, either to protect, or to co-ordinate with rail services. In spite of the Commissioner's request[63] that the Minister should decide on this matter of principle, the latter failed to do so. ATLB case-law was under ministerial attack but little, evidently, was to be put in its place.

Any confusion caused by the ATLB's being overruled on matters of both policy and judgment was only added to by the failure of Commissioners to adopt a consistent attitude to the Board. Appointed *ad hoc,* usually from the ranks of retired judges and civil servants, the Commissioners tended to take approaches that differed but reflected their individual previous experience. Some were reluctant to interfere with the ATLB but others considered that they should review decisions quite freely. Thus Sir John Lang clearly felt no reluctance to overrule the ATLB's specialist judgment.[64] In 1969, after the ATLB had refused a winter inclusive tour application (B85272) in order to protect BEA scheduled services, Sir John was persuaded that extra traffic would be created and recommended allowing the appeal. In spite of the ATLB's having, for some years, monitored the question of diversion on the Malta route, Sir John heard argument and, on this very issue, substituted his judgment for theirs.

In contrast, some Commissioners felt that an onus had to be displaced before the expert tribunal would be overruled. Sir Ralph Hone indicated[65] that in the absence of new evidence, he was unwilling to interfere with the Board's 'reasonable and proper conclusions'.[66] Similar support for the Board came in an appeal of 4 November 1966 on a more contentious matter. The ATLB, with a Labour administration in power, had licensed a private operator (British Eagle) on the Bremen route in preference to BEA.[67] The Board was upheld, however, by Sir John Evans, who said:

> . . . the appellants have failed to show that the Board was in error in appraising the matters before them or that their decision was against the weight of evidence or otherwise wrong. It follows, in my opinion, that the Board's decision should stand.

It was, however, 1971 before any open discussion of the Commissioner's role took place. This involved an appeal by BEA and Caledonian/BUA against the licensing of Channel Airways for a Glasgow to Stansted route.[68] Mr D. Henry for Channel said that the central issue was a question of judgment on the effect of diversion and the weight to be put on it— 'a matter peculiarly within the Board's competence.'[69] He argued that before a Commissioner allowed an appeal, he ought to be satisfied that the licensing board, with all the material and background, was wrong in its judgment.'[70] The Commissioner, Sir Dennis Proctor, conceded the weakness of his position:

> A commissioner who comes to the individual case without any
> accumulated knowledge . . . has no competence to pass judgment
> on a decision which has only been reached by the Board itself
> after a most careful review of the issues. . . . Nevertheless . . . it
> appears to me that a Commissioner has a duty . . . to exercise his
> judgment . . . and to deliver his own recommendation.[71]

He denied that he needed to find that the Board's decision was
wrong in order to allow an appeal—his judgment might simply
be different.

With some Commissioners supporting the ATLB and some
less inclined to do so, the ATLB was placed in a confused
position.[72] It feared being treated as a stepping stone en route to
the minister but this it virtually became. The position was
eventually reached when BOAC in 1968 argued (albeit unsuccessfully) that major policy decisions should be taken on appeal
rather than at first instance.[73] Clearly preferring decisions by the
ATLB to those of a Labour Minister, the independent operators
replied that there was nothing in law to suggest that the Board
was not entitled to decide major policy.[74] Matters were made
worse by Commissioners' and Ministers' inconsistency on
whether cases should be re-heard by the ATLB. On some occasions it was asserted that this should be done so as to give the
specialist body the final say,[75] at other times or at different levels
of decision, it was decided that to re-hear would create too much
expense and delay.[76] In many instances, moreover (e.g. both
cases just footnoted), the Commissioner and Minister disagreed
on this issue also.

When ATLB and ministerial policies diverged and the re-
hearings procedure was used, there were almost farcical results.
On 4 December 1963 the ATLB, in the face of objection by
Starways Ltd., granted Cambrian Airways a licence for the
Liverpool to Cork route, allowing ten flights a week. This decision was based on Starways' past failure to satisfy demand.
Starways appealed and, in March 1964, the Commissioner
recommended rejection of the appeal. On 8 July the Minister
ordered the ATLB to re-hear the case and this the Board did on
5 August, reaffirming its original decision.

Starways (who had become British Eagle (Liverpool) Ltd in
December 1963) then appealed against the re-hearing on the
basis of diversion and lack of demand. The Commissioner, Sir

· John Lang (who had not heard the first appeal), recommended supporting the ATLB decision but the Minister[77] did not accept the recommendation. He considered that Cambrian's ten frequencies constituted wasteful duplication and that the fairest solution would be to grant both operators three flights a week. Few would have predicted the outcome of this protracted case.

By 1971 the ATLB was prepared to admit (Eleventh Annual Report para.8) that appeals had 'gone far to undermine' its authority. It argued that new evidence should not be allowed to be introduced before the Commissioner and urged that, since it was in a better position to judge any new evidence that did arise, a re-hearing should be ordered in those cases. It emphasized the need for a future authority to have some opportunity of answering the case made by an appellant against a decision. However painstaking commissioners were, said the ATLB, they were also:

> ... bound to be unaware of some of the background that underlies a decision by the Board.[78]

Whatever premium is to be placed on the consistency and coherency of policies it is clear that the Board was overruled too often on matters both of major policy and of specialist judgment for these objectives to have been achieved. Rules of evidence and airline practices did not help. Thus, for instance, because new evidence was admissible on appeal, many operators deliberately held back evidence from the ATLB so that they could use it later. Ministers and Commissioners, instead of offering support for the Board, only complicated and extended the decision-making process. What the history of the ATLB perhaps showed more than anything else, was the amount of confusion that could be generated by a procedure in which those at one level of decision-making had little respect for the status or expertise of those at others.

Conclusions

It is clear that, simply in terms of the co-ordinating of functions, the ATLB experienced major difficulties in working alongside a central government department. In large part these problems stemmed from the way ATLB members saw the Board as a traditional tribunal. Because of such a conception, they saw no need to increase their secretariat and so their expertise (judges hear arguments, they don't research). They demanded independence of a formal kind from the Department but were in no position to sustain this. It was perhaps ironic that shortly after the ATLB had been set up, Professor M. H. Bernstein was criticizing American agencies, for their over-judiciality, saying:

> The inability to come to terms with the political character of regulation has been glorified as an honourable escape from politics, and it has sanctified the drive towards further judicialisation of administrative regulation.[79]

In British civil aviation regulation the same mistakes were then just about to be made. As the ATLB grew older its independent stance took on a personal dimension and this encouraged the movement to judicialization and formality instead of a system based on specialization, flexible procedures and coherent policy-making. Finally the ATLB was swamped by a Departmental control that it constantly fought to resist. The position was summarised by Mr Michael Noble, Minister for Trade, n debating the 1971 Civil Aviation Bill.

> The ATLB regarded itself as a quasi-judicial body. There was no contact between the ATLB and the Department of Trade and Industry or the Secretary of State at the time or the President of the Board of Trade either. There was no consultation or agreement about how anything should be handled.[80]

In the end it was plain how badly a regulatory system could be made to work when appeals lay from a 'court-substitute' tribunal to a political decision-maker by way of inexpert intermediaries.[81] Such procedures realized nearly all permutations of inconsistency and undermined the ATLB's legitimacy. It was to be expected therefore, that the agency's whole relationship to Government was to be central to any restructuring of the licensing system.

5
Case Law, Rule-making and Justiciability in the ATLB System

Whether or not the phrase 'quasi-judicial' is helpful to administrative lawyers, that was the term used by ATLB staff in describing the Board. This, in their view, was a court-like body that
very much accorded with Franks' view of the tribunal as part of
the 'machinery provided by Parliament for adjudication rather
than as part of the machinery of administration'.[1] Adjudication
by trial-type procedure was seen as central to ATLB policy-
making and it is therefore fair, in looking at the match between
the Board's procedures and functions, to examine whether aviation licensing issues proved justiciable.

This question asks whether those issues were appropriately
dealt with by court-like procedures (i.e. adjudication on the basis
of evidence and argument delivered adversarily).[2] There are two
debates combined here: one concerns political legitimacy, the
other the competence of legal techniques. The first asks: Does
there remain a politically acceptable amount of discretion in the
decision-maker's hands after the application of legal rules and
principles? The second centres on procedural practicalities: Is it
possible for legislators to put policies into statutory form so that
standards, rules and principles will be defined with precision?
Will the trial-type process operate efficiently and discretions be
circumscribed?[3]

Fortunately there are shorthand versions of the political and
legal issues: (1) Will politicians tolerate the delegation of such a
discretionary power to this kind of body?; (2) Can trial-type
procedures be used without losing their coherence and legitimacy? Already we have seen that the ATLB encountered
political problems: the use of a tribunal in close harness with a
government department did create considerable tensions and we
will see below how the ATLB eventually met its political demise.
To answer the legal question it is necessary to see whether the

ATLB was able to adjudicate on licensing issues in accordance with standards, principles and rules[4] and whether the public hearings procedure was put to appropriate use.

Even by the time that the ATLB was created it was clear that it was no simple matter to allocate economic decision-making to a body adjudicating by trial-type procedures. In the case of one celebrated example, the Restrictive Practices Court, which had been set up in 1956 to decide issues relating to trade agreements, two distinguished commentators were to say:

> The British Act . . . in seeking to have both the advantages of a less dogmatic approach to the effects of competition and also the advantages of the judicial process, has failed to achieve the latter. . . . The failure to appreciate the nature of the judicial process led Parliament in 1956 to commit to judges the type of tasks which even American judges, far more accustomed to handling matters of an economic and political nature, would assume were beyond their competence . . . the Restrictive Practices Court is required to involve itself in a process of evaluation and decision-making which does not appear to be peculiarly suited to the judicial process or causally related to the peculiarities of legal logic or legal relevance.[5]

When we ask if the ATLB's procedures for adjudication were any better suited to its own functions it should be remembered that those licensing procedures were not new but had been modelled on the system that had operated in road transport licensing for nearly thirty years. It had been hoped that, just as rules, principles and policies had been developed by the Traffic Commissioners in conjunction with either the Minister (in passenger appeals) or the Transport Tribunal (in goods appeals),[6] the ATLB would develop a case law that would serve as a guide to short and long-term aviation policies.[7]

To this end, the ATLB stated from its inception that, in the absence of detailed statutory guidance on policy, it would set out its reasons for decisions at length 'wherever an important point of principle or the construction of the Act is involved, even though less exhaustive reasons would serve the needs of the particular case'.[8] Clearly, both agency and sponsoring Minister thought that licensing could be made in some sense justiciable on the basis of rules and policies set down in case decisions.

To see how such a way of dealing with economic issues[9] worked in practice, we will look at policy-making via case law in relation to certain key issues in regulation: scheduled service competition; the ATLB's supervisory role and inclusive-tour charters. Methods of developing policy other than via case law (e.g. by rule-making) will then be considered. Before looking at the substance of case law however, something should be said of the role of trial-type hearings in the ATLB system.

Only one in forty applications to the ATLB was decided after a public hearing. Such figures, however, are misleading as a guide to policy formulation. In accordance with the regulations[10] all applicants and objectors were entitled to a hearing (which was to be held in public unless the ATLB decided otherwise). In practice the vast numbers of routine and unopposed applications (mainly concerning inclusive tours and charters) were granted without hearing. These were held whenever an objection was lodged against an application or, in rare cases, when the Board wished to satisfy itself of an operator's suitability for a route. Procedure before the ATLB resembled that encountered in a minor court of law, with parties supplementing written evidence with oral submissions given in adversary fashion. Cross-examination of witnesses was allowed but it was rare for counsel to be employed by airlines - usually a non-lawyer member of the airline's licensing staff would prepare and present the case. No statutory provision was made for the awarding of costs at hearings, which were conducted by a panel comprising at least three ATLB members and usually between seven and ten. In accordance with the Board's legalistic approach to regulation, the question whether or not to hear a case did not prove problematic or the subject of a bargaining process. As with appeals, the fact that major policy issues tended to involve objections, and so public hearings, meant that the relatively small number of applications heard in public were, in policy terms, of crucial importance. This should be borne in mind in considering the role of case-law in policy-making in relation to the first of three central issues.

(i) Scheduled Service Competition

The ATLB assessed the level of competition that it would allow by reference primarily to section 2(2) subsections (d), (e) and (f) of the 1960 Act. On such a basis the first general principle governing competition licensing was set out in the 'European

Case' of November 1961. What became known as the 'growth formula' allowed the licensing of a second operator if the growth of traffic within three years would by itself be adequate to support a second carrier at a reasonable frequency. The principle also covered UK domestic routes considered in 1961 and, under this formula, Cunard Eagle was given daily scheduled service licences from London to Glasgow, Belfast and Edinburgh but was refused routes to Manchester and Liverpool.

In its 1961–62 Annual Report (para. 8) the Board expanded on the principles set out in the European case saying that 'material diversion' under the Act was not regarded as a bar to the grant of a licence since this approach would 'freeze' the existing route structure and give a result unenvisaged by the Act.[11] A clear distinction was drawn between diversion that reduced present traffic and diversion that merely retarded the growth of a competitor's traffic.[12]

The 'growth formula', though it implied minimal protection for Corporation investments, was firmly established. In its third Annual Report (para. 36) the Board stated that it would continue to license more than one operator on a route if traffic was judged to be sufficient to allow competition. Even with a Conservative government in office until 1964, however, some tension existed between the ATLB and the Department, with the Board favouring competition to an extent that the government sometimes considered to be unacceptably damaging to BOAC and BEA. When the Minister allowed BOAC's appeal against the licensing of Cunard Eagle to New York in 1961 (on the grounds of diversion and wasteful duplication) it was against a background of BOAC losses of 16.5 million in 1961–62.[13]

On the Labour Party's coming to power in 1964, it was to be expected that the new Minister, Mr Roy Jenkins, would act to reduce competition and thus counter the thrust of the ATLB's first four years of decision-making. Sure enough, his parliamentary statement of 17 February 1965 set out policies on domestic routes (no increases in the independents' permitted capacities) and on international ones (no further double designation) which stood in potential conflict with the ATLB's 1961 'growth formula'.

In 1967 the ATLB confronted this problem. It stated that reasons were given in individual cases but that a general statement of policy was desirable 'as applicants should know the criteria we have in mind'. Referring to the 1961 'growth formula' the Board explained that, though often referred to in subsequent hearings, it was, in the light of experience, disposed to attach less importance to it.[14] The circumstances of earlier cases were unlikely to be repeated, said the Board, and in recent years it had tended to move away from a 'theoretical approach' and to reach conclusions on the basis of 'practical considerations'. A revised and looser formula was offered: in future competitive applications it would consider the absolute volume of traffic available; the effect of competition on growth and the practical circumstances of the route and the operator concerned. It noted the Minister's statement but repeated that cases would be considered on their merits. This produced a situation after 1967 in which the 'growth formula' had been diluted to the point of abandonment and in which the 1965 policy statement was of swiftly diminishing relevance. Even in 1967 BEA complained that the ATLB had granted competitive licences to independents against the Jenkins policy. On the major domestic trunk route to Glasgow the first appeal after the 1965 statement had contradicted that statement by adding a competitor for BEA and extra frequencies. The appeal on BUA frequency increases in 1967 was not used to stop them[15] and in November 1970 the ATLB finally granted BUA unrestricted frequencies on the Glasgow route, stating that the time had come for BEA to face the full rigours of competition on equal terms with its rivals.[16] By that time the relevance of the 1965 statement appeared to have been lost and decisions on the basis of 'practical considerations' offered little guidance to applicants. The ATLB had destructured its discretion and adopted an *ad hoc* mode of decision-making instead of taking steps to devise principles of sufficient breadth to guide applicants and to plan for the industry.

If broad principles of competition policy had dissolved by the late 1960s, those looking for the consistency or the structured discretion commonly called for in trial-type procedures (see *infra* Chapter 11) would have looked for those more detailed policies or standards that had been developed by the ATLB. An examination of some of these also reveals difficulties: let us take, for example, the more precise question of when an existing operator would be penalized for failing to satisfy public demand: this was perhaps a sufficiently narrow and recurring issue to have created some expectation that standards would be developed.

Protection of the Existing Operator.

It was of vital importance for airlines operating any route to know whether their markets would be protected. If they had invested in a loss-making route in the expectation of a profit after, say, three years, or were considering further developing a route, the advent of a competitor to share the market would come as a rude financial shock. Protection was to be derived from sections 2(2)(e) and (f) of the 1960 Act which required the Board, in considering applications, to look at the 'adequacy of any similar service' as well as any 'wasteful duplication of or material diversion' of traffic from licensed services.

Although the 'growth formula' had made it clear that an operator's *absolute volume* of traffic, not *growth* of traffic would be protected, a more detailed statement of policy was given in a major decision on the Glasgow route in 1965.[17] British Eagle had, in response to BUA's application to revoke their licence, argued that, in terms of section 2(2), their services merited protection. They had invested £500,000 in the services and had only ceased to operate temporarily following the Minister's 1965 statement. The ATLB commented that, although in ordinary circumstances a licence would offer some security:

> It should be open to any operator at any time to seek to persuade us that the interests of British civil aviation will be better served by the grant of new licences accompanied by the revocation of existing licences on particular routes . . . such cases are for consideration on their merits.'[18]

The ATLB said that it would be wrong to infer from the Act that the substitution of one operator for another could never be justified or that it required one to demonstrate 'that the old services were intrinsically bad or culpably mismanaged'.[19] More was said on the issue of protection in November 1963 when BUAF competed with Channel Airways for a cross-channel service.[20] The Board stated that where operators were in the process of recovering initial expenditure they would be given a degree of protection from interference and that they were reasonably entitled to protection in the case of an investment which had served to develop UK civil aviation. Having been described thus, however, the policy was not applied consistently. After the Board had licensed a second operator on the London to Manchester route in 1964, the Minister allowed an appeal on the grounds that BEA had not been given sufficient time to recover development expenditure on the route.[21] On this basis, it was difficult for operators to judge whether they would have to face competition or not. Thus, if BEA feared an independent rival, it might rely on the 1965 statement which restricted private sector frequencies but the statement declined in influence, was not openly acknowledged by the ATLB and was subject to numerous exceptions 'on the merits'. In August 1965 it appeared, after the Glasgow case, that an operator might be removed from a route without fault being shown. When considerations of blame are examined further, the picture becomes even more confused.

A common situation in licensing is the application by one operator for a licence to fly a route already allocated to another airline: is the original licensee to be protected even if it has shown itself reluctant to use its license? Under ATLB regulation, 'wasteful duplication' or 'material diversion' under the Act referred to traffic which was 'being, or is about to be, provided under any air service licence already granted'.[22]

In its 1961–62 Annual Report the ATLB said that 'about to be provided' here meant 'really was going to be provided' and not 'merely contemplated'. This statement only partly solved the problem of the airline that abandoned a route but recommenced operations when another operator applied, or who only started operating when a competitor approached or who pleaded that 'plans had been made' to operate the contested route. (Although the Board did receive information on operators' future plans this was not supplied in sufficient detail for use as a bar to such arguments.) The Board's dilemma was that, though it was not part of its functions to penalize operators,[23] it did want to discourage practices which were detrimental to the service enjoyed by the public.

The Board attempted to clarify policy in its 1962–63 Annual Report where it stated that little weight would be attached at a hearing to objections based on: letters (as opposed to a parallel applications) informing the Board of interests in operating similar services in the future; competing applications lodged just before the hearing, or, existing licensed services not operated or in prospect of operation at the time of the hearing.

The problem with enunciating such considerations was that, in its decisions, the Board failed to apply them explicitly. This was a case, in Daniel Gifford's terms, of a body failing clearly to disclose the factors taken into account—the 'decisional referents'—in its decision-making.[24] The British Eagle case of August 1965 involved such a difficulty. BEA supported BUA's application to revoke Eagle's Glasgow licence, stating that the company 'did not sufficiently consider the public interest'. Though Eagle argued that their withdrawal from the route had been temporary and that they had resumed the service, they admitted that a 'factor in their recent thinking' had been BUA's application.[25] In its decision, the ATLB stated that it attached no importance to the newly restored Eagle operations and that:

> The abrupt withdrawal of British Eagle's services in February 1965 . . . even if explicable, was clearly a disservice to the public.[26]

The ATLB commented that, but for the BUA application, Eagle would not have resumed their service and added . . . 'no question arises of punishing British Eagle for any deficiencies in their performance. The stop-go nature of British Eagle's services however, must be a matter for concern'.

The Board thus revoked Eagle's licences and gave BUA the routes, introducing a 'use it or lose it' clause in the licences given to BUA to ensure their automatic expiration if not used. The real reasons for this decision were not made clear. The Board said that it attached 'little importance'[27] to Eagle's plea that it had spent half a million pounds in developing the routes and, on the question of the interrupted service, stated that the suitability of Gatwick versus Heathrow was a consideration outweighing any importance attached to Eagle's position as the existing licence holders.[28] The ATLB denied that it would punish Eagle but concluded that the interruption of a service, whether culpable or not, was a factor to be taken into consideration in licensing.[29] Eagle's licence was taken away ostensibly on the grounds of the airport used but there were undertones of an ulterior reason. The opportunity to state a clear ruling on the consequences of a failure to serve the public was lost and little effort was made to indicate the weight to be given to the various factors in such decisions.

Soon after the Glasgow case, British Eagle International became the challengers to the non-operating licensee. They applied for a London to Bremen route (application A5253) and a month later BEA responded with a similar application (A5274).

The ATLB heard the applications together and stated that, though BEA held a cargo licence to Bremen (A3177), they had neither operated it nor applied to vary it so as to allow carriage of passengers:

> On both these points we have received acceptable explanations from BEA and we attach little significance to them except in so far as they further indicate a rather more advanced state of readiness by British Eagle to embark on the new service.[30]

The Board gave the 'balance of advantage' to Eagle in spite of BEA's argument that Bremen enhanced their network of 16 German routes—an argument that had been said to have given BEA a 'strong case' for approval in 1968 when Eagle had ceased to operate. BEA appealed unsuccessfully,[31] saying that the ATLB, to be consistent with the principles set out in its 1962–63 Annual Report, should have disregarded the 'readiness' point altogether. Again the residual feeling was that the ATLB would favour the initiator on a route. The incentive system seemed to be at tension with the ATLB's denial of a 'first come first serve' preference system.[32] For fear of being considered punitive, the Board was inclined to justify decisions on grounds other than an operator's failure to serve the public. This led to an opaqueness of reasoning that was not the case where, for example, the existing operator had offered a deficient service rather than completely failed to operate.[33]

Over a ten year period ATLB case law on scheduled service competition might be described as patchy in the extreme. A number of factors made consistency difficult: clearly the ATLB's relationship with government was an impediment, appeals were allowed, traffic rights were often not forthcoming, fares structures were interfered with and unwanted guidance was given. Even considered in themselves, however, the ATLB's decisions were inconsistent. In the absence of broader policies many decisions were made *ad hoc*, 'on their own merits' or as exceptions to rules. Reasons for decisions were often contradictory or evasive and, even when the need to decide on the basis of 'practical considerations' was asserted, the ATLB failed to develop or disclose clear standards. Whether or not such 'flexibility' was desirable, it was not the model of decision-making aimed at by the ATLB or by the agency's designers. The tribunal-like body encountered not merely political difficulties but problems in developing a coherent case law at all.

(ii) The ATLB's Supervisory Role

Since the 1960 Act empowered the ATLB to consider the financial resources, abilities and organization of the applicant when licensing, a question arose as to the extent to which the Board would take over from the operator the responsibility for judging a route's potential or its viability, or would seek to protect operators from their own optimism. Again this was a recurring issue on which developed principles or standards might have been thought possible.

Dealing with tariffs, the ATLB did not on profitable routes make a general ruling on what constituted a reasonable rate of return. It pointed out in its 1963 Report that such problems did not arise since 'unfortunately . . . losses on domestic routes are the order of the day'. It saw its expertise as the ability to set levels of fares after hearing arguments from parties: the airlines had to justify fares application on figures and evidence and could not merely tell the Board that they had decided on a certain fare level.

A different rule was made in 1963 for unprofitable services. On routes served for social or long term purposes, the ATLB endorsed the airlines' practice of minimizing losses by charging 'what the traffic would bear'. It stated in its Annual Report of 1963 that in the detailed application of this practice it would rely mainly on the commercial judgment of the operators. This major concession to the airlines' own powers of management was an acknowledgement of the operators' closer knowledge of the degree of cross-subsidization inherent in a service, of costs and of the potential demand on a loss making route.

As K.M. Gwilliam[34] has pointed out, this policy was not consistently applied for on 24 February 1965 the Board refused a number of domestic fare increases on the grounds that the airlines would approach closer to break even point on the existing fares structure. BKS were not allowed to put up fares on Teeside and Dublin services in spite of the Board accepting that the routes would remain unprofitable for some time. Rejecting another application (from Dan Air) the Board had said that the applicant would be better off accepting the existing, reasonably satisfactory, results rather than jeopardizing traffic by raising fares. Having admitted the superiority of the operator's position to judge fares on loss-making routes in their 1963 and 1964

Annual Reports, the Board had substituted its own judgment for theirs in 1965.

This issue eventually went to appeal when in 1967 the ATLB prescribed tourist and standby fares on British Eagle's loss making Liverpool, Chester and Glasgow routes in excess of those asked for by Eagle.[35] Sir Ralph Hone recommended allowing the appeal. He agreed with the airline that the ATLB's aim had been to rationalise tariffs rather than decide on the specific evidence. He then said that, with their special knowledge and experience on the routes, the judgment of Eagle was to be preferred to that of the ATLB, adding:

> I doubt whether, in the case of a well established airline . . . the Board has any duty, so to speak, to save British Eagle, from themselves by forcing them to charge on a particular route fares higher than they deem economically justifiable.[36]

He considered that the lower fare would be in the public interest and, following his recommendation, the appeal was allowed.

The 1971 Domestic Air Tariffs decision[37] in which the Board refused fare increases on loss-making routes in order to make a stand against inflation did nothing to increase clarity on the matter. That case was successfully appealed by nine operators[38] who argued that the ATLB was wrong to overrule their judgment and give the fight against inflation priority over the welfare of the industry.

Matters could hardly have become more confused. On its role as tariff supervisor the ATLB first made a ruling on its own position; it then acted in variance with the principles expounded in its Annual Reports; in pursuance of a new policy it was overruled on appeal in favour of the operator and near the end of its life it once more overruled the operators' judgment only to be reversed again on appeal. Because of confusion between the ATLB and Minister, and because, having set out a policy, the ATLB simply failed to adhere to it, the airlines (and airline users) were deprived of intelligible principles. If the ATLB's failings in other areas had resulted from a failure to develop broad policies, here the error was far more a matter of sheer inconsistency.

In the case of route licensing there was similar confusion on the Board's role. The original rule was that evidence of need, demand and viability should be put to the Board which would

decide whether to licence a route or not. Having stated that
operators would have to make a case for a service with hard
evidence (Annual Report 1964–65) the Board then proceeded to
allow exceptions. It allowed BUA to 'put their commercial judgment to the test' on South American routes after expressing
doubts as to viability[39] and, in similar circumstances, gave BMA
a licence to Strasbourg.[40] In contrast, the ATLB decided in 1968
not to allow Caledonian Airways to take a risk on the North
Atlantic route because it considered that failure would involve
loss of prestige.[41] Operators, by the late 1960s had come to view
ATLB responses on such issues as something of a lottery.

(iii) Inclusive Tour Charters

A major objective of the ATLB in the 1960s was to prevent
cut-throat competition in charter services and to see that these
did not harm scheduled operations. It was thus concerned to
regulate the minimum prices of inclusive tours and generally did
so by inserting 'Provision 1' into licensing conditions to provide
that tour prices should not be lower than the corresponding
return scheduled service fare. Final control of tariffs still rested
with the Minister who approved international fares under section 2(5). He could, therefore, set guidelines for the Board by
approval or amendment of the IATA fare resolutions on which
'Provision 1' was based. First application of fares policy to
individual cases was, however, the task of the ATLB.

Apart from the general problems of controlling 'affinity' charter abuses and airline finances, the ATLB had difficulty in
developing clear principles to guide its inclusive tours decisions.
It started off by declaring in its 1961–62 Report that it would
adopt a liberal licensing policy on inclusive tours. (A major
reason for this policy was that tour organisers would resort to
foreign charter operators if the British airline they proposed to
use was refused a licence.)[42] So as to regulate overall capacity on
international tours the Board declared in 1963–64 a policy of
hearing all summer inclusive tour applications together and for
the ATLB's first four years a liberal licensing policy ran
smoothly. In his 1965 policy statement, however, Mr Jenkins
stated that it was not desirable to apply restrictions to inclusive
tour charters and the ATLB, in general, agreed with him. In its
1964–65 Annual Report it said that there were alternative

theories concerning tour charters: that they created new traffic by converting people to air travel or, that they diverted from, and harmed, scheduled operators. It, however, inclined towards the former view, stating that it had found little evidence of harmful diversion.

In the industry there appeared, in the early years, to be some agreement on charter policy but, by 1966, the first indications of discontent had emerged. The British Independent Air Transport Association (BIATA) raised the question of the duration of inclusive tour licences and of minimum price regulation based on 'Provision 1'. They considered the latter to be too restrictive and creative of anomalies and made a submission in these terms to the Board under section 4(1) of the Act.

The ATLB published the representation (CALN 256 pt. III) and invited evidence on the matter. It favoured adherence to 'Provision 1' control but reformulation of the IATA fares structure to eradicate frustrating anomalies (e.g. the application of 'Provision 1' to short winter and long distance holidays). It asked the Minister to press for these changes in the fares structure and to consider such applications sympathetically on appeal. In response, the Minister published his views and those of the ATLB (CALN 287 pt. VIII). He stated that he would consider applications on their merits but he opposed departure from 'Provision 1' since that was the only guiding rule on tariffs and it applied also to foreign operators. He urged the ATLB to be aware of this approach.

There was thus open disagreement between the ATLB and Minister over long-distance tours. Divergence of policies for shorter distances was less clear cut. On 12 December 1967 a BEA appeal was allowed against the granting of sub-'Provision 1' fares to Palma and Genoa. The Minister instituted 'Provision 1' prices, following the Appeal Commissioner in refusing to accept the ATLB's judgment that the application justified exceptional treatment.

The Minister then relaxed 'Provision 1' conditions in 1968, allowing the pre-devaluation rates to continue into the summer. He introduced, for the winter of 1968–69, a minimum tariff for inclusive tours of 50 per cent of the normal IATA tourist class return fare. On 4 April 1968 he stated that 'Provision 1' ought to apply to most applications for the summer of 1969.

Towards the end of 1968 the ATLB decided a key case

involving thirteen independent operators and over 140 routes, divided into groups to be debated under eight 'test cases'. All applications were for prices below 'Provision 1'. The ATLB favoured one of the test cases, but refused to allow the other tours at prices below 'Provision 1'. It made an attempt to set standards by upholding 'Provision 1' in spite of the anomalies the rule created on certain routes. 'Provision 1' should be upheld, the Board said, to prevent price cutting, protect organizers' profit margins, stave off financial difficulties for airlines and avoid undue diversion from scheduled operations. It added:

> These risks are by no means remote possibilities, and, if price control were abandoned, they could quickly become a threat to the tour industry, to the public and to the stability of British civil aviation.[43]

Six companies appealed against the decision, arguing to Sir Dennis Proctor that they sought to abolish, not 'Provision 1' control, but the anomalies caused by its application. One representative said that the ATLB had just decided to keep 'Provision 1' and then had rationalized with a 'hotch-potch of reasons'.[44] In defence of the ATLB decision, Mr Scarlett of BEA argued that the proposed exceptions from 'Provision 1' were so numerous that to allow them would result in the virtual elimination of control. He urged that the decision of the experts, the ATLB, should be respected.

Sir Dennis did not think that to allow the appeals would remove control, but considered that if eradication of the anomalies would have that effect, then 'Provision 1' did not offer a suitable control structure in the first place.[45] He said that, whatever the case law of the ATLB, he was an independent judge who should decide strictly on reference to the Act. Recommending allowing the appeals, he added:

> The Board appears to have regarded the applications before it as departures from a general doctrine which could only be countenanced if there were overwhelming arguments in their favour, whereas to me they appear to be commonsense adjustments which are obviously desirable unless there are overruling objections to them.[46]

For his part, the Minister noted that holidays had been advertised at the prices originally applied for and, not wishing to apply minimum charges which would result in surcharges at a later date, he allowed the appeals.[47]

The decision was a major set-back for the ATLB's effort to give clear guidance on prices. They had reviewed the issues of diversion and competition and had come to a considered judgment. The Commissioner overruled that judgment with severe effects on ATLB pricing policy. The Board responded by using its Ninth Annual Report (1968–69) to repeat the reasons for its decision. It remarked that the degree to which departures from 'Provision 1' should be allowed was a question of judgment and argued that were it to make other tariff provisions save exceptionally, it would 'undermine the foundations' of British civil aviation policy (para.31). It concluded by saying of the 'test case' appeal:

> . . . we believe that the Board of Trade decision created a situation where rational control over inclusive tour charges in 1969— has been shown non-existent.[48]

Confusion became worse after an appeal was allowed a year later[49] in which different decisions were made at each level, from Board to Commissioner to Minister. The result of that case (the Minister allowing a low fare that had been rejected by the ATLB and Commissioner) was, in ATLB eyes, the 'collapse of price control' over short winter holidays in 1970.–71[50] By the end of the ATLB era, licensing control over inclusive tours had thus reached a parlous state and even the ATLB admitted this. Operators could not predict with any reliability such matters as whether 'Provision 1' price control would be applied because clear policies had either failed to emerge or had been undermined. A primary cause was the lack of any division of responsibility for policy between Board and department. This deficiency was exemplified in appeal decisions. Even taken in themselves, however, neither ATLB nor appeals decisions offered a coherent approach. Again an aggravating factor was the ATLB notion of itself as a judicial tribunal; this ruled out an expansion of research activity which, in turn, meant that the ATLB was not able to identify precisely the scheduled service routes requiring protection from charter competition. Structural policy could not therefore be devised or set out. The problem was not simple inconsistency but the ATLB's lack of authority. The difficulties encountered in inclusive tour regulation summed up the general failing of the ATLB licensing system.

Conclusions: ATLB Case Law and Justiciability

Assessment of ATLB case law can be put in a comparative context by recapping on those respects in which the Restrictive Practices Court (RPC) proved inadequate. Stevens and Yamey argued in dealing with that body:

> . . . it is not normally assumed that in the course of such indus-
> trial investigations the judges will have to choose between con-
> flicting economic predictions, and make value judgments involv-
> ing the conflicting interests of different groups or competing
> policy objectives.

They concluded:

> The Restrictive Practices Court is called upon to make the type of
> decisions the Supreme Court has insisted are "value choices of
> such magnitude" that they are "beyond the ordinary limits of
> judicial competence".[51]

The RPC, then, was criticized not so much for encroaching on the political province of Ministers as for its lack of competence to decide certain types of issue. The ATLB, however, fell down on both counts. Political interference undermined its policy-making and the Board failed to develop its competence adequately to produce decisions of sufficient quality and to sustain its legit-imacy. Inconsistency, as has been argued by Robert Summers,[52] can evidence non-justiciability and, although the ATLB could not have been expected to achieve the same results as the courts of law, its failings were such as to undermine its authority.

The ATLB clearly failed to develop a mixture of principles, standards and rules which might be termed a consistent or coherent body of case law and it did so for a number of reasons. In regulating competition it set out to establish guiding princi-ples, but abandoned these in favour of '*ad hoccery*' in 1967. In setting out its supervisory role it was guilty of plain incon-sistency, and, on the issue of price control over inclusive tours, it became hopelessly embroiled with the appeal authorities. Hav-ing said this, it should be asked whether the ATLB set out to develop a case law at all. Mr Noble, we have seen, envisaged it doing so and from 1961 to 1963 the Board had promised to give detailed policy guidance via decisions and had stressed the importance of predictable decisions to airline investors.[53] The ATLB at no time, however, bound itself rigidly to precedents. It consistently ruled that the doctrine of *res judicata* did not apply to its decisions and that cases would be treated on their merits.[54] If a prior decision was cited, the typical ATLB reaction was to stress the merits of each case and to reject the notion that prior decisions bound it in any way.[55]

Thus stated, the ATLB approach seems a moderate compromise. After all, to treat cases on their merits and reject the binding nature of precedents is not to rule out some form of policy-making by a flexible case law. The real problem for the ATLB was that, instead of being a body of expertise and flexibility, it produced legalistic policies of jelly. A feature of its decision-making was the extent to which both it was prepared, and that circumstances drove it,to grant licences on an exceptional basis. Treating cases 'on their merits' thus proved expensive in terms of policymaking.[56] On a number of occasions operators pressured the Board into exceptional licensing decisions by 'pre-emptive advertising' of an, as yet unlicensed, charter flight, or by submitting a late application.[57] On these occasions the Board would act to avoid inconveniencing passengers, but major breaches in such rules as 'Provision 1' were allowed.[58]

Apart from the dilution of simple exceptions there were other reasons why the Board had, by 1967, abandoned the hope of adhering to longer term principles and standards. A number of factors militated against regulatory decision-making by a tribunal ill-equipped to develop policies other than through the trial-type process. Conditions in the industry were changing rapidly. Governmental strategies were always shifting. On individual routes and in relation to central policies, the economic climate constantly varied. Even by the time of its 1963–64 Annual Report (para. 9) the Board was saying that reasons for decisions had, with the passage of time, to be considered against the changing traffic patterns and other features of the route in question, the changing circumstances of the British civil aviation industry as a whole and changes in the operation and structure of the applicant company.

The Board's small resources meant that it could not impose order on the chaos of decisions by means of well-researched medium or long-term policies. Nor did its regulatory powers allow it to avoid airline abuses of the licensing system. Relations with the Government meant that longer-term plans could not be sustained, nor could these be supplied by the Board of Trade.

Given these failings, were ATLB reasons for decisions of any value at all? Certainly in major decisions the Board lived up to its promise to give full reasons. On giving BEA a licence (A300/4) to Malta as late as 8 March 1967, the Board described at length its criteria for licensing a second operator on the route[59] and, in refusing North Atlantic scheduled services to British Eagle and Caledonian Airways on 22 May 1968 (applications A7146, A7154) the Board set out detailed 'considerations of policy' in a 275 paragraph decision. (When, in 1972, British Caledonian successfully applied for North Atlantic licences, arguments in that case were largely based on the considerations set out in 1968).

Such an approach might have aided consideration of individual routes or decisions (especially those involving prestige services) but it failed to give operators longer term guidance. They would have wanted to know:[60] firstly, the relevance of any ATLB standards or principles (e.g. whether the 'growth formula' applied); secondly, the broader policy applicable (e.g. the ATLB long term policy on scheduled/charter balance, dual designation, etc.); thirdly, the degree to which any particular decision was intended to guide any future decisions, and fourthly, the findings of fact upon which the decision was based and those aspects of the Board's own knowledge relied upon.

The non-emergence of principles or standards and the Board's decline into *ad hoccery* largely accounts for the lack of the first three desiderata. On the fourth count, there were further problems. The Regulations gave the ATLB a duty to give reasons for decision, but stated that there should not be a requirement to disclose any information either received under section 2(3) consultations with the Minister, or required from any person (in pursuance of Regulation 9) and which was regarded as confidential.[61] An ATLB statement in a tariff decision of 9 December 1970 indicated its reliance on voluntary disclosure. It said that as the airlines were unwilling that these financial details should be made public, it could refer to them 'only in general terms'. In the absence of such disclosures, parties to a case were in no position to challenge submissions or ATLB findings. The problem was especially severe for non-parties to the case (e.g. independent members of the public challenging fare increases). A final hurdle was finding out which figures the ATLB had accepted as valid in making its decision. Of necessity the Board did not disclose commercial information of a confidential nature, but where information was not of this kind, its approach varied. In some cases e.g. North Atlantic decisions, it would offer its own assessment of traffic saying e.g. 'We reject the applicant's figures as too optimistic; we think that growth will be between 5 and 8 per cent per annum'. In other cases it might merely note that the estimates were 'over optimistic' or traffic 'insufficient' and so would fail to offer guidance for future applications. Again, a root cause was the ATLB's lack of a research-base: a great deal depended on its knowledge of a particular operation. It did not have data covering all routes, consequently, when it relied on parties to the case for figures or information, it would be less able to give a clear indication of its own position. Its tendency to use its specialist or 'judicial' hats to disguise contentious decisions (as either 'matters of judgment' or as issues on which it claimed the final say) further inhibited the supply of detailed reasoning.

The ATLB came up against a set of variables to be encountered in many systems of industrial regulation, these included: technological innovations; changing economic conditions and aims; changes in governmental policies and variations inherent in describing any problem of great complexity. In the face of these, the case law system failed as a method of developing regulatory policy. In road transport licensing a similar system had already survived for over thirty years but aviation proved a more difficult field for a number of reasons: the variables noted above all existed in more acute form; each decision involved larger sums of money and was therefore more contentious; the parties affected by any decision were a close-knit group, well-equipped to contest ATLB rulings and aviation decisions were both more politically contentious than and more closely connected to departmental activity than road transport issues. It has not been demonstrated, however, that the aviation licensing questions of the 1960s were inherently non-justiciable in the sense that no body using trial-type procedures could have developed lasting and legitimate decisions or policies.[62] A realistic conclusion is that the ATLB with its particular package of procedures and attitudes failed to *render* them justiciable. This might have been done had the Board been able to research problems in depth and sustain policies against governmental opposition. As it was, its public hearings were used to some (mainly symbolic) effect, but the Board lacked the resources, legal powers or breadth of perspective that might have helped to harness them effectively into the wider system of regulation.

Policymaking Outside the Trial-Type Hearing

If case law failed to give operators any lasting guidance as to regulatory policies were there other methods of disclosing licensing objectives in the ATLB system? The role of four principal devices should be considered in this context.

(a) *ATLB Announcements on Policy*

The ATLB would, on rare occasions, use their 'Civil Aviation Licensing Notices' (CALN) for consultation or to make announcements of policy. Thus, in the summer of 1966, they published the BIATA representation concerning 'Provision 1' (CALN 256) and followed this, on ministerial orders, with publication of their own, and the Minister's views (CALN 287). Such a procedure, however, involved a formal exchange of views followed by a pronouncement of policy rather than any proper consultative process (neither the 1960 nor the 1964 regulations set down any procedures to govern rule-making by the Board).

The publication of ATLB policies in CALN notices was not, however to avoid challenge. When, after a number of 'test cases' on the 1 in 20 tour organizer concessions, the Board published a notice of policy (CALN 474) stating that the concession would not normally be allowed on holidays over three nights long, Court Line challenged this on appeal.[63] The airline argued that the ATLB had not considered the case on its merits but had expected applicants:

> ... to convince them that a policy which they had promulgated in their licensing notices—giving no reasons for it—was wrong.[64]

Court Line urged that the case should be decided by reference to those considerations set out in the 1960 Act. As we have already noted, Sir John Lang agreed with the appellants that the Board should have given reasons for ending a well-established policy and recommended allowing the appeals.[65] The appeal was allowed and, though the ATLB might have been at fault in failing to consult on or justify its new policy, the appeal did deal a blow to the Board's attempts to structure its discretion.[66] Sir John came close to finding that the ATLB's deciding on the grounds of a policy unsupported by reasons was *prima facie* evidence that they had not considered the merits properly. In any case, the ATLB's efforts to indulge in rule-making were defeated. It did not attempt to use a pronouncement of this kind again, but preferred to announce policies and reasons in its Annual Report.

(b) *Annual Reports*

The ATLB used its reports to perform a number of functions: to set down rules and principles for future guidance; to publish or clarify rules or principles laid down or implied in cases and to argue the Board's point of view against that of the Board of Trade. The Second Report of 1961–62 was the first one to be put to such use and dealt with issues arising out of decisions, including: relations with the Minister; pooling agreements; surface carriers; ministerial directives; cross subsidization; potential services; 'wasteful duplication'; 'material diversion and the 'growth formula'. Some of the principles discussed were of major importance, for example, the ATLB's statement that it would close its mind to any 'persuasive implications' received from the Minister.[67] Others gave useful details on policies stated less clearly in case law, thus 'wasteful duplication' was broken down into five further considerations.

A year later the Third Report (para. 28–9) disclosed further particulars about the principles used in domestic tariff decisions. The problems involved were discussed at length and the Board's conclusions set out in detail. This was clearly intended to guide airline applications; so much so that in the Board's Eighth Annual Report of 1967–68 the ATLB stated that it had based its policy on those principles set out in 1962–63. The 1967–68 report proceeded to examine how far the Board had managed to put the principles into effect and discussed at length (49 paragraphs out of a total report of 109 paragraphs) the problems encountered in developing tariffs policy. As well as setting down principles, therefore, the annual report was used in an effort to explain the thinking behind policies.

The ATLB employed its reports to justify its own policies as in 1968–69 when, following an adverse appeal decision, it repeated its arguments in favour of 'Provision 1' price control and contested the wisdom of the Minister's decision.[68] In this manner the Board often used to argue for changes in the Minister's approach. Early reports all criticized the lack of overall policy direction given by the Government and repeatedly urged that the government should directly subsidize the operator on 'social service' routes (these promptings went unheeded until the 1971 Act). When proposals for changing the licensing system emerged (e.g. the Labour Government's White Paper of 1969) Annual Reports were used as a means of comment (see Tenth and Eleventh Reports).

Did the reports provide the guiding principles lacking in case law? Certainly they clothed a number of principles in greater detail, but examination of these reveals a high mortality rate. The principles of the second report largely amplified those rules of competitive licensing set out in case law and suffered a parallel decline in the years to 1967. Those domestic tariff principles set out in the third report were shown, even by the ATLB's own review of their operation, to be largely unhelpful. Thus, topics considered in the 1967–8 review had included: airline efficiency; the level of 'reasonable profits', and policy on loss-making routes. The Board admitted that when the issue of efficiency had come up in a recent case the evidence received had not been conclusive enough to make this a factor in its decision.[69] It conceded that, due to the airlines' general failure to make profits, the need to define 'reasonable profit' had not arisen,[70] and in two respects little was achieved in policy on loss-making routes: whereas the ATLB had urged the Government directly to subsidize loss-making areas and had said that it would rely on the operator's judgment as to the most suitable level of fares on such routes, the Government had not directly subsidized and the ATLB had overruled the operators on tariff levels in 1965.

The Annual Reports served a certain purpose in publishing and developing rules or principles or in explaining and arguing for policies but they enjoyed no greater success than did the case law in setting down lasting guidance. Such principles and standards as emerged met the same obstacles as those arising out of cases, namely, the contradictions of ATLB and departmental policy, the problems of rapidly changing economic and political conditions, the lack of a research base, the complexity of the subject-matter and the pressures towards flexibility and exception.

(c) *Ministerial Policy Statements*

It has already been noted that Mr Jenkins' policy statement of 17 February 1965 had no basis in law; it was meant, however, to provide guidance for the ATLB. Did it do this?

BEA and British Eagle considered the statement to be of some importance. In doing so they had an eye open to potential appeals and to the Government's role in allocating traffic rights. The ATLB, on the other hand, treated the statement as having no force and its Chairman told the 1967 Select Committee that he was not interested in the Minister's policy. Nevertheless, it seems that with a few exceptions, the ATLB acted in conformity with the statement, dropping its 'growth formula' and dealing with competition more on the merits of each case. To this extent the ministerial statement may be seen as guidance, but, for it to have been of real significance at the time, the airlines would have to have seen the ATLB taking cognizance of the new policy. With successive Annual Reports denying the relevance of the Minister' statement, this would have demanded great perspicacity. As the years passed, the statement, which was couched in terms of the near future, lost relevance as economic conditions changed. Thus, for example, BUA gradually did increase its frequencies on the major domestic trunk routes and a number of international routes were given in double designation. A further factor was the advent of the Edwards Committee which in 1968–69 was considering the shape of 'British Air Transport in the Seventies'. The Committee espoused competitive policies more akin to those of the early ATLB than to those of the Jenkins policy statement. Consequently, the looming presence of the Committee tended to counter any weight left in the restrictive policies of the 1965 statement. If the latter did give any real guidance then it did so only for a short period of time, it did so unacknowledged by the ATLB, subject to exceptions and without much long-term reliance being placed upon it by airlines.

There were no other such statements during the life of the ATLB. The Minister, however, was given an opportunity to state his inclusive tours pricing policy after BIATA had made a (section 4) representation to the ATLB on minimum price control in Autumn 1966. His statement appeared together with the slightly divergent views of the ATLB, but though it may have had some influence on operators, it was not adopted wholeheardedly by the ATLB who continued to pursue their own policies on 'Provision 1' price control. The resulting confusion has already been described. The other opportunity for ministerial statements of policy, was, of course, provided by the appeals system. This, however, served to fragment rather than co-ordinate policy-making. In all, Ministers conspicuously failed, by any method, to impose on the licensing system those consistent objectives missing from ATLB decision making.

(d) *Informal Communications*

The licensing staff of the airlines gained a degree of insight into ATLB decisions through the grapevine of a closely knit industry. They obtained a more complete understanding of ATLB decisions than was available from the written page by seeing and hearing the Board's responses to certain arguments. Those experienced in appearing before the Board have indicated that they developed a 'feel' or 'working understanding' of ATLB policies, based on a combination of formal and informal sources. Thus, for example, the attitudes of individual Board members towards certain arguments would be noted as background for future applications and hearings.

Operators looked at case law and appeal rulings, not in meticulous detail, as a lawyer might, but as part of a general scheme allowing the experienced advocate to judge, sometimes accurately, the Board's approach. Except in relation to a few specific matters (e.g. financial safety) the ATLB did not use informal negotiations as a part of the licensing process. They would not, for example, tell an operator that, if a certain action was taken, a licence would be given. Nor would an operator be warned that non-use of a particular licence placed it in jeopardy. The ATLB would await the application and discuss the matter at a formal hearing. In this respect the ATLB's concept of itself as acting 'quasi-judicially' restricted its use of informal control methods. Nor could it be said that informal communications served to disclose longer-term policies to operators—the Board itself had difficulty enough in predicting the lifespan of individual policies.

At most, informal methods served to explain, more fully, attitudes on individual decisions or on particular routes.

It must be concluded that none of the four 'ancillary' methods of developing or disclosing policy that were used in the ATLB system amounted to a coherent rule-making system or managed to substitute to any real extent for the lack of either a lasting ATLB case law or overall policy guidance from the Minister. In many respects they only constituted further elements in a fruitless contest between an 'independent' tribunal and a government department.

6
Conclusions: Regulation by Tribunal

The Board faced massive problems on its political and judicial fronts. Was it, in spite of these, able both to regulate in the public interest and to structure the aviation industry efficiently? It seems not. In a number of respects the ATLB was unable to exert positive control over operators because it lacked the required information, resources or expertise. This was especially so in the financial areas where the Board had two principal aims: to ensure that operators were financially viable and to impose economic direction over the industry in its licensing decisions.

The first of these objectives involved something of a contradiction. The ATLB was precluded by sections 2(4) and 3(4) of the 1960 Act from considering safety matters in licensing, but it did attempt to ensure that licences were only issued to operators enjoying a sound financial base. To this end the Board, from its earliest days, used its Regulation 9 and 18 powers to require applicants to furnish information relating to financial competence.[1]

Regulation 18 powers were used selectively to require certain operators to submit quarterly profit and loss accounts, balance sheets and estimates of cash flow. The Board often required licence holders to explain this information and held private discussions with them where commercially confidential information was involved.[2] They warned that they would not normally grant licences to operators who failed to submit up-to-date accounts.[3]

Apart from the difficulty of obtaining figures in the first place, the absence of a common accounting system among the smaller airlines limited the value to the ATLB of such information. The Board annually expressed concern at the precarious state of operators' finances. In 1961–62 ten operators ceased to operate and, in the following year, four more failed. The Board, in 1963, began to refuse licences on the grounds of financial unfitness, but operators continued to drop out (two in both 1964 and 1965).

By 1967 the ATLB's central concern was the financial soundness of the tour organizers associated with airlines for inclusive tours. In that year it approached the Association of British Travel Agents (ABTA) and requested voluntary disclosure of organizers' financial details at licensing hearings. The ATLB had no power to order the supply of such information and, in 1968, noted the lack of response from tour organizers.[4]

The problem of stability proved haunting: in 1968 two more operators went into liquidation and the Board described its financial responsibilities as 'a source of continual anxiety'.[5] After the demise of a larger operator, British Eagle, together with the fall of Transglobe Airlines, the Board admitted in 1969 the need for financial control and supervision of a kind that, with its limited information and resources, it had been unable to offer.[6] By 1972 a total of over 31 ATLB-regulated airlines had ceased to operate.

Although, by pressure to increase paid-up capital, the Board was able to secure some strengthening of tour organizers' finances by 1971 and was then able to publish aggregate profit and loss figures for 57 of the larger tour operators, it still had to warn them that their margins were too small and that some were indulging in 'suicidal price cutting'.[7] The ATLB, however, did at no point in its life fight for the increased resources that it would have needed in order to impose real control in the area of financial safety.

As far as general economic control of the industry was concerned, the Board was in no better position. In issuing licences to operators it relied, to a great extent, on figures submitted by applicants or objectors whether in writing in advance of, or actually at, a public hearing. It was never able to build up a workable picture of operations for its own use by collating information from operators. It did accumulate some statistical information by use of Regulation 18 powers (this resulted in operators having to send the same figures to both the ATLB and the Ministry), and it stated, in its Third Report, that it wished to publish this in order to supplement the Ministry of Aviation's Annual Abstract of Statistics' and the 'Monthly Digest of Statistics' prepared by the Central Statistical Office. Operators objected that disclosure would damage them commercially but the ATLB negotiated a compromise.[8] The result was the introduction, in 1964, of the Ministry's new publication 'Operating and Traffic Statistics of United Kingdom Airlines'. Detailed traffic and operating statistics, previously given only for scheduled services, were provided for charter flights in quarterly bulletins.

In spite of the acquisition and limited publication of a certain amount of information, the ATLB always lagged behind the operators. In no sense did it lead or structure the industry by positive regulation. It failed to research route or price structures in depth. This meant that cases were decided *ad hoc* and, instead of building up networks of services, the operators applied for individual licences only to end up with a hotch-potch of routes. The ATLB could not invite applications, e.g. to fill networking gaps, nor could they, by such means, promote the supply of regional services. They could only await applications from airlines. They could not judge the suitability of any particular route to an operator since they were more concerned to see that an airline had short-term viability. Long-term structuring of the airlines' different roles was not possible and neither could the growth rate of the overall industry be predicted. Since the Board's supply of information was insufficient, it could not, given competing applications for a route, tell which of the two operators was the more efficient.

If any innovations (for example in types of service to be supplied) were required to meet future market conditions then any movement towards these had to come from the airlines—the ATLB found it difficult enough to assess the existing market. New developments in licensing forms and conditions did evolve in the 1960s, for example: ITX fares (low fares for tour excursions by scheduled services); tour organizer concessions; split charters (flights able to be shared by more than one charterer); relaxation of 'Provision 1'; multiple journey 'E' cargo licences and automatically expiring licences, but in the case of none of these could it be argued that the ATLB was the instigator of change. Though the ATLB was liberal in approving licence changes it responded to, rather than instituted, innovations. The Board's relationship with the Government meant, moreover, that any change in a licence condition (e.g.'Provision 1') tended to be fraught with delays and confusions.

Over the broad area of financial regulation the picture was of a

Board unable to control the finances of the airlines or tour organizers in an effective way. The legal framework of the 1960 Act largely overlooked the financial-safety connection and failed to give the Board powers of routine economic direction. The main difficulties were: the small size of the ATLB staff; its inability to prepare financial data fully; the nature of the industry (many operators relied on seasonal charter traffic which provided an unstable demand and financial data soon became outdated); the lack of a common accounting system among airlines; airlines' failure to submit up-to-date accounts and the Board's inability to publish full financial data for public scrutiny.

That the ATLB failed to co-ordinate its functions is now clear. Although the individuals making up the ATLB and their staff were highly respected in the industry, the ATLB did achieve the worst of a number of worlds in combining its various powers. Politically, it failed to co-ordinate with the Government to create a workable division of functions. As a result, domestic and international tariffs were at odds and the appeals system destroyed the coherency of ATLB policy without replacing it with anything else. Even safety regulation was inadequately co-ordinated. Air Operators Certification was not considered in conjunction with air transport licensing and the advantages of examining the relationship between an operator's financial and operational safety records were neglected.

As a body attempting to combine expertise with adjudicative functions, the ATLB also failed. This was not merely the result of political interference. The Board did not have the resources to be able to develop its own policy. Such a principle as the 'growth formula' could not be sustained without extensive research into the markets involved and the charter/scheduled service balance could not be resolved without research into the effects of charter flights on each of the scheduled services. Even free from ministerial interference, the ATLB would have needed greater resources to have been able to structure its decision-making in a viable manner. Its regulatory failures reflected the difficulties it encountered in attempting to make aviation licensing issues justiciable. Barry Boyer has summarized the general problem of approaching complex economic or 'polycentric' problems with trial-type procedures:

... it might be asked whether some problems are inherently and irreducibly polycentric, or, on the other hand, whether polycentric problems are simply situations in which standards of decision have not been formulated. On the theoretical level, it seems likely that most of the problems confronting administrative agencies would prove capable of solution through application of general principles—if social and value preferences were well established ... and if the state of knowledge were sufficient to provide theoretical constructs that would adequately account for all relevant variables. When these conditions do not exist, however, the agency confronted with a polycentric problem must seek to find the optimal—or at least an acceptable—trade-off. Frequently this task must be performed in the context of administrative adjudication; yet trial-type procedure may well be inherently ill-suited to the job.'[9]

In the case of the ATLB little attempt was made to develop a level of expertise and a stock of 'theoretical constructs' that would have served to account for all relevant variables. Its adjudication lacked a developed context, its independence was ill-defined and its expertise insufficient. This was an agency offering a modest combination of powers and resembling previous tribunals: when subjected to political rigours, however, it failed in its blinkered moderation.

7
From Tribunal to Regulatory Agency

It was argued in Chapter 1 that British governments, administrators and academics have failed to pay sufficient attention to the kinds of machinery used to control industry: in particular, it was said that the regulatory agency has been neglected. Civil aviation, however, has been to some extent exceptional: some thought has been given to the problem of machinery. It is thus necessary to examine how, in the late 1960s, a new regulatory system came to be devised, how the deficiencies of the ATLB were perceived by legislators and parliamentarians, and how proposed changes in agency framework were intended to cure the ills that proved fatal to the ATLB.

The first major criticism of the ATLB system of licensing came in the report of the Select Committee on Nationalized Industries (BEA) of 1967,[1] which looked at the efficiency of the ATLB and in particular the effect of its licensing regime on BEA.

A great deal of evidence was submitted to the effect that the decisions of the ATLB were unpredictable: BEA said that they were made *ad hoc* and 'without regard for the long-term planning requirements of either Corporation or the private airlines'.[2] Since Appeal Commissioners could not look at the 'wider aspects' of licensing, the situation on appeal was said by the Corporation to be as bad as at first instance:[3] the system had resulted in 'a permanent state of uncertainty for all British carriers'.[4] Private operators made similar criticisms: Sir Myles Wyatt, Chairman of BUA referred to the independent airlines' 'complete uncertainty as to the future'[5] and noted that, in both ATLB and appeal decisions, there had been 'an element of capriciousness'.[6] He asserted that the system achieved the worst of two worlds. Independents were allowed to equip for competition but were too frustrated by the licensing procedure to be able to operate properly.

The committee accepted that the ATLB had failed to create policy via case law,[8] and so had not provided stability for British civil aviation. It was emphasised that the interests of the industry could not be met 'unless each airline operator has reasonable certainty as to how he is able to conduct his operations'.[9]

On the issue of ATLB independence, evidence was submitted of the Board's 'arm's length' policy and of ensuing difficulties. As has been noted, witnesses from the ATLB and the Board of Trade disagreed as to whether the former had actually followed the guidance offered by the Jenkins policy statement of 1965. Of one thing, however, the committee was sure:

> . . . the inherent uncertainty of the whole situation has been clearly and publicly demonstrated.[10]

When the committee suggested, as a solution, the introduction of a departmental system of licensing wholly within the Board of Trade, witnesses from that department, surprisingly perhaps, defended the existing structure, arguing that fairness and openness demanded appeals to an outside body. They said that to abandon the appeals system would be unacceptable to operators and that the creation of an independent appeal body would not be tolerated by the government.

The Committee, however, was not impressed with the argument that an appeals system was necessary in order to promote confidence in the licensing decisions reached (Report IV paragraph 50). They felt that drastic changes were required and concluded that the Board of Trade should regulate competition with the Corporations. As for the use of an independent agency, they said that a 'façade of independence' would not promote confidence and that 'actual independence in implementation had been seen to result only in confusion' (Report IV paragraph 52). They proposed that matters of air safety should be left with the Board of Trade, that operators should fix their own fare levels and that, since the ATLB would then be left without functions, it should be wound up (Report IV paragraph 56).

In spite of its radical recommendations (perhaps because of them), the Select Committee report, which was published in October 1967, did not have enormous impact on civil aviation regulation. This was due, firstly, to the Committee's consideration of the ATLB from a narrow 'Corporation' viewpoint, and, secondly, because it was overshadowed by the President of the

Board of Trade's announcement in July 1967 that he was setting up a committee under Sir Ronald Edwards (Chairman of the Beecham Group) to enquire into the financial and economic prospects of the civil aviation industry and to examine methods of regulating competition.

The subsequent report *British Air Transport in the Seventies*[11] dealt with the major problems of regulation in detail, making particular suggestions as well as giving broader guidance on substantive policies. Of twenty chapters only one dealt specifically with licensing but others considered problems of central importance to regulation (e.g. the role of private airlines).

The Edwards Committee and ATLB Licensing

Edwards noted the 1967 Select Committee's recommendation that the ATLB should be wound up but stated that their own evidence showed the faults to lie in the licensing system rather than the Board itself.[12] Ten main criticisms of ATLB licensing were set out: an absence of clear statements of policy and a lack of case law had hindered operators in predicting the results of cases; insufficient opportunity had been given for airlines to develop viable route structures; the Corporations had been over-protected; insufficient attention had been given to developing regional air services; insufficient investigation of airlines' general finances had been undertaken in licensing; the Board had not insisted on the submission by airlines of sufficient statistical data on which growth and performance could be judged; applications had taken too long to be processed; the difficulties of obtaining traffic rights had been ignored in licensing international routes and too little attention had been paid to the safety implications of the ATLB's financial investigations.[13]

Edwards accepted in part an ATLB contention that it had been limited by its terms of reference but considered that it had interpreted these 'too narrowly'.[14] On the other hand, the Committee were impressed by the clarity of those ATLB reasons for decisions that they had studied and thought that many criticisms of the ATLB were based on a misunderstanding of the purpose of the 1960 Act which, they said, had not been to give private operators complete freedom at the expense of the Corporations.[15] As far as criticism of the Board's failure to issue policy statements or to take initiatives (e.g. to improve route structures), the ATLB's defence again presupposed a court-like role: it asserted that the 1960 Act did not provide for it to do such things; it was merely obliged to hear individual applications with reference to the Act. The Board pointed to two main defects in the system for developing policy: there was no method by which a matter of policy arising in a case could reach the Minister unless a party appealed; and, there was no compulsion on the Board to follow ministerial appeal decisions.[16]

Edwards concluded that, no matter how the licensing system was to be administered, there was 'an imperative need for future licensing policy to incorporate provisions by which all statements of policy are formulated by the Government from time to time and are published in a statutory instrument as the legally binding guidelines upon which licensing policy should be based'.[17] It was considered that this innovation would solve the appeals problem and improve procedure. As far as appeals themselves were concerned, it was felt that airlines had increasingly come to regard the ATLB hearing as no more than a 'preliminary round in any major case':[18] Edwards proposed a much stricter limitation of the grounds for an appeal, and the use of the courts or a special tribunal, rather than Ministerial Commissioners for hearing them.[19] Limitation of grounds was to be achieved by reference to the statutory guidelines already mentioned and by limiting appeals to either points of law (e.g. assertions that the Board had acted *ultra vires*), or to allegations that decisions were perverse (i.e. that they could not reasonably be brought within the declared policy of the Government as set out in the statutory instrument). No new evidence would be permitted on appeal.

Edwards was confident that in both types of appeal there would be issues that could be decided by the courts, or by a special legal tribunal.[20] The choice between ordinary courts and an appeals tribunal was left open, but the Committee would have been happy to see an appeals system similar to that operating for decisions on Air Operators Certificates (in which the appellate tribunal was appointed by the Lord Chancellor and might include assessors).

A further advantage claimed for the system of declaring policy was that it would cause policy statements to be written 'in terms sufficiently clear to be generally understood and, if necessary, to stand the test of judicial interpretation'.[21] In order that the

Government might modify policy in the light of a particular decision, it was suggested that the Board of Trade should have power to direct the licensing authority to suspend a decision pending a reappraisal of, and if necessary, a change in the statutory guidance.[22]

The ATLB had used no pre-hearings process but Edwards recommended that the new authority should follow the American Civil Aeronautics Board (CAB) and adopt such a practice. This would streamline procedure by sifting evidence, by disposing of differences of fact and by isolating the relevant issues.

The future authority was to improve on the ATLB by introducing a more positive regulatory role into licensing procedures, with the agency itself initiating proposals for change in the route structures of airlines and by ensuring that the relationship between technical standards and financial resources was kept constantly under review. Here the Committee differed from the 1967 Select Committee, which had thought that technical safety could be left with the Board of Trade and that airlines should be allowed to regulate their own finances. Edwards considered that financial weakness and safety were related and noted that, on five occasions in the ATLB era, the withdrawal of Air Operators Certificates had not been found necessary because the operator had gone out of business for financial reasons.

The Committee was not satisfied with the division of duties between the Board of Trade and the ATLB. In the ATLB system, responsibility for tariffs had been divided but Edwards wanted all tariff functions to be the responsibility of one authority since domestic, international, inclusive tour and charter pricing policies interacted and should be considered jointly, since the staff required to develop positive tariff policies would be more economically deployed under one authority, and because there was a good case for requiring certain aspects of international tariff regulation to be subject to public hearings.[23]

It was thought that traffic rights should also be the responsibility of the new agency. Edwards was not, however, unaware of the tension involved in hiving-off important functions, and yet retaining governmental control:

> We recognize that traffic rights negotiations may sometimes involve issues and interests which run beyond civil aviation, and also that negotiations may well involve important issues of policy, which are the prerogative of Ministers. Nevertheless, in the inter-

ests of keeping the whole task of supporting and developing British civil aviation in one set of hands, we recommend that the Authority should be in a position to carry the main weight, in association with the Foreign and Commonwealth Office, of these negotiations in most cases. We recognize, however, that some of the major negotiations may go to the root of policy and that the sponsoring department which will remain responsible for general policy must reserve the right to concern itself with these'.[24]

The range of functions given to the new authority was thus to be:[25]

(1) The issue of route licences and enforcement of their terms.
(2) Route structure reviews.
(3) The main work in negotiating traffic rights.
(4) Regulation of operator and tour operator finances and accounting procedures.
(5) Consultation with and advising the Government on regional aviation (including subsidies).
(6) The review of airline mergers and consequent licence variation.
(7) Co-ordination of economic and technical safety regulation.
(8) The collection, preparation and issue of statistical and financial data for the industry on a standardized basis.
(9) The making and publication of economic studies on important aspects of air transport.
(10) The consideration of consumer representations.

The new body was to be a Civil Aviation Authority (CAA). In contemplating the framework of the CAA four alternative ways to produce an improved agency had been considered: (1) to create a strengthened ATLB; (2) to place economic and technical regulation in two separate bodies outside government;[26] (3) to have all regulation within the government; (4) to place all regulatory functions outside the government in one Civil Aviation Authority headed by a board working to policy instructions. Whichever structure was selected, the Government was to formulate general aviation policy.[27]

The first choice, involving minimum change, was rejected as perpetuating the problems of dividing technical and economic regulation. The idea of two boards was abandoned since the difficulties of separating technical and economic regulation would have remained and some issues would still have fallen between two stools. A government department might have regulated and co-ordinated efficiently but the Committee stated that:

> Independents fear that they might not get a fair deal from a government department responsible also for the financial health of the nationalized Air Corporations.[28]

They were also concerned that a departmental pay structure would not attract personnel of sufficient calibre for the job.

It was by a process of elimination, therefore, that the single independent authority the CAA was chosen. Policy was to be made openly and the CAA was to be free to advise the Government on its formulation. It would have its own staff, pay structure and public relations and, though finances would be supplied initially by the Government, it was to aim, in time, to support itself by licence revenues.[29] The new Authority was envisaged as firmly committed to research, it was to advise the Government on airport planning and would be responsible for the provision of Air Traffic Control Services (ATCS) and the former Air Registration Board (ARB).

Edwards stated that the statutory guidance they advocated might be elaborated by White Papers (which would lack the force of law) and that hearings would be regulated by a publicly-known machinery. They noted the difficult 'parliamentary and constitutional issues' involved in their proposal but 'took courage'[30] from the Fulton Committee's mention of air traffic control as a possible area for 'hiving-off' from central government.[31] In doing so they did not distinguish between hiving-off a regulatory as opposed to an operational function but the problem of laying down written policy guidance for the Authority was not overlooked. The committee recognized the difficulty of separating policy formulation from its daily administration.[32] They argued that the CAA 'should obviously be in close touch with the department'[33] but noted that the proposed division of functions would depend on the department's working 'on the broader front' and not reviewing the CAA's day-to-day decisions.[34] The Authority would thus be left to exercise its licensing powers with reference to statutory provisions or directions on policy issued by the department, extra-statutory documents issued by itself and minor regulatory powers, or bye laws, where Parliament had authorized the Authority to make these.

The body proposed by Edwards was thus to be very different from the ATLB. It would combine many functions formerly separated, it would act in consultation with the Government and it would lead the industry by positive action. This was the respect in which it was to resemble not so much the British tribunal as the American independent regulatory commission. It was to combine trial-type adjudication with expert management and both of these with policy-making in a politically contentious area.

Proposals on the Shape of the Industry

Edwards did not believe that there was a case for denationalizing the Air Corporations since the ownership of BOAC and BEA was held to have had little effect on their efficiency—the existence of competition was considered more important in this respect. The committee accepted a 'mixed economy' view of the future industry but rejected as 'inhibiting' a system of quantitative regulation between the two sectors (as found in Australia).[35] The Corporations and independents, it was said, should be treated equally before the Authority and, although the Corporations would bear the burden of technical innovation and international representation, there was a place in the industry for privately owned airlines and for airlines of mixed ownership.[36]

Having rejected a monolithic structure for the industry as creating more problems than it would solve,[37] it was recommended that a 'second force' airline should be set up. This was predicated on the argument that, if it was possible to have an alternative source of management and innovation, without significant loss of scale economies, this was worth doing.[38] They believed that a 'second force' could be created without seriously affecting the Corporations' prospects and envisaged the future industry as consisting of: a long-haul airline based on BOAC; a European and domestic airline based on BEA; a second force airline licensed to operate a viable structure of long-haul and short-haul routes and serving as the second UK operator in those cases where double designation was in the British interest;[39] a group of provincial airlines to operate secondary domestic and some European routes and a small number of inclusive tour and other charter specialists.

On the matter of the private airlines, Edwards said that in 1975, following rationalization (needed to counter underfinancing), they should carry about a third of British traffic (compared with a quarter in 1968). To serve as a spur to the Corporations the 'second force' airline would have to be able to compete in the world market and thus a minimum size of fleet was necessary. Edwards concluded that British United Airways (BUA) and Caledonian Airways, operating in association, presented the best chance of such an airline.[40] Plans for the second force were discussed with BUA who argued that a transfer of routes to them from BOAC would be required to establish the operator. The committee believed that a balance could be negotiated,[41] and argued that, in return for the transfer of routes, the proposed National Air Holding Board (the holder of the Corporations' assets) would be given a stake in the 'second force' relating to the size of the transfer.

Space here does not permit a detailed review of the many economic issues discussed by Edwards. An outline of the committee's general approach should, however, be noted. They favoured competition but, after review, concluded that, of domestic routes, only one (London to Newcastle) might develop sufficiently to justify competition within a decade. Internationally, they urged that competition should be allowed on the prestigious New York sector but, in Europe, the only routes justifying competition were said to be those to Paris and Brussels. They agreed with the ATLB that regional services ought to be directly subsidized by the government (with local Authority contributions) and said that routes in the difficult Highlands and Islands of Scotland ought to be operated by a British Air Services (BAS) subsidiary.

Existing policy on the minimum price control of charter tours was not endorsed: the Board had been 'too restrictionist'[42] and Edwards argued that regulatory policy should set out so as to define those scheduled routes requiring protection for public policy reasons and to allow more liberal policies to be applied to other routes. They recommended an experimental period in which price control would be abandoned and, instead of using price control to protect the public from the failure of operators, they wanted a system of bonding for inclusive tour licence holders. On tariffs for scheduled services, they saw no alternative to these being agreed at IATA conferences. They did, however, advocate that financial data submitted in domestic tariff cases to the Authority should be published.

The Labour Government's White Paper of 1969

The first official response to Edwards was a White Paper presented to Parliament in November 1969,[43] a document that was 'intended to provide a new charter for the industry for the next decade'.[44] It admitted that the 1960 licensing system had not been as successful as had been hoped and that justified criticisms had been made, especially concerning the absence of a full statement of aviation objectives and the ATLB's *ad hoc* approach to licensing.

The Government accepted the Edwards proposals for a new CAA to be placed beyond the detailed supervision of Ministers and the departmental system: a separate organization would allow a comprehensive expertise to be developed in aviation matters and CAA staff, therefore, ought to be outside the Civil Service. It was accepted that the agency would be responsible for all aspects of safety regulation (so as to co-ordinate economic and safety controls) and for civil air traffic control.

The CAA was to be established as a corporate body under a board appointed by the Board of Trade. One independent member would be responsible for consumer interests. Licensing would be by hearings, the procedure for which was to be governed by the Council on Tribunals. The new policy guidance proposal was also accepted: provision would be made for the appropriate instruments under the Act and it was cautioned that, for the sake of stability, changes in such policy would have to be infrequent.

Appeals were to be allowed from CAA decisions, but the Government was not prepared to go as far as Edwards in freeing the new agency from ministerial control. It was conceded that, as with the ATLB, appeals on grounds of law should be allowed before the courts, but the White Paper 'saw difficulty' in Edwards' recommendation that the courts or a judicial tribunal should hear appeals based on the consistency of a decision with declared policy. It was stated:

> The formal policy statement, being concerned with essentially economic criteria, is unlikely to be expressed in terms lending themselves to judicial interpretation. The consistency of the Authority's decision with the policy can best be judged by the Board of Trade, which will have drawn up the policy statement in the first place.[45]

This was a significant difference of opinion. Of this renewed support for ministerial appeals the ATLB rejoined:

> ... there must be the seeds of dissatisfaction and confusion in a system which, in the first place, accords the responsibility of deciding appeals against the decisions of a judicial tribunal to a member of the Executive, which we have always considered wrong and which, moreover, when the tribunal's decisions have been taken in conformity with declared Government policy, allows the retrospective adjustment of that policy to contrive their frustration.[46]

The government also declined to accept Edwards' recommendations that the CAA should be the main traffic rights negotiator and the authority for setting international tariffs. It was accepted that the CAA should be closely involved but it was stated that 'international negotiations ... must remain the responsibility of Ministers'[47] such questions were too closely related to civil aviation policy to be removed from Board of Trade control. The CAA's role would accordingly be to advise the DoT and to send members to attend international negotiations and meetings.

In the Government and civil service those involved were clearly aware that such an authority involved 'a number of constitutional and administrative innovations'.[48] It was to have substantial discretion but, as the White Paper put it: 'The essential feature of [its] status will be the separation between policy formation and the detailed application of policy.'[49] The Board of Trade was to be responsible for matters involving 'wider considerations than the Authority would be competent to decide'[50] but within its jurisdiction, the CAA would have a 'wide discretion'. Regarding broader issues, it would participate by advising the Government.

On shaping the industry, the White Paper largely accorded with Edwards though it differed on some significant points. The new Airways Board, it was argued, should be set up but should control BOAC, BEA and BAS rather than merely hold their combined assets. The second force airline was to be allowed but not at the expense of transferring a significant portion of the Corporations' routes. As far as the idea of an experimental abandonment of minimum price control on inclusive tours was concerned, the Government preferred the more modest course of an examination of the routes involved, followed by a gradual relaxation of restrictions.

The Conservative Party Response

Although no full parliamentary debate on the White Paper occurred until 1971, indications of Conservative reactions to the Government's proposals appeared at an earlier date. The Conservative Political Centre published John Seeking's booklet *Guidelines for Airlines* in 1970 and the trade magazine *Flight* gave an account of Conservative policy as expressed by Mr Heath in its issue of 19 February 1970.

The Tory Party wanted as independent a CAA as was possible, desiring for airlines an environment lacking political interference on matters of short-term significance and hoping to minimize opportunities for ministers to protect the British Airways Board from private sector competition. They differed from the Labour White Paper in advocating (in accordance with Edwards) that the CAA should be responsible for both international traffic rights and the approval of international fares.

On the public/private sector balance, the parties were generally in agreement—the White Paper had, after all, subscribed to the notion of freer competition for independents. As far as the second force airline was concerned, however, Conservatives agreed with Edwards, as against the White Paper, that route transfers might be necessary to set it on its feet. They accepted in the main the machinery of control proposed by Edwards and the idea of a written policy guidance system was not contested.

Conclusions

For those concerned with the administrative process, the key items in the change from ATLB to CAA regulation were the movements from a tribunalized body to a broadly-powered agency, and the choice of a system of written policy guidance as the means of yoking that agency to the governmental machine. Although, as will be seen below, debate on the guidance device took place later in Parliament, the crucial step was taken by the Edwards Committee. They saw the new guidance system as a cure for many of the ATLB's deficiencies and as somehow providing not only for the agency's freedom to develop expertise and coherent policies but also for its submission to general political control. Considering its 'innovatory' status the device was not examined in great detail. Edwards noted that there would be difficulties in separating the formulation of policy from its application but, apart from this, the wide range of problems purportedly solved by such a device was left undiscussed. It remained to be seen whether guidance could be reconciled with either the development of expertise by the agency or with the continued use of trial-type licensing procedures.

8
A New Way to Regulate:
The CAA is Created

Central to the Edwards plan was the fostering of a 'second force' airline to compete with the British Airways Board in world markets. Without such an operator it was considered that any new agency would have had little choice in major licensing decisions.[1] Before setting up the CAA, therefore, it was important for the Labour Government to ensure the birth of such an airline. The advent of the new operator was, however, beset with confusion.

In September 1969, and acting on the strength of Edwards, BUA aimed to establish itself as the 'second force' by applying to the ATLB to take over a number of BOAC's African routes. After the 1969 White Paper[2] was published, the Chairmen of BUA and Caledonian Airways met the Minister of State at the Board of Trade to discuss the possibility of a merger. BUA asked for assurances that substantial transfers of BOAC's routes would be given to the new operator but, when such promises were not forthcoming from the Labour administration, BUA withdrew its application for the African licences.

In January 1970 BOAC approached the President of the Board of Trade, Mr Roy Mason, and sought approval for the purchase of BUA (the initiative for this move had come from the principal BUA shareholders). Mr Mason announced on 5 March 1970 that the merger was acceptable to the Government in principle, a statement that resulted in Caledonian applying to the ATLB for all BUA's main domestic services and in BEA's application for BUA's European and North African networks. The ATLB deferred hearing these cases pending the outcome of BUA's ownership, which became an open question after the Board of Trade had temporarily halted BOAC's acquisition of BUA and encouraged Caledonian Airways to re-open negotiations with BUA.

At a later date (18 March 1970) Mr Mason told the House of Commons[3] that he had been misled into believing that a merger between Caledonian and BUA was not possible and that, soon after 5 March, he had discovered that negotiations were continuing. He had, therefore, decided to withhold approval for the BOAC–BUA merger on 17 March pending clarification of the position.

Caledonian and BUA continued to negotiate. In June 1970 a Conservative government was formed, one which feared that BUA would fall into BOAC hands unless the desired transfer of routes was made. In August the Government announced that Caledonian was prepared to take over BUA and that between 5 and 6 million pounds worth of BOAC routes would be transferred to the new airline.

Mr Noble, the Minister for Trade, introduced the Civil Aviation (Declaratory Provisions) Bill in the autumn of 1970 in order to give the Government powers to make this transfer. No compensation was to be given to BOAC for the consequent loss of revenue and Labour MPs were furious. Mr Roy Mason promised that his party would not be bound by 'this shameful act' and would, on return to office, restore the routes to BOAC and BEA without compensation.[4]

The Bill received the Royal Assent on 17 February 1971 and, by Statutory Instrument,[5] the transfer of a number of BOAC's African routes to Caledonian/BUA was effected. In May of that year the ATLB granted Caledonian/BUA a West African licence and deleted a number of locations from BOAC's licence. This decision was based largely on the Government's policy as set out in the instrument. The 'second force' was set on its feet and CAA regulation was further to secure its position.

The 1971 Civil Aviation Bill

In looking at the CAA as a particular type of regulatory agency it is important to bear in mind how its place in government was perceived by those involved with the 1971 Bill. What is striking in retrospect is the extent to which there was agreement between the parties on the CAA's kind of relationship to the Minister, which both major parties acknowledged involved novelty and which has since been radically changed. In moving the Bill's second reading in March 1971, Mr Michael Noble argued the case for a unified body to control economic, financial, safety and traffic aspects of aviation, and then stated of the new Authority:

> It is of course a constitutional innovation. The key point perhaps is that we are in this Bill hiving off a regulatory function. Ministers remain responsible to Parliament for policy, but detailed decision rests with the Authority.[6]

The kernel of the Bill was to be clause 3 which provided broad objectives for the CAA and for more detailed guidance to be given in writing subject to Parliament's approval. The Authority, Mr Noble said, would have discretion in balancing the objectives since the Government could not lay down guidance on each matter in advance without putting the Authority in a strait-jacket. This meant, however, that the objectives and the guidance would be in general terms, mainly about economic considerations and would 'not be suited to ultimate decision by the courts'. Appeals, he said, had therefore to be with the Secretary of State.[7]

For similar reasons, he considered that the grounds of appeal could not be limited to consistency with the guidance since it would be 'impossible to give policy sufficient precision for this to operate'.[8] Mr Noble assured MPs, however, that the Government did not intend regularly to substitute its discretion for that of the CAA and that the Secretary of State would on appeal uphold the decision of the Authority 'unless there are clearly major reasons for departing from it'.[9]

The Opposition, after objecting to further route transfers in favour of Caledonian/BUA, agreed that the Bill largely accorded with their own White Paper's ideas of a powerful and comprehensive regulatory authority. Mr Mason noted that the Authority, with all its regulatory powers was a 'major constitutional innovation' and a 'new form of corporation'[10] but he complained that the Bill was 'riddled with Ministerial interference'.[11] He was supported by Mr Rankin who argued that the Department of Trade and Industry (DoTI) would be given more power than it had had over the ATLB: it would control international fares and traffic rights, items that Edwards would have delivered into CAA hands.[12]

In Committee[13] Mr Millan outlined the difficulties of dealing with criteria in an (as then) unpublished policy guidance White

Paper but he successfully introduced an amendment to make the issue of guidance subject to a duty to consult the Authority. When the question of appeals arose, it was clear that severe difficulties were met in assessing the level of generality at which the guidance should be pitched. Mr Millan wanted to make inconsistency with the guidance the only ground of appeal.[14] and cited both Edwards and the 1969 White Paper on the point. He conceded that the Government, rather than the courts, should rule on issues of consistency, but warned that if an unlimited right of appeals was given: 'we shall repeat all the misfortunes and unfortunate history of the ATLB.'[15]

Mr Noble, said this 'essentially a legal point',[16] and repeated the arguments made at second reading: to allow such restriction the guidance would have to be laid down 'in very precise terms . . . which contained no possibility of conflict'[17] and this could not be done 'consistently with leaving the Authority any real discretion as to the matters covered in the guidance'.[18] He asserted that guidance about economic policies did not lend itself easily to precise drafting: 'We tried it and we failed.'[19] In any case, he said, the Secretary of State would be responsible to Parliament for his control of the Authority. Then, in words perhaps unfortunately echoing those of Mr Sandys in 1960, Mr Onslow added that:

> The Minister is, in any case, obliged to give his reasons for turning down appeals, so that a kind of case law ought to be built up.[20]

The Bill received the Royal Assent on 5 August 1971.

Establishing the CAA

The CAA assumed responsibility on 1 April 1972 under Lord Boyd-Carpenter, former Conservative MP, practising barrister and Minister for Transport and Civil Aviation. Close ties with the Department were secured with the appointment as Deputy Chairman of Mr Robin Goodison, formerly a Deputy Secretary in the DoTI concerned with aviation. The CAA staff also started work at Aviation House, Kingsway, on a basis of familiarity with governmental aviation policies: they had, after all, been recruited largely from the civil servants of the DoTI and were to work on secondment until finally offered contracts by the

Authority in July 1974. Continuity was ensured by the apppoint-
ment to the CAA board of Mr John Lawrie, who had chaired the
ATLB from 1970 onwards. The ATLB's small staff of twenty-
four joined the CAA's Economic Policy and Licensing (EPL)
Division, the head of which, Mr Raymond Colegate,[21] had formerly been an Assistant Secretary in the DoTI and had been
closely involved in devising the first policy guidance for the
CAA.[22] Total CAA staff concerned in economic policy and statistics was by 1973 around the 150 mark.

The Civil Service reaction to the hiving-off of aviation was
defensive. In his memoirs Lord Boyd-Carpenter commented:

> Whitehall as a whole quite clearly resented and feared the setting
> up of the CAA and the removal of work and staffs from the
> central Government machine. This showed itself very quickly.[23]

As for financial independence, the Authority was set up with a
grant-in-aid but the Government aimed to reduce this progressively until the CAA became self-sufficient.[24] It was given broad
responsibilities in addition to air transport licensing. The CAA
took over the regulation of air safety from the department both in
respect of the aircraft themselves (airworthiness) and their use
(operational safety). To this end the Airworthiness Requirements Board (ARB) was set up to advise the CAA's Controller
Safety on standards of design, construction and maintenance as
well as on the issue of Air Operators Certificates (AOCs).
Licensing of personnel (pilots, crew, etc.) was made the
responsibility of the CAA's operational safety division.

The vast majority of CAA staff (around 80 per cent) were
concerned with the provision of National Air Traffic Services
(NATS) and telecommunications; this again was a function
formerly under departmental control. The CAA was made governmental advisor on airport planning policy and was given
responsibility for setting up (by 1 April 1973) an Air Travel
Organizer's Licensing (ATOL) system.[25] (The purpose was to
protect the public from the risk of being stranded abroad by a
tour organizer's failure and also to minimize exploitation by
unscrupulous agents.) Ownership and the management of Aberdeen (Dyce) Airport plus eight smaller aerodromes in the highlands and islands of Scotland was another CAA function as was

responsibility for consumer interests,[26] the publication of statistics and ensuring the conformity of airline pricing with governmental pricing policies.[27]

For the purposes of this book, however, the CAA's noteworthy function was the regulation of the civil aviation industry by licensing. To this end it was given four general objectives in section 3 of the Civil Aviation Act 1971 (the 1971 Act): to secure the satisfaction of all substantial categories of public demand at the lowest charges consistent with high safety and both an economic return to operators, as well as the sound development of the industry; to secure that at least one operator, not controlled by the British Airways Board, should participate in those services; to encourage the industry's contribution to the balance of payments and (subject to the above) to further the interests of users of air services.

Provision for policy guidance was made in section 3(2) and (3) which empowered the Secretary of State for Trade and Industry to 'give guidance to the Authority . . . with respect to the performance of the functions conferred on it'. To be of effect such guidance had to be in writing and had to have been approved in draft by a resolution of each House of Parliament.[28]

Beyond mere 'guidance' the Secretary of State might, under section 4, give 'directions' in the case of imminent or actual war or national emergency. After consulting the Authority he might also direct on a number of other grounds, namely: in the interests of national security; in connection with foreign relations or with regard to international obligations of the UK; in order to deal with noise, vibration, pollution or other disturbances.

The CAA was as we have seen, given a number of functions formerly allocated to the Department or other agencies, (principally: air safety control; NATS; airports management and planning) the Department retained, however, a number of important tasks including: the decision of appeals; international traffic rights negotiating; environmental and noise control; the licensing of foreign operations to this country and accident investigation. Fares on international services had, in ATLB days, been finally approved by the Department, but although no statutory transfer of functions took place, the Secretary of State in 1972 administratively delegated responsibility for this task to the CAA.

The Task Ahead

The most immediate problem facing the new CAA was that of combining its different functions to create a comprehensive organization out of a number of separate bodies.

In the area of economic regulation the Authority set out to control an industry made up of two Corporations, a new second force and a number of other independent airlines at a time when growth exceeded demand. On international routes there were three major issues. There was a need, on scheduled services, for lower, cost-related fares to be set out in a rational pattern. The rules concerning charter flights required to be changed so as to provide alternatives to the much abused 'affinity group' charters. Finally, there was the question, inherited from the ATLB, of whether Laker Airways' walk-on 'Skytrain' service should be allowed on the North Atlantic route. These problems were rendered more acute by the excess of capacity already being offered on the premier scheduled routes.

On the matter of inclusive tours, the Authority faced both the need to allow the flexibility necessary to satisfy demand and also the dangers of price cutting and heavy losses. Similarly, on domestic scheduled services a major issue was the need to reconcile a flexible fares system with the control of prices in a time of inflating costs. In addition, the CAA confronted the perennial problem of sustaining the development of provincial services.

As far as the airlines themselves were concerned, the central issue was the role of the 'second force' airline. How was it to be supported in developing as a competitor for the Corporations, and how much of a privileged position was it to enjoy in relation to the other independents? Of all questions to be answered by the independent agency, these were to be the most politically contentious and the most dependent on the policy guidance system.

9
Regulating Under Government Constraint

If the CAA had to do one thing better than the ATLB this was to co-ordinate its regulatory activities with overall policy control in a manner that was politically viable. As David Coombes has said:

> It has been repeatedly explained that, if public agencies combining an adjudicative and an expert approach are to be successful, then security both in their existence and in government support for their judgements is essential.[1]

It, furthermore, had to avoid some of the practical deficiencies so clearly exhibited by the ATLB with its inconsistency and its failure to bring expertise to bear. Favouring a closer understanding with the Government was the recruitment of CAA personnel who were familiar with departmental policies and procedures. In addition, the balance of staff had also shifted in favour of the agency, whose employees outnumbered the Department in licensing and economic matters by four to one. These factors militated in favour of a body better able to resist ministerial interference than the ATLB.

Working against harmony was the Whitehall suspicion of independent power of which Lord Boyd-Carpenter spoke in his memoirs.[2] In the CAA's early years, its Chairman had a generally co-operative relationship with Ministers but one that was subject to periods of tension on specific matters. The most senior CAA officials worked in relative harmony with 'old friends' at the DoT, yet at this and lower levels there were still disagreements in particular areas (e.g. international licensing), especially where strong personalities were involved. On general policy issues the relationships of that time tend to be referred to as 'productive'. Because the CAA and the department worked in close contact on a number of issues (e.g. traffic rights negotiations and airports developments), there evolved an unavoidable process of consultation which led by the end of the seventies to a considerable degree of mutual dependence and respect. One CAA official commented:

> It is one of my jobs to ensure good relations with the Department. If these broke down and we were confined to a formal footing that would be a loss to the working of the whole system.

Staff of the CAA and DoT frequently meet to discuss policy issues 'over a beer', a process made easier because the CAA has not seen itself as a wholly 'judicial' body in the way that the ATLB did. A senior member of CAA staff has indicated that the Government was and is 'a constituency as much as any other: views have to be considered but that does not mean they are binding on the Authority'.[3] Such a comment displayed both a confidence and a breadth of views that had been missing from the CAA's predecessor.

The way in which the CAA is connected to the government machine can best be described by looking at the policy guidance system in operation, the appeals system, the traffic rights negotiating process, judicial review of the CAA and the other ways in which the Authority can be controlled or called to account.

(i) Policy Guidance

Those drafting the 1971 Act clearly intended policy guidance to do three things: to provide for government influence over broadest policy; to structure the considerations used in licensing decisions and to encourage regulatory consistency. Success or failure on the last two fronts will be judged in the following chapters, here the use of guidance in shaping the CAA's relationship with the Government is examined. A central question is whether written guidance encouraged forms of governmental control that were consistent with the CAA's developing its own approach to regulation.

Departmental officials drew up the first guidance[4] and this was laid before Parliament by the Secretary of State for Trade and Industry (Mr John Davies) in February 1972. As had been promised, general terms were used so as to allow the CAA's staff some discretion in working out detailed policies. As a general principle the Authority was reminded that it should act to serve the public needs and that it 'should aim always to impose the least restraint upon the industry'. It was urged to secure a high standard of safety and to have due regard to military and civil interests in providing air traffic and navigation services. In licensing it had to encourage services that would foster the development of UK trade or tourism and strengthen the balance of payments; to ensure that the scale and character of airlines' operations were within their resources; to allocate suitable patterns of routes and to seek to provide that efficient operators in both public and private sectors would have the opportunity to operate profitably (paragraphs 10–12).

It was not to reserve any particular type of operation to a particular sector of the industry nor to try to balance the two sectors. Entry of airlines to particular types of operation might have to be 'controlled in order to avoid undue fragmentation of effort' but it was, in general, said to be desirable that more than one airline should engage or be available to engage in each type of operation (paragraph 13). A viable network of scheduled services was to be developed so far as was necessary in terms of the CAA's statutory objectives.

The British Airways Board airlines were to remain the 'principal providers of scheduled services' (paragraph 15) and British Caledonian (B.Cal.) was to remain the principal independent scheduled airline. These airlines were to be given adequate opportunities to compete and thus the CAA was advised to limit, 'at least for some years to come', the grant to other British independent airlines of licences to serve additional international scheduled routes.

Competition was governed by paragraph 16 which provided that, subject to the limitations imposed by international relations, more than one British airline should be licensed to serve the same scheduled service route whenever the Authority was satisfied that: (1) traffic would be sufficient to support competing services profitably within a reasonable time; (2) the choice and standard of service would be increased more rapidly than would otherwise be likely.

The most controversial instructions were those providing for the 'second force' airline and are worth repeating:

> The Authority should bear in mind the need to give British Caledonian Airways adequate opportunities to develop its route

network particularly during this airline's formative years. The Authority should therefore give preference to British Caledonian Airways when licensing an additional British airline to serve an existing scheduled service route. The Authority should also give British Caledonian Airways a measure of preference over other airlines in allocating licences for new scheduled service routes and for non-scheduled services where the number or capacity of British airlines needs for the time being to be restricted. The Authority should however, in every case take account also of the considerations in paragraphs 10, 11 and 12 above and the effect of its decisions on the development of other airlines; it is not the Government's intention that any preference should be automatic or complete. (paragraph 17)

The Debate on the First Guidance

Mr Noble sought parliamentary approval for the first guidance on 13 March 1972.[5] Apart from brief preliminaries the whole debate centred on paragraph 17 and the 'second force' airline. The Opposition, only a few weeks beforehand, had been incensed by the ATLB's decision to grant B.Cal. a 15-year licence to compete with BOAC on the North Atlantic.[6] Mr Millan saw this as a 'scandalous'[7] dying shot against the Corporation and he objected to further routes being taken from BOAC. Mr Noble assured him that there would be no more transfers.[8]

On the general level of guidance, there were few strong feelings. Mr Millan thought that, apart from paragraph 17, the guidance was vague and 'platitudinous' but in contrast, Mr Michael McNair-Wilson considered that it was too rigid.[9] In winding-up, Mr Noble did not apologize for the 'second force': his party had foreseen the requirement to give B.Cal. the resources needed to set it on its feet and was not ashamed of its policy.[10] The guidance was approved.

This document might have thrown up more problems had not those who were later to interpret it been closely involved in its drafting. Lord Boyd-Carpenter was to agree with the Chairman of the Select Committee on Nationalized Industries in 1975 that the prior involvement in DoT drafting of the 1971 Act of the CAA's later Head of Economic Department, Mr Raymond Colegate, had gone far in ensuring that the Authority did not misunderstand its objectives.[11] Mr Colegate himself considered the guidance system to be innovatory: unlike the ATLB the CAA would not operate in a policy vacuum and, if the Government desired to alter policy, he said that it would not tinker around with appeals but would openly change the guidance.[12]

When the guidance emerged it did not take the form of a precise statutory instrument (as Edwards had advocated) but, as we have seen, was set out in broader terms. As a result, it proved to be of limited assistance as a guide to individual cases. As shall be clear from the review of CAA case decisions in Chapter 11, each paragraph could be countered by quoting another, and 'escape clauses' were provided. Thus the paragraph 17 preference for B.Cal. was not 'automatic or complete' and was subject to other paragraphs: the rights of other 'efficient operators' to profits might be considered under paragraph 11 or BAB's position as 'principal providers' of scheduled services under paragraph 15. The guidance did not define precisely those cases where competition would be allowed: traffic had to be 'sufficient' within a 'reasonable' time service 'improved' and total UK share of traffic 'increased'. It was up to the Authority to lend some precision to such general rules, principles and standards.

On certain issues the guidance was fairly specific, but only for a limited period. The paragraph 17 preference for B.Cal. was to be a determining factor[13] in the CAA granting, against opposition, that airline's applications for scheduled services to Toronto, Singapore and Boston/Atlanta/Houston[14] in 1973. Later in that year licences were issued 'on the same basis' for services to Brussels and Algiers.[15] Once B.Cal. had received these services to add to those West African routes already gained either by statutory transfer or from ATLB licensing, it was generally considered that the preference had been used up and, after the Brussels case, B.Cal. representatives did not rely heavily on paragraph 17 as a basis for argument before the CAA.

In decisions other than those involving paragraph 17 the first guidance offered information of little more value than had been contained in the ATLB's early policies. Some assistance, however, was given for the investment planning of the larger airlines: B.Cal. was told that it would be protected sufficiently to allow it to secure its 'second force' position; BAB was told that it would remain the principal provider of scheduled services. Little help was given either on short and medium term policy or to smaller operators. This lack of detailed policy largely flowed in the early years, from the CAA's level of expertise which then was not such as to allow it to supplement the guidance with its own policy rulings.

As far as the CAA was concerned, the job of the guidance was to serve as a formal limitation of its discretion that superseded other, more covert, forms of government control. To some extent this was the case: in a review of the Authority's first three years of operation[16] Lord Boyd-Carpenter emphasised that the CAA's position as an independent body made it necessary for the Government to work out and state its policy clearly and publicly in a way not done in the past. Again differing from the ATLB, the CAA Chairman saw the development of expertise as a precondition of real independence. Five months later he indicated the CAA's intention to accumulate experience and information to an extent 'never available before either to the ATLB or to the relevant Ministry'.[17] Given that the independent agency was attempting to build up continuity of expertise and policies, the greatest threat to it lay in the shape of an over-hasty change in guidance, whether this was to arise from a turn-about in the approach of one administration or from a change in the party of government. The Authority and the guidance system faced such a change with the installation of a Labour government in March 1974 and its re-election in October of that year.

The 'Shore Review' of Civil Aviation Policy

The new Labour Secretary of State for Trade, Mr Peter Shore, began a review of civil aviation policy in early 1974. Some feared the execution of those threats made by Labour MPs (e.g. Mr Mason) in 1971 to give back to BOAC the West African routes transferred to B.Cal. Indeed the Parliamentary Secretary, Mr Clinton Davies, told the Commons, on 25 March 1974, that this was one of the matters under review.[18]

In December, 1974, Mr Shore announced that his policy review would consider what changes were desirable in the first guidance in the light of the economic and financial position and prospects of the industry.[19] He indicated that the organizations most closely interested had been offered opportunities of making their views known to the reviewing committee and he invited other organizations or individuals to make representations.

Although the DoT was primarily responsible for the review,

the CAA played an important part. Apart from discussions, CAA participation involved the submission of a considerable volume of detailed research studies to the team of DoT civil servants who were conducting the review. These documents covered the whole range of CAA responsibilities under the first guidance and the operation was taken by the Authority as an opportunity to mount a major reappraisal of many of the policies it had developed in its first three years. These staff reports were not merely outlines of policy but the results of a long period of continuous work in analysing markets and forecasts: they were intended to provide the basis for future CAA policies.

The range of questions examined by the CAA was extensive: it was known from the start that central issues would be the position of B.Cal. as the 'second force', and the level of competition to be allowed on international routes, but when, at a later date,[20] it emerged that Mr Shore also intended the Laker's 'Skytrain' issue to be reviewed, the CAA responded with further studies. As well as these topics the CAA dealt with such matters as: the charter/scheduled services division; private/public sector balance; strategies best served to maximise UK airline earnings; the economics of domestic services; the interaction between European scheduled and inclusive tour markets; the development of Gatwick airport and regional and airports policies.

The importance of CAA input to the review is appreciable when it is considered that the CAA in its Economic Policy and Licensing (EPL) and Economics and Statistics (ES) branches had twice the manpower of the DoT's civil aviation divisions. A mass of information was offered for analysis to a controlling body hardly as well equipped for this purpose as the supplying agency.

DoT staff studied the submissions of the CAA, the airlines and others and, after consulting those closely involved (primarily the CAA, British Airways (BA) and B.Cal.), they submitted their confidential report to the Secretary of State for Trade in May 1975. The impression prevalent in the industry was that this policy review report, although reformulated according to 'the DoT line', owed a great deal to the reviews and submissions of the CAA.

By this time, the DoT, in conjunction with the CAA, and, in anticipation of the review, had been engaged for some months in consultation with BA and B.Cal. to see whether changes could be made in the roles of the two major airlines. It was apparent that the need for new policy guidance would depend to some extent on the outcome of these consultations. The CAA was again involved at the highest levels and these consultations, both on route rationalization and the general policies of the review (including 'Skytrain') continued into the summer of 1975. During this period of consideration the industry grew nervous— one journalist was to write:

> The desire for a period of calm in which to conduct serious planning for the future is almost a desperate one in the air transport division.[21]

B.Cal. did not know whether its position as the 'second force' would be secured or undermined and feared anything from nationalization to gradual decline. The independent charter operators feared that BA might take over B.Cal. and swamp the tours market. The DoT was known to be considering a broad spectrum of options ranging from nationalizing B.Cal. to preserving the status quo.

Although airlines were invited to make submissions for consideration in the review, and limited discussions with the airlines took place in the DoT, there was considerable dissatisfaction with the manner of its undertaking. Some operators, notably B.Cal., made it clear that they felt the whole exercise to be unnecessary. Michael Donne commented:

> For the first time in many years a major change in the structure of civil aviation is being planned virtually in secret. It is this situation which is giving rise to much of the criticism, for it is seen by many as part of the current Whitehall trend away from 'open government'. Nobody outside the DoT knows what is in the report or even the names of all the officials involved in compiling it—there has been no announced intention of publishing all or any part of it.[22]

Anxiety lingered. A solution was proposed by B.Cal.: that the Government should take a minority shareholding in the airline. In the House of Commons the Secretary of State was asked when he would publish his review and he was reminded of the industry's uncertainty.[23]

The Second Guidance

On the 29 July 1975, Mr Shore made a statement on future

aviation policy to the House of Commons.[24] He proposed a number of changes to be incorporated in a new policy guidance for which he would seek Parliamentary approval in due course. He argued that existing civil aviation policy was largely modelled on Edwards, which had assumed the expansion of the industry throughout the seventies. This had not happened; in 1974 traffic had fallen by 10 per cent and B.Cal. had been forced to cut their staff and services, including the North Atlantic route.New guidance would take care of this by not permitting competition on long-haul scheduled service routes, by giving B.Cal. a 'sphere of influence' for its long-haul services, within which it would continue to be the preferred operator and by not allowing Laker's proposed 'Skytrain' service to commence operations.

The Shore policy was thus to replace the competition philosophies of Edwards and the CAA with a 'spheres of influence' approach. Although Conservatives made mild protests about the treatment given to B.Cal. they were generally happy to see that airline's confirmation as the 'second force'. They were not pleased, however, with Mr Shore's 'downgrading' of the CAA[25] or his 'personal management' of CAA policy.[26]

After the July statement a new working group was set up in an attempt to gain BA and B.Cal. agreement to the route rationalization necessary to produce Mr Shore's spheres of influence. This was seen as a precondition of presenting the new guidance for parliamentary approval. The CAA was closely involved in this group which was headed by the Deputy Chairman of the CAA and the Deputy Secretary of the Civil Aviation Division of the DoT. It contained officials from BA, B.Cal., the CAA and DoT and, in the period before Christmas 1975, considered many refinements and combinations of route swaps. Matters moved slowly since BA, at one point, was unwilling to give anything to B.Cal., saying that Mr Shore should make the exchange himself on an openly political basis.[27] The Corporation's hard line softened following the appointment of Sir Frank McFadzean to replace Sir Henry Marking as BA Chairman from 1 January 1976. Rationalization plans were also discussed by a more formal interdepartmental committee comprised of representatives from various government departments (e.g. Employment, Environment, Trade and Scottish Office) but the main negotiations went on through the working party.

By early 1976 the airlines, with some reluctance, had accepted the route exchanges proposed by the DoT and the way was clear for Mr Shore to set out his new policy guidance. B.Cal's Managing Director, Alastair Pugh, was by now commenting that the review 'made nonsense' of long-term planning and investment.[28] His company had given up its 'Cannonball' routes to Boston and Toronto[29] (for which it had been licensed in 1973 but had not received traffic rights), the routes to New York and Los Angeles (which had been licensed by the ATLB in 1972 and operated from 1973 until their withdrawal in November 1974 for financial reasons) and its exempt charter service to Singapore (which was being operated). For their part, BA had given B.Cal. routes to Caracas, Bogota and Lima in South America, and B.Cal was allowed Central and West Africa as its sphere of influence. With the routes rearranged, Mr Shore laid the new guidance before the House of Commons on 11 February 1976.

Part I of his White Paper set out the economic case for a change of policy. It was argued that in a period of slow growth virtually no route was such that dual designation[30] would increase total British earnings and that long-haul competition would therefore be stopped. The Government had considered making Laker's 'Skytrain' an exception to this rule but had decided to cancel Laker's traffic rights designation since 'Skytrain' would divert from other low fare services and because its introduction would jeopardize arrangements made with the United States to control capacity on the North Atlantic.

Part II constituted the detailed guidance, and put the new 'no competition' policy into effect. It provided that the CAA should not license more than one UK airline to serve the same long-haul route. B.Cal., under paragraph 7, was made the 'preferred' airline for routes within its sphere of interest (as defined in Annex A to the guidance) and BA was to be preferred on all other long-haul routes. Where a long-haul was not already operated by a preferred airline, the CAA was 'only in quite exceptional circumstances' to license this to another operator against the objection of the preferred airline. The CAA was also to review existing licences in the light of this paragraph and to take appropriate action.

Concessions to Concorde were made in paragraph 8, which provided that nothing was to prevent the licensing of any airline to serve a long-haul route with that aircraft, or the licensing of any airline to operate a scheduled service, provided that the consent had been given of the airline preferred for the relevant sphere of interest. As for short-haul international routes (i.e. to Europe and North Africa) the CAA was not to license more than one operator on routes other than those to London (paragraph 9). On these and domestic routes a second operator was to be allowed only if the CAA was satisfied that traffic would be 'sufficient' to support competing services 'profitably within a reasonable time' and that the choice and standard of service available was 'likely to be improved' (especially regarding choice of London airport). There was a further condition of international routes: that satisfactory arrangements had been, or were likely to be, made with the other country as to the introduction of a second carrier. The Authority was furthermore ordered to 'make public' the factors it would take into account in applying short-haul competition policy.

Two significant advances were contained in these instructions. Firstly, the availability of traffic rights was made a positive factor in the licensing process (this had only been a 'background' consideration beforehand). Secondly, the CAA was invited to engage in administrative rule-making and lay bare its licensing criteria. The CAA, in its early years, had not pretended to offer such guidance but, after studying short-haul routes in detail (particularly the European scheduled service market) and, after four years of collecting information, it was in a position by 1975/6 to offer its own precise guidance for airlines. The rule-making instruction in paragraph 9 was thus the reflection of a new confidence among CAA staff.

The guidance was expected to last, unchanged, for a number of years and favouring stability was the fact that the new policy on long-haul routes (including 'Skytrain') was the only major departure from CAA thinking. On that issue the CAA wished to retain its option to license competitively and was not so inclined as Mr Shore to preserve the North Atlantic status quo. In February 1976, the CAA Chairman made this point in a letter to Mr Shore that subsequently appeared in House of Commons Written Answers.[31] Lord Boyd-Carpenter expressed appreciation for the attention paid to CAA representations by the DoT and stated that, with a 'substantial exception', the Authority was content with the new guidance. He continued:

> The Authority, dissents from the provisions of paragraph 7 of the draft of the new guidance insofar as they are intended to and would have the effect of inhibiting the Authority from granting,

even in the most exceptional circumstances, an air transport licence to more than one British airline on the same route. This would severely limit the use of the licensing system to secure improvements in air services over the main air routes otherwise than at the discretion of the monopoly carrier. It would also inhibit, *inter alia,* the licensing of experimental services such as 'Skytrain', and remove the possibility of the Authority using its licensing powers to deal effectively with circumstances at present unforseen unless and until further amendments were made in the Guidance. ... I have therefore to inform you that the Civil Aviation Authority disagrees with these provisions.

Displayed in the letter was a degree of concern at any challenge to the CAA's autonomy and expert status. Lord Boyd-Carpenter had had doubts as to the legality of such peremptory guidance at an early stage; he was to write in his memoirs:

I warned Ministers that in seeking to restrict the CAA in this way they were going against the spirit of the 1971 Act, and that if they really wanted to claw back so much of our discretion they should legislate to amend the Act. Politically this could have been awkward for them. However, Peter Shore did not take the advice I gave him, in two long talks, on the legality of what they sought to do. The Government preferred the advice of Board of Trade officials—who unhappily, in the rump left behind when the abler ones with knowledge of civil aviation went to the CAA, did not include anyone of experience.[32]

Mr Shore sought approval for the second guidance from the Commons on 26 February 1976. He repeated the Government's reasons for cancelling the designation of 'Skytrain' and argued that it was not possible to leave the CAA free to institute competition on long-haul routes 'without introducing an undesirable element of uncertainty which would disrupt the long-term planning of both BA and B.Cal'.[33] He referred to a booklet produced by his department to accompany the debate.[34] This stated that an American 'Skytrain' would match Laker's service and worsen the net balance of payments deficit by at least 2 million annually.[35] Such an analysis was that of the DoT alone and did not represent CAA opinion (which favoured keeping the 'Skytrain' option open even given such possibilities).

The Opposition protested. Mr Tebbit argued that the guidance was likely to last, not for a decade or so, as most people hoped, but only until market conditions changed. A motion was put forward rejecting the Secretary of State's decision to cancel Laker's designation and also his instruction to the CAA to revoke the 'Skytrain' licence. This was, however, defeated and the guidance approved. In the House of Lords on 15 March 1976, the guidance was also endorsed but this time a motion was carried calling upon the Government to withdraw the instruction to the CAA to revoke the 'Skytrain' licence.

At this point in the history of the second guidance, the 'Skytrain' question became central. In an attempt to bring their innovatory service into operation Laker challenged the legal validity of key sections of the new guidance and began the process of its decline.

The 'Skytrain' Decision

'Skytrain' was a new type of 'no frills' scheduled service first proposed by Laker in 1971. It was to operate initially from London to New York on a walk-on, no reservation basis. By eliminating trimmings, Laker proposed to offer flights at a very low fare (£37.50 in 1972) so as to cater for the 'forgotten men' who could not afford to travel on normal scheduled services. It was argued that 'Skytrain' would develop new traffic rather than divert from existing operations.

The first application for a 'Skytrain' licence[36] was rejected by the ATLB in 1971. On appeal, the Commissioner recommended allowing the service but the Secretary of State, wishing to avoid anticipation of the CAA decision on the matter, refused the appeal.

Laker applied to the CAA in August 1972 and was opposed by BOAC and B.Cal. on the grounds of diversion and the dangers of American retaliation. The CAA, however, was attracted to the 'Skytrain' concept. Its licensing panel accepted the need for a 'no frills' service, felt that the service's prospects were good, believed that licence limitations (including flying from Stansted) would restrict diversion to limits acceptable under the first guidance and granted a 10-year licence from 1973 to 1982. As for retaliation, the CAA doubted whether other IATA operators would react with similar operations. The Authority believed that the US authorities would allow the designation of Laker as a UK carrier on the route under the Bermuda air services agreement and considered 'Skytrain' to be compatible with other low fare

proposals such as Advanced Booking Charters (ABCs). When
B.Cal. appealed against this decision, the Secretary of State
decided that they had not made a case sufficient to justify revers-
ing the CAA.

After the appeal, Laker invested in three DC 10 aircraft to
operate 'Skytrain' but traffic rights approval from the US Civil
Aeronautics Board (CAB) was slow to come. The British Government designated Laker as a carrier under the Bermuda air
services agreement by an exchange of notes on 26 February 1973.
In spite of pressure from the British Government the American
authorities, in what the CAA was later to refer to as 'unconscion-
able procrastination',[37] failed to grant traffic rights. Sir Freddie
Laker's biographers were later to comment: 'No stone was left
unturned, no obstacle unraised, in an effort to find something,
anything to block Laker's path.'[38]

With 'Skytrain' still on the ground, BA applied to the CAA for
revocation of Laker's licence at a hearing on 21 and 22 January
1975. The Corporation argued that the market of 'forgotten men'
had disappeared, that there would be diversion, US retaliation,
an adverse effect on the UK balance of payments and that ABC
charters had arrived to satisfy demands for cheap North Atlantic
fares. Laker replied that they had invested £31 million in
aircraft and other provisions for the service, that the Bank of
England had approved their aircraft purchases, that the Department of Trade had allowed the aircraft into the country
duty-free for the 'Skytrain' operation and that the Government
had fought hard to gain American permission.

The CAA accepted the evidence of a decline in the post
fuel-crisis market and that both diversion and the possibility of
retaliation would be on a larger scale than in 1972. It stated that
1975 was not the right time to start 'Skytrain' but considered that
it would be wrong to go back on the decision to license Laker. It
decided not to revoke the licence but cautioned that the service
should not be commenced until the market resumed growth. No
earliest date suitable for operation was set down but the CAA
stated that this was unlikely to be for at least twelve months.
Thus, in early 1975 Laker Airways still had a licence to fly, they
had no traffic rights permission but had received 'advice' from
the CAA not to start for a year. Six months later Mr Shore, in his
July policy review statement, said that 'Skytrain' would divert
traffic away from the existing services and, in particular, damage

BA. He announced that he had told Laker Airways that, in these circumstances the 'Skytrain' service could not be allowed to start.[39] Somewhat ironically, the *Sunday Times* reported a few days later that the Americans had relented and that President Ford had been on the verge of telling the CAB to allow 'Skytrain' when Mr Shore had made his statement.[40]

Laker produced a booklet, 'Skytrain: A National Scandal?', in late 1975 contesting the Shore Committee findings, emphasizing their $71 million investment and accusing Mr Shore of exercising 'arbitrary power'. On 10 February 1976, the Secretary of State informed Mr Freddie Laker that, though cancellation of the 'Skytrain' licence was a matter for the CAA, he was going to withdraw Laker's designation under the Bermuda agreement.

Laker brought an action in the High Court and was granted declarations that paragraphs 7 and 8 of the second guidance went beyond Mr Shore's powers and that the Department was not entitled to withdraw designation. Mr Justice Mocatta said that the Secretary of State could not undermine the CAA's statutory licensing responsibilities, either by use of 'guidance' or by use of a prerogative power in relation to the Bermuda treaty.[41] In the Court of Appeal Lords Denning, Roskill and Lawton were essentially in agreement in dismissing the Department's challenge.[42] 'Guidance', said Lord Denning, could explain or supplement the CAA's statutory objectives, but it could not reverse or contradict them.[43] Paragraphs 7 and 8, he stated, were so peremptory as to constitute 'directions' rather than 'guidance': they could not be allowed to overrule the law of the land and were ultra vires.[44] Lord Roskill stressed that the 1971 Act gave very limited powers of direction in section 4 and said that 'guidance' could not be used to stop the CAA carrying out its 'quasi-judicial functions'.[45] Like Lord Denning, he concluded that paragraphs 7 and 8 were inconsistent with the CAA's statutory criteria and were ultra vires.

On Mr Shore's power to withdraw designation, their Lordships said that the prerogative could not be used to circumvent the procedures and protections set out in the 1971 Act.[46] Parliament could not have set up an elaborate licensing code, subject to limited powers of direction, only to allow the Crown an unfettered prerogative power to render licences useless.[47] It was thus declared not only that paragraph 7 and the proviso to paragraph 8 of the guidance were outside the Secretary of State's powers, but also that, in terms of the 1971 Act, the Department was not entitled to withdraw designation of Laker until the expiry of the Bermuda Agreement or the lawful termination of Laker's licence, whichever should be earlier.

It is arguable that the judges involved in this case failed fully to appreciate the way the policy guidance was intended to work. It had been clear since 1960 that the Government would have the final say on major competition policy. The guidance gave a method of setting this government policy down clearly rather than using a messy combination of appeals, section 4 powers or withdrawals of designation. The judges of the Court of Appeal strove to protect the CAA's discretion and to cut down what was (admittedly very clumsy) ministerial interference but in doing so they conceived of the CAA as a traditional body with 'quasi-judicial' functions.[48] They saw it as a court giving licences with rights to be protected by legal due process and as a judicial body deserving protection from executive interference.[49] They failed to see the significance of the CAA as a new form of multi-faceted agency of government, attempting to combine judicial and executive methods in a delicately balanced legal framework whilst acting in a politically contentious area. In attempting to preserve for the CAA an independent judicial status the judges may have sought to achieve the impossible. No-one expected the CAA to be fully independent of government in the manner of a court—as was pointed out in the Court of Appeal the government could always control the agency in ways other than by using guidance. This decision could be said to have jeopardized a system of balance based on compromise because the method of control fitted no neat jurisprudential category. Whatever the judges' reasoning and, whether, on the facts, Mr. Shore's clumsiness did justify the decision, the Court of Appeal's ruling did put into question the feasibility of governmental guidance.[50]

Consequences of the 'Skytrain' Appeal

On 14 February 1977 the Secretary of State for Trade, Mr Dell, told the House of Commons that the interpretation placed by the Court of Appeal on section 3 of the 1971 Act might cause difficulty in the field of licensing policy. He proposed therefore to introduce legislation, when parliamentary time permitted, to clarify the situation but did not think it would be helpful at that stage to issue new guidance for the CAA.[51]

Although, when Mr Dell spoke, the Labour Government's

policy remained one of single designation on long-haul routes, the new UK/USA air services agreement (Bermuda 2) was shortly afterwards signed in July 1977 and provided for dual designation on two routes to America. Under this treaty the 'Skytrain' commenced operations to New York in September 1977. This eased the problem, as Mr Dell explained on 16 January 1978:[52]

> In this new situation the uncertainty surrounding paragraph 7 of the policy guidance is much less significant than it was since the United States was the only country where the designation of more than one airline for a long-haul route was a real possibility. In view of this I have decided not to introduce . . . an amendment to Section 3 of the Civil Aviation Act 1971.

The CAA was, however, involved in some embarassment. Since paragraphs 7 and 8 of the 1976 guidance sanctioned protection for the 'preferred' airlines, BA and B.Cal., in their respectively defined spheres of interest, it was questionable whether the two operators could still rely on those provisions in resisting a competitive challenge.

The Authority considered its position in three major licence applications. When Laker Airways applied in March 1976 for a licence to operate 'Skytrain' to Los Angeles and to revoke B.Cal's licence on the route, both parties argued that paragraphs 7 and 8 should be disregarded. The CAA panel chairman, Mr Colegate, stated that, though the Court of Appeal had held those paragraphs to be *ultra vires*: 'It did not necessarily follow that the paragraphs were invalid for all purposes and in all circumstances.'[53] Two years later[54] the CAA took the view that the Court of Appeal decision had related only to the case then before their Lordships and that no judicial decision governed the preferences enjoyed by BA or B.Cal. It was accepted, however, that the guidance was *ultra vires* in so far as it denied to the CAA the discretion to license in 'quite exceptional circumstances' a non-preferred airline to serve a destination in the sphere of interest of a preferred airline in spite of the latter's objection.[55] The Secretary of State upheld the CAA on appeal,[56] and, whatever the extent of any nullification by the Court of Appeal, all parties clearly held the view that the CAA held a residual discretion to licence competitively. The position was summarized by the CAA when Tradewinds Airways applied to operate a cargo service in BA's sphere of interest in April 1979:

. . . the Authority subscribes to the generality of the spheres of interest policy; but feels able to depart from it if a sufficiently compelling and acceptable case is made.[57]

Since the 1976 guidance was based largely on the CAA's own policies and departed substantially from these only in attempting to remove the option of competitive licensing on long-haul scheduled routes, the effect of the Court of Appeal decision was almost to tailor the guidance to the CAA's views. As Mr Dell noted, the opportunities for dual designation long-haul were so restricted that the potential areas of contention between a Labour Government and the CAA were minimal. Since almost any such case could be treated on a 'quite exceptional basis', then any governmental attempt to restrict the CAA on such a matter was liable to be construed as the kind of undermining of CAA discretion that the Court of Appeal had termed 'direction' as distinct from 'guidance'. The CAA was, therefore, not to be restricted on the issues of greatest contention: those concerning long-haul competition. An argument had emerged that the guidance was redundant.

When a Conservative Government came to power in 1979 the utility of the guidance system was reconsidered in the light, *inter alia*, of those restrictions imposed on the device by the Court of Appeal. The decision was then taken to abolish governmental policy guidance in favour of statutory objectives in combination with CAA-issued policy statements. Since this decision and an assessment of the overall role of guidance should be viewed against a fuller account of CAA decision-making, an evaluation of guidance and the decision to abolish it will be deferred to Chapter 13 after such an account has been given. What can be said at this stage is that, simply in terms of the relationship between the agency and the Government, the policy guidance system did, between 1972 and 1979, succeed in placing control on a public basis in a manner that had never before been achieved. Whether or not the 'Skytrain' decision was to destroy the policy-making system, it could not be doubted that until 1979 affairs had been conducted with a new openness.

(ii) Appeals

The appeals system created for CAA decisions reflected the use of policy guidance as the main tool of control over CAA policy.

In the introduction to both policy guidance documents it was stated that the Secretary of State would, on appeal, uphold the Authority's decision unless there was 'clearly a substantial reason' for departure.[58] In contrast to the ATLB's procedures, new evidence has not been permitted on CAA appeals[59] and written appeals have to be made directly to the DoT without the intervention of a Commissioner. As suggested by the ATLB,[60] the new CAA regulations permitted the Authority to supply expanded reasons to the Secretary of State.[61]

Standard procedure has been as follows: a party has 21 days in which to appeal. Written submissions of the parties and the CAA are considered by the Civil Aviation Policy division of the DoT which receives from the CAA a transcript of the CAA panel hearing, the original applications, objections and submissions of parties together with CAA decision and reasons and all the evidence submitted to the panel, including confidential material that may have been debated in camera.

The CAA and DoT adopt a formal relationship once any question of appeal arises: on notice of appeal both sides will 'clam-up' and no informal communication occurs on the case. Because of potential resort to the courts of law,[62] DoT staff record in a formal manner the internal minutes, ministerial advice and general progress of the appeal.

Since CAP division, with about 30 staff headed by an Under-Secretary, cannot match the detailed expertise of the CAA's 150 specialists, it does not conduct extensive researches into the merits of each decision appealed. Their broad approach is to examine the *vires* of a CAA decision. The Authority's figures will also be reviewed for blatant errors. Neither the policy founding the decision nor the judgments involved have been questioned in detail. The DoT has looked to the criteria and the guidance as defining the CAA's discretion and, following both guidances, has placed such a heavy onus upon those challenging the CAA's decisions that, in the 23 appeals decided from 1972 to 1980, no CAA decision was reversed and on only two occasions was a re-hearing ordered.

The Secretary of State conveys his or her appeal decisions in letters which are published in the CAA's Official Record and the appeal function of the Secretary of State has been summarized in a letter to the CAA dated 5 March 1981:

... to decide only whether the Authority was justified on the facts before it, or in law, in coming to the decision it did. It is not his function to hear new evidence and to usurp the Authority's role by deciding whether on the merits of a case a licence should be granted or revoked.[63]

Thus the standard reason for refusing an appeal has been that, given government promises of support for the CAA, the appellant had not made a sufficient case to justify reversal of the CAA's decision.[64]

Secretaries of State have supported the CAA in a number of ways on appeal. Politically contentious decisions have been contested but the Authority has been upheld on major decisions by governments of differing persuasions. Thus, the CAA's decision to license Laker's 'Skytrain' to New York was supported on appeal to a Conservative government in 1972[65] and a Labour administration similarly supported the licensing of a Los Angeles 'Skytrain' service in 1978.[66] In August 1973, during Conservative rule, the CAA gave BA a Concorde service to Johannesburg as an exception to its 'spheres of interest' policy and, an appeal by B.Cal., the normal West African carrier, was unsuccessful.[67] Nor have Conservative Secretaries of State been above warning the CAA against undue liberalization. When, by way of compensation for B.Cal. shortly after the Johannesburg decision, that airline was given services to Boston, Dallas, Singapore and Toronto (the 'Cannonball' routes)[68] the CAA was upheld on appeal and the Secretary of State indicated that, though the CAA might, under the guidance, license a second operator on a route in certain circumstances he: 'would . . . expect such circumstances to occur comparatively rarely'.[69] This was the first warning that there were limits to the competitive licensing policies that would be supported on appeal.

In fact, that limit was not reached in the period to 1980. It was clear that on matters involving longer term planning Secretaries of State preferred to review the guidance than allow an appeal. Thus, after the CAA changed the conditions on 117 international scheduled service licences, in December 1974, to convert these into 'part-charters' the Secretary of State refused the appeal but indicated that he would examine the matter in his forthcoming policy review.

Perhaps the most rigorous tests of CAA independence have been British Airways' appeals to Labour Governments. No such appeal has succeeded in spite of the CAA's having decided against the Corporation in a number of important cases: British Midland Airways (BMA) were preferred to BA for a Copenhagen service in 1975;[70] the CAA allowed, against BA opposition, a 'Gatwick discount' and imposed on BA a higher fare than the Corporation desired on the London/Glasgow service in October 1975;[71] Thompson/Britannia were licensed for very low fare 'Wanderer' inclusive tours in September 1975 when BA protested that these unfairly attacked their scheduled service market;[72] British Air Ferries (BAF) were given a Manchester/Rotterdam service in 1977 in spite of diversion from BA's Amsterdam route;[73] BMA were given a £5 'differential' on their Gatwick/Belfast service in 1977 against BA pleas of diversion;[74] Laker Airways were permitted to sell vouchers for 'Skytrain' tickets in 1978 after BA had argued that this would erode their scheduled market;[75] BA were refused charter services to Strasbourg in 1978[76] and, when BA and B.Cal. put in competing applications for Dallas/Fort Worth/London services in 1978, the CAA licensed B.Cal. and not BA in spite of BA protests that the route was both within its sphere of interest and offered a rare chance to use Concorde.

Procedurally, appeals have served the function of encouraging CAA precision in reasons for decision and have allowed a re-hearing to take place in exceptional circumstances. Opportunities have been taken to endorse the CAA's own licensing principles. In the very first appeal approval was given to a CAA statement that 'a most powerful case' would be required before a route would be taken from an efficient operator.[77] Such endorsement has served to reinforce principles and the Secretary of State has on occasion gone so far as to explain CAA policy. Thus, after British Island Airways (BIA) and Dan Air had been refused a number of European services from Gatwick in favour of BA in September 1977, the Secretary of State disabused appellants of a misconception. He said that, according to the CAA's own principles as set out in its reasons for decision, BA as holders of a Gatwick licence did not have to satisfy such of the CAA's licensing criteria[78] as applied to a *new* service in order to retain an *existing* licence.

Precise reasoning and the resolution of conflicting evidence have been called for when the Secretary of State has considered himself badly informed. In one case he asserted:

... more attention might be given in future cases, where the issue is of importance, to the reconciliation of different forecasts either at hearing or in the Authority's exposition of reasons for decisions.[79]

The first order to the CAA to re-hear a case involved similar dissatisfaction with evidence. Cambrian Airways appealed on the grounds of diversion, against the licensing of Dan Air and BIA on Isle of Man routes.[80] In these cases the Secretary of State considered that failure by the CAA to quantify diversion from Cambrian or to evaluate the inconvenience suffered by users of present services made it difficult for him to form a view on the key issues.

The CAA re-heard the application[81] (BIA having withdrawn) and ruled that it was for the objector, not the CAA itself, to quantify diversion. It was in adopting such an approach that the CAA took refuge in its status: it did not adopt a judicial posture normally but in difficult cases could demand that airlines rather than its own staff should make out a case. That the Secretary of State accepted the CAA's model of its procedure as adversarial rather than inquisitorial emerged in a later appeal in which it was stated that the Authority's role was 'to consider evidence brought before it and not to adduce evidence itself'.[82]

Conclusions on the Appeals System

That no appeal succeeded in the period 1972–80 said much about the CAA's licensing freedom. Even on re-hearing a case the CAA tended to adhere to its original position. The ATLB experience was not repeated and appeals, though they were used to indicate governmental attitudes, were not used to regulate CAA policy. This is not to say that the effect of appeals was insignificant: CAA staff, in writing decisions, did so with an eye very much on the Secretary of State. Such pressures led to greater precision and coverage both of evidence and reasons. The need to justify every detail of a decision to the appellate body (and thereby to minimize the opportunities for reversal) perhaps served as a greater spur to informative reason-giving than any desire to inform future applicants of relevant policies or to show consistency of policy.

Only in the case of one major decision before 1980—that to allow Laker's 'Skytrain' to New York—did a Government seek to reverse the CAA. That a method other than the appeals system was used on that occasion serves as some indication that the lessons of the ATLB era had not gone unheeded.

Considered in 1980, it was not unlikely that at a future date some appeal would be successful. Since policy guidance, according to the 'Skytrain' decision, had to leave the CAA a discretion covering exceptional cases, the possibility remained that a government would disagree with the CAA. Such an appeal decision, if allowed on an exceptional basis (and not couched in wide policy terms), was not liable to undermine CAA policy-making. Experience to 1980 indicated that appeals had not been disruptive to CAA policies but the continuation of such a limited role for appeals depended on there being other ways to control CAA policy. As will be seen below in Chapter 13, there is evidence that the abolition of the governmental policy guidance system in 1980–81 left the appeal as a more tempting medium of policy control.[83]

(iii) Traffic Rights Negotiation

The negotiation of air service agreements (ASAs) has long provided governments with a way to influence policy, one that in the ATLB system was used to the detriment of the licensing board. Although Edwards had wanted the CAA to carry the main weight of ASA negotiations, both Labour and Conservative governments retained this function within the Department of Trade in the seventies. The two policy guidances, however, ordered the CAA to 'maintain a close working relationship' with the DoT in all international matters and to provide staff and expertise for international discussions.

When an ASA is to be discussed a negotiating team is appointed. In major discussions (such as the 'Bermuda 2' ASA, reached with the USA in 1977) CAA staff are heavily engaged at all stages. Where less important agreements are negotiated abroad, the team tends to comprise DoT staff only but the CAA is always represented at pre-briefing sessions with the team in London where a written CAA brief is submitted. In recent years the CAA has tended to become more involved in negotiations, especially where there is a competitive issue involved, and the CAA staff take a prominent role in putting forward the technical arguments in support of the UK's aviation policy line. The DoT and Foreign and Commonwealth Office look to broad issues of international relations, the CAA supplies the negotiating team with relevant statistics on such items as 'bilateral balances' (i.e. UK shares of a market) and it outlines the licensing policies that will be affected by the ASA.

In pursuance of each licensing decision the CAA advises the Secretary of State of the kind of traffic rights conditions that will be acceptable in terms of industrial and users interests. The Authority attempts also to define the 'maximum price' that should be paid in negotiating traffic rights. This advice is based on evidence presented in the licensing case and is disclosed to parties so that it may be challenged on appeal. In the case of negotiations straying into areas unforseen in the CAA's advice, the decision on acceptability will now be made after consultation between the CAA and DoT.

As for DoT advice on the negotiating prospects of a potential CAA decision, this is sought by the CAA before a hearing and is incorporated verbatim in the brief submitted to the CAA hearing panel by the CAA's International Section.[84] This is often released to parties but the Secretary of State will not usually reveal confidential communications with foreign governments or airlines. It is the Secretary of State who is the final judge of how much information will be released to the CAA and, for this reason, a suggestion that DoT staff should be cross-examinable by parties at CAA hearings has been rejected by the Secretary of State.[85]

From the DoT aspect two difficulties can follow a licensing decision: firstly, that when rights to fly exist in an ASA the licensing decision may provoke a dispute with a foreign government and secondly, when rights are not contained in an existing ASA, that these may not be obtainable on acceptable terms.

Although CAA staff appear confident that the DoT will generally do its best to obtain rights for a licensee, there have been occasional cases of governmental failure to obtain agreements and airlines have dubbed the negotiation process 'the third licensing system' (i.e. after licensing and appeals). B.Cal. received a Singapore (trade name: 'Cannonball') licence in 1974 and, failing to obtain traffic rights, at no time operated the service. Referring to the 'Cannonball' services and the Labour Government's lack of sympathy for B.Cal., Lord Boyd-Carpenter said of the failure to designate:

The excuse was that a 'review' of Civil Aviation policy would soon be undertaken. But it was bad administration and, as the Laker case indicated, of doubtful legality.[86]

In spite of the DoT's having to consider policy matters in, for example, renegotiating an ASA so as to allow a second operator on a route, there has ('Cannonball' apart) been only one case in which traffic rights designation has been refused for openly political reasons. That was the removal of designation for 'Skytrain' in 1976. As Lord Boyd-Carpenter has noted, and, as we have seen above, the legality of using the prerogative power deliberately to frustrate the CAA was denied by the Court of Appeal.

The 'Skytrain' decision might properly be restricted in application to use of the designating power to overturn a licensing decision on doctrinal grounds rather than on the merits of the individual case. Unless this were so, the DoT would be obliged to designate whatever the costs of securing international agreement. The CAA inclined towards the former construction when, on Laker's application for a licence to operate a Los Angeles 'Skytrain',[87] they were invited by B.Cal. to express a view on the Secretary of State's duty to make his decisions on designations consistent with CAA licensing decisions. Referring to the Court of Appeal judgement, the CAA said:

> It does not necessarily follow that it would be an improper exercise of the prerogative to refuse designation to a licensed airline.[88]

The Authority stated that it would, however, be 'less than satisfactory' for conflicting decisions to be taken, especially as there were no formal procedures set out for designation decisions. Then, in a plea that designation should not be used as a covert reviewing procedure, the CAA said that it had set out 'in great detail the relevant facts and its own reasoning'[89] and that if the Secretary of State was to reach different conclusions on such facts, the Authority hoped that this would be brought out fully at the appeal stage (assuming there was any) and that the designation decision would be consistent with the appeal decision.[90]

Where the DoT advice to a CAA panel has inclined towards a particular result the Authority has been wary of having its decisions pre-empted. If the CAA, on normal licensing criteria, has favoured competition on an international route but has been warned by the DoT that this might provoke retaliation or the extraction of a high price by a foreign government the CAA has been strongly disposed to adhere to its licensing policy on the principle that failure to call either the DoT's or foreign governments' hand would diminish the authority of the licensing system.

In one such case the whole question of the CAA's licensing discretion was at issue. This involved the granting to B.Cal. of permission to serve Scandinavian routes in October 1977.[91] The CAA favoured dual designation to Scandinavia with BA operating on their existing licence from Heathrow and B.Cal. starting Gatwick services. The Scandinavian governments considered such competition for SAS to be unacceptable and denounced their ASAs with the UK. BA appealed against the CAA allowing B.Cal. to compete with them and, on 10 July 1978, the Secretary of State directed the CAA to reconsider its decision in the light of developments. A new ASA was reached in December 1978. This allowed only one designated airline from each country on each city pair and became effective from 1 January 1979. The CAA re-heard the case in March 1979, having sought the DoT's advice and after circulating this to parties. In making its decision the Authority summarized to DoT advice as stating that the new ASA:

> ... precluded the United Kingdom from designating B.Cal. for services between Heathrow or Gatwick ... and any one of the three Scandinavian capitals ... either in addition to British Airways or in its stead.[92]

The problem was whether the CAA could re-hear the case with any freedom at all. On the above DoT advice the Authority commented:

> If this were indeed so, there would be no point in the Authority's considering the case any further: the only decision that could stand would be to confirm British Airways as the sole British operator. ... The issue would in effect have been decided in the course of the negotiations on the Air Service Agreement and not by the Authority under the licensing procedures laid down in the Civil Aviation Act 1971.[93]

An escape route emerged. The CAA disagreed with the DoT's interpretation of the ASA, stating that, though allowing only one designated airline, the airline was not specified and so the CAA could licence B.Cal. as sole operator. The CAA stated that, in the light of the Laker Airways decision, it would assume this licensing discretion in the absence of a (section 4) direction from the Secretary of State.

In the event, the CAA found that replacement of the existing operator, BA, was not justified in the circumstances and B.Cal. was not licensed from Gatwick.

Although the Authority reserved for itself the option of licensing B.Cal. as sole operator on the route, the renegotiated ASA, in providing for single designation, did limit CAA discretion. With an eye on the courts, the Authority said of the general problem:

> The extent to which the Department in the course of international negotiations did, or can properly, pre-empt licensing decisions which under the 1971 Act are to be made by the Authority is a question which may fall to be decided elsewhere; indeed it is one which might usually be clarified. . . .[94]

It is perhaps too much to expect a clear definition of what constitutes pre-emption. In favour of the CAA it may be said that, whatever the concessions made by the Authority in the Los Angeles 'Skytrain' case, the Court of Appeal decision did give some protection from clear pre-emption and the Scandinavian case did arise from exceptional circumstances that are unlikely to recur with frequency. From experience to 1980 it may be concluded on the issue of traffic rights that neither the courts nor the Authority will readily bow to pre-emption of the CAA's licensing discretion.

The CAA now manages to license more intelligently concerning international matters than did the ATLB. The DoT, at least in the period 1972–80, no longer had to use traffic rights as a policy lever and it may have been deterred from such use by the Court of Appeal. The system is not perfect, however, and it may be useful here to contrast procedures in the USA with the British system of allocating licences in advance of traffic rights negotiations. In the United States it is usual for traffic rights for unspecified carriers to be negotiated in advance of licensing by teams made up of representatives of the Civil Aeronautics Board, the Department of Transportation and the Department of State. Assuming that traffic rights exist, a number of carriers then apply for licences to the CAB (at whose hearings the Departments of Transportation and State may be represented), and one or more is selected. In accordance with section 801 of the Federal Aviation Act of 1958 such a CAB decision must be presented to the President for review. The President may disapprove certification only on the basis of foreign relations or national defence and not on economic or carrier selection grounds: public reasons for disapproval must be given within 60 days of submission. The advantage of such a system is that, apart from separating economic from security issues and bringing intra-governmental disagreements out into the open, it maximizes the national bargaining power. One senior staff member in the US Department of Transportation said of the British system:

> Your negotiating position will always be weakened when the government staff have the carrier needing the rights sitting next to them at the table.[95]

The British reply to this point is that having the licensing decision and carrier section in advance of traffic rights negotiation gives negotiators a much more precise idea of the price worth paying for those rights. Lord Boyd-Carpenter has advocated a simple way of co-ordinating both functions, saying:

> ... now that the greater part of the expertise in the highly international world of Civil Aviation is to be found in the CAA it would make sense if the convention were allowed to develop that the Secretary of State relied on the officers of the CAA as his advisers and negotiators in international negotiations affecting aviation. This would prevent the present duplication of staffs, and secure that those conducting the negotiations did so with full background knowledge of the interests of British civil aviation.'[96]

It may be a long time, however, before governments will give an independent body the power to conduct treaty negotiations that are bound up with national prestige, security and broad economic considerations. What can be expected in the short term is that the CAA and government will continue to work towards clear and more efficient co-ordination of their respective functions. In the seventies, although there were occasional cases where tension was exposed, co-operation on a semi-formal basis appeared to have produced a workable regime. The CAA was not frequently compelled to make hasty adjustments to its international policies to accord with traffic rights considerations. As in the case of appeals, however, the 1980 abolition of policy guidance might be expected to place greater pressure on governments to control CAA policy via traffic rights powers. This is a process, therefore, to be monitored closely in the future.

(iv) Judicial Controls and the CAA

In the decade 1972 to 1982 the CAA's licensing procedures and decisions were subjected to no legal challenge in the courts. The 'Skytrain' case of 1976–77 concerned the actions of the Secretary of State rather than those of the CAA and Laker's attempts in 1981 to reduce a CAA decision not to license them on 660 routes to Europe (on the basis that this contravened the EEC's competition rules) fell with the collapse of Laker Airways in February 1982.

Such lack of resort to law is noteworthy given the degree to which other British agencies, such as the Commission for Racial Equality,[97] have been subjected to judicial review and is the more remarkable when set against the extent to which the American courts control agency procedures.[98]

There are a number of reasons given by those in the industry to explain why the CAA has not been taken to court. First, they say, there is a general reluctance to go to the expense and delay of judicial review when in the long term this might not affect an operator's overall share of routes. Gains made by legal challenge today may be lost by another's challenge tomorrow and the licensing process would slow down dramatically. Second, this is a close community in which operators have a continuing relationship with each other, the CAA and the Department— there may be occasions on which it is politically inopportune to go to law. In any event, it might be that a victory at law would achieve little since an unwanted decision might well be re-made by the CAA or by the Secretary of State. Insofar as some airlines have in recent years come to view the 'political' appeal as all-important, their motivation to challenge 'legal technicalities' in CAA procedures may be reduced. The appeals system is indeed seen by some as the most important reason why the courts have not been resorted to. If dissatisfied with a CAA decision on procedural or substantive grounds, an operator will appeal to the Secretary of State in the hope of having the decision reversed. Success on that front makes up, in the airline's view, for any defects in the CAA process. The appeals system also allows many complaints to be redressed. Regulation 16 of the

1972 Regulations permitted appellants to serve notice on the Secretary of State giving reasons why the CAA decision should not be upheld, the CAA has a duty to furnish expanded reasons for decision to the Secretary of State and appellants are given 14 days in which to reply to the CAA's reasoning. This procedure has often allowed those who, say, think that an argument put by them has not been considered properly, to make this complaint and either to have the CAA remedy this or to have the Secretary of State's ruling on the matter.

The CAA's legal advisers have the function of seeing that licensing procedures comply with the rules of natural justice and *vires* and the quality of their advice may affect the number of challenges by operators. Thus, in spite of the absence of contests so far, the rules of administrative law do have considerable bearing on the practices of an agency of mixed functions. It is therefore necessary to note briefly those areas of the law that particularly affect agencies that are distinguishable from traditional tribunals by their policy-orientation and developed expertise.

In broad terms the CAA has to meet its duty to act fairly. The law has come some way from the position in which courts refused to apply the rules of natural justice (in particular the duty to hear), to administrative bodies exercising licensing powers. The notion that the duty to act fairly only applied to bodies acting judicially[99] or those concerned with *rights* as opposed to *privileges*[100] has given way to more particular consideration of a licensing authorities' functions and duties and a realistic assessment of the economic effect of a decision on an individual.[101] In the gaming case of *Benaim and Khaida*, Lord Denning rejected the view that the rules of natural justice did not apply to licensing agencies such as the Independent Broadcasting Authority or the Gaming Board. These bodies had to act 'fairly' but in such cases, he said, 'it is not possible to lay down rigid rules as to when the principles of natural justice are to apply: nor as to their scope and extent. Everything depends on the subject matter.'[102]

The conceptual approach reappeared, however, in *McInnes* v. *Onslow-Fane*.[103] Viscount Megarry said in the Chancery Division that there were three kinds of licensing case: (a) those involving *forfeiture* of an existing right or position; (b) where an *application* for membership or a licence is refused and; (c) where the applicant for a licence has a legitimate *expectation* that the application would be granted (this included renewals of licences or re-elections). In forfeiture cases there was clearly the right to know the charges and to be heard. In application cases nothing was being taken away and so there was no requirement to hear. Where someone sought a licence for the first time, therefore, there was only *hope* not *expectation* and there was no right to be heard, nor was there, in the absence of any statutory requirement, a duty on the licensing authority to give any reasons for a decision at all: this was the legal position, at least, where refusal of an application left no slur on the applicant's character and where there was a general licensing discretion as opposed to a statutory duty to decide upon a defined issue.[104]

As for bodies like the CAA, two general conclusions can be drawn from the cases:[105]

(i) Non-renewal of an existing licence may be viewed more seriously than refusal to grant in the first place.[106]
(ii) If the licensing authority is constituted as a distinct tribunal, or is expressly required to entertain representations or objections or appeals or to conduct hearings when deciding whether or not to grant a licence (particularly if its discretionary power is limited) the presumption must be that it is to act in accordance with natural justice.[107]

The real difficulties arise when an agency uses public hearings within the wider policy-making context. In aviation licensing there are a few points in particular that may give rise to problems and these should be considered.

(a) *Non-disclosure of CAA Panel Briefs*
The parties to CAA hearing do not have an opportunity to contest any of the information contained in the staff brief given to CAA hearings panels[108] except in so far as they make the relevant points in argument with each other. The legality of the brief thus turns on whether it is viewed as background knowledge in the light of which the parties are examined or as evidence upon which the CAA decides the case. In *Wiseman* v. *Borneman*[109] the issue arose when taxpayers claimed that they were unable to reply to a counter-statement of the Inland Revenue Commissioners which was taken into account by a tax tribunal. The tribunal had no power to pronounce a final judgment and the taxpayers lost but Lord Reid stated that had the

tribunal been given such a power 'justice would certainly require that [the taxpayer] should have a right to see and reply to this statement.'[110]

The courts have consistently been reluctant to require the disclosure of inspectors reports in planning cases[111] and in the *Bushell*[112] case have refused to allow parties to cross examine civil servants on the subject of figures used by the Department at a public inquiry. On the other hand, it could be argued that there is still a duty on the CAA to disclose information where reasons of public interest[113] or confidentiality do not rule this out. Lord Denning said of the Gaming Board in *Benaim* and *Khaida*:

> They can and should receive information from the police in this country or abroad who know something of them. They can, and should, receive information from any other reliable source. Much of it will be confidential. But that does not mean that the applicants are not to be given a chance of answering it. They must be given the chance. . . .[114]

The 1972 regulations[115] gave the CAA a duty to furnish parties to cases with a copy or summary of 'any information in the possession of the Authority which has been furnished in connection with the case or which the Authority has reason to believe will be referred to at the hearing of the case'. This requirement has not been read as demanding the disclosure of the CAA's analyses (as opposed to evidence submitted by the parties) and, as we shall see, these analyses are not explicitly referred to at hearings. Legally the brief is on relatively firm ground if it is used not as evidence (as was the case of the information at issue in *Benaim* v. *Khaida*), but is limited to the role of background knowledge, as was the case of the forecasts in *Bushell*. Where a specialist agency looks at forecasts in the light of its own computations, however, the line between evidence and own knowledge may be a difficult one to draw.

(b) *Policy-making and Adjudication*

A policymaking body that exercises statutory discretions courts a number of dangers.[116] In the case of the CAA, issues revolve round the place of CAA policy initiatives that are debated at public hearings: can new policies be challenged and has the CAA fettered its discretion in relation to a particular application?

We will see in Chapter 11 that some airlines have protested that new policies are difficult to challenge at hearings but what of the law? Judicial review of those policy decisions on their own merits seems unlikely: the courts are reluctant to interfere where Parliament has clearly allocated specialist policy-making to a particular body—a strong thread in the 'Skytrain' case was the fact that air transport policies were matters given to the CAA to decide, not the Secretary of State (or the courts).[117] If a CAA policy cannot be shown to be unreasonable it may be argued that a licensing discretion has been fettered—if, for example, a licence is refused by the CAA because it has adopted a new policy of limiting licences in that class.[118]

It is clear that bodies exercising discretion may develop policies to guide in particular cases[119] and that to exercise a discretion without fettering involves a willingness to consider the particular merits of individual applications.[120] Whether or not parties affected by a policy have a right to be informed of that policy and to argue against it is not clear. The leading text argues that there are 'indications pointing in this direction'.[121] Lord Reid said in the *British Oxygen* case:

> I do not think there is any great difference between a policy and a rule. There may be cases where an officer or authority ought to listen to a substantial argument, reasonably presented urging a change of policy. What the authority must not do is to refuse to listen at all.[122]

In the pioneering case of *R* v. *Liverpool Corporation Ex. p. Liverpool Taxi Fleet Operators Association*[123] a Corporation committee resolved to increase the number of city taxi licences and did so in breach of a public undertaking not to do this. The Court of Appeal prohibited the Corporation from acting on the resolution without first hearing representations from those interested. This involved policy-making, as opposed to a specific determination, but still there was a duty to act fairly. Lord Denning was clear:

> . . . suppose the Corporation proposed to reduce the number of taxicabs from 300 to 200, it would be their duty to hear the taxicab owner's association: because their members would be greatly affected. They would certainly be persons aggrieved.[124]

As for changes of policy, it could be argued on the basis of *HTV* v. *Price Commission*[125] that the CAA could not change

policy direction without cause if this would prejudice a licensee.
Lord Denning said:

> 'it is in my opinion, the duty of the Price Commission to act with
> fairness and consistency in their dealing with manufacturers and
> traders. Allowing that it is primarily for them to interpret and
> apply the code, nevertheless if they regularly apply the code in a
> particular way—they should continue to interpret it and apply it
> in the same way thereafter unless there is good cause for depart-
> ing from it.[126]

Such statements might make agencies nervous when adapting
their policies to new circumstances but they might comfort licen-
sees, especially those with legitimate expectations of renewal.

It remains to be seen whether the procedural duties of policy-
makers will be developed further. For bodies like the CAA, who
already consult widely, this may not make much difference to the
way that they operate, but any expansion of the rules of fairness
may render them more liable to legal challenge.

(c) *The Duty to Decide*

The specialist agency has difficulties even after a trial-type hearing is completed. Instead of simply deciding between two sets of
arguments, the quality of evidence has to be reviewed in the light
of the CAA's own calculations and the policy implications of the
available licensing options may have to be considered by the
decision-making panel in committee with other CAA staff.[127]
Questions arise as to whether the rules of natural justice are
breached by these practices and whether the decision-maker, by
reference to committee, may fail to exercise a discretion.

On the first point it appears from the field of planning that
Ministers, having heard the arguments for and against a compulsory purchase order, should hold themselves aloof from parties from the case but may consult with other Departments on
matters relevant to their decision whether or not to make the
order.[128] If the courts were to treat agencies as tribunals
rather than as policy-making bodies, however, the courts might
impose more rigorous standards on them: perhaps to expose any
information supplied by agency staff to the parties' criticism. As
with the use of briefs, the CAA can seek to avoid review on this
front by treating staff advice as analysis rather than as new
evidence—as an aid to decision-making as opposed to a reopen-
ing of the case.

On the legality of combining public hearings with policy discussions there are similar issues. If it was to be shown that the CAA licensing panel had acted under the dictates of its policy committee then it might be held to have declined jurisdiction by failing to decide the issue itself[129] or to have decided by reference to a pre-ordained policy rather than given consideration to the merits of the case.[130] This, however, is an area in which a properly advised agency may easily avoid legal challenge. (In any case the problems of proof for the aggrieved would be almost insurmountable.) A CAA decision might indicate that a certain policy has been 'taken into account' in a decision but, since each decided application is checked by CAA lawyers, it would invariably stress that the merits of a particular case had been fully considered.

To summarize on judicial controls over the CAA: these all exist in potential form. There are however certain problem areas that policy-oriented bodies have to negotiate and this derives from their use of a hearings system in a field where policies are constantly developed and in which judgments as to the quality of evidence have to be made with the assistance of others. The CAA is content not to put its own forecasts and calculations at issue in hearings. Until now there has been no great pressure from the airlines to have such disclosure. There are two reasons for this: the CAA's general policies and marketing approaches are available from sources outside the hearing such as CAA published statistics and policy statements (see Chapter 11) and the operators realize that any method of having the CAA's own case argued at public hearings (as happens with the US CAB)[131] would involve substantial and costly lengthening of the trial-type process. An expanded system of judicial review that penetrated to the merits of licensing policies would prove unpopular with the airlines: given the choice between an aviation strategy devised by the CAA (even as amended on appeal) and one devised by the courts, they would opt for the lesser of two evils.

(v) *Other Methods of Calling the CAA to Account*
Apart from the channels of control noted above, the CAA is subject to those political controls normally associated with any public corporation. These are principally: the appointment of members to the CAA board; financial controls; formal directions; informal directives and parliamentary control through select committees, questions and debates.

Though numerous these controls have not been used to great effect in policy terms. This is largely explicable in terms of the CAA's depth of expertise and because it sees its adjudicatory functions as demanding a degree of independence from government. Whereas in the United States appointments to the chairmanship of agencies have been used openly to influence policy[132] this has not happened in the case of the CAA. Up to 1982 there were two Chairmen of the CAA: Lord Boyd-Carpenter, who fought vigorously for CAA independence from Whitehall and, from March 1977, Sir Nigel Foulkes, former Chairman of the British Airports Authority. The latter was appointed by a Labour Government and has commented:

> I arrived clearly as a professional businessman and by no stretch of the imagination as a politician suitable for the objectives of the government's aims at the time. . . . My own reputation is of being a difficult chap who doesn't like civil servants or politicians. You couldn't have a less 'political' appointment.[133]

On the need to preserve agency independence from departmental interference, Sir Nigel argues that the relationship of a nationalized industry or regulatory body to government depends on how dangerous the administration of the industry can be to that government.[134] Mining is thus a more contentious area than that covered by the CAA or British Airports Authority (BAA) and the main task of an administrator is to minimise political upheaval:

> The Government want to forget the area and merely want advance notice if there is a really bad political shock in store. . . . You have to avoid politically embarrassing the Government, and so have to know what causes embarrassment.[135]

Financially, it was the aim of the 1971 Act and the guidance[136] that the CAA should pay its own way. Although the Authority has received substantial grants-in-aid from the government (£13m in 1978–79; £24m in 1979–80; £36m in 1980–81) the purpose of these has been to offset the expenses of 'uncontrollable' operations (UK airspace traffic services and Scottish aerodromes). As far as operations where charges are controllable by the CAA (airports, safety and economic services) the Authority was given the task of breaking even by the year 1977–78 but achieved this objective by 1976–77 and in these areas has continued to profit (£1.9m in 1978–79; £81,000 in 1979–80; £1.5m in 1980–81).

The grant-in-aid has not been used as government leverage over economic policies of the CAA, nor would the Authority deem this to be a proper course of action.[137]

The Court of Appeal did suggest that the Secretary of State might have used directions under section 4 of the 1971 Act to stop 'Skytrain'. Such directions, however, are permissible only in relation to 'a particular thing' rather than general policy (section 4(3)) and may be used only in the interests of national security or in connection with either foreign relations or international obligations.

The Thatcher Government issued four such directions to the CAA between April 1979 and April 1980. Only one direction had previously been issued in the CAA's lifetime. If the revived use of such directions indicated anything it might have been that the DoT saw direction or interference with the CAA as a less extreme course of action than it did formerly.

As far as informal control over the CAA is concerned, this is limited by the Authority's status as an expert adjudicating body. In relation to licensing hearings and appeals, the Authority adopts an independent position and does not tolerate interference from government. As already noted, when an appeal is imminent relations between CAA and DoT become formalized. Having said that, it is clear that the CAA does in some areas work in close harmony with the DoT. Authority staff adopt the attitude that they may freely discuss policies with government, airlines or public as their constituents but that this process places the CAA under no obligation to act in a particular manner. One CAA member told the author:

> You take the views of people, attach weight to them and say openly what the policy grounds are. There is no reason not to discuss policies with the government.[138]

Thus, in accordance with the guidance, co-ordination between traffic rights negotiations and licensing has been pursued by means of consultation. Similarly the DoT, being responsible for licensing overseas operators coming to this country, has acted to ensure a working parity of licensing conditions between UK and foreign operators. Again it should be noted that such co-operation as exists does not amount to influence over CAA policy-making via the 'lunch-table directive': because the CAA has been deliberately distanced from government in order to

treat private and public operators on an equal footing it does not
take its independence lightly. Unlike the ATLB it has the muscle
with which to resist interference.

Sir Nigel Foulkes has indicated that he mets the Secretary of
State for Trade three or four times a year face to face, the
Parliamentary Under Secretary two or three times a year and the
Permanent Secretary twice as often. He said:

> I don't see it as my business to be constantly in touch with the
> civil servants and politicians. Only when political embarrassment
> is likely. I would only see them if I thought I should warn them
> that we might embarrass them or vice versa. That is very rare, I
> do not badger the Secretary of State with trivia.[140]

In the case of CAA staff other than the chairman, contact with
the Department is necessarily more frequent. Sir Nigel stressed
that his Group Director of Economic Services, Mr Colegate, was
'acutely aware of the political effects of our and of government
decisions' and so was in regular communication with the civil
servants. This was not seen by any CAA staff member as pre-
judicial to the CAA's functions.

As far as parliamentary control is concerned, there is limited
scope for calling the CAA to account. The Minister's policy
guidance provided the main forum for debate of aviation policy.
Since the guidance had to be approved by both Houses of
Parliament, considerable scope for debate was given and taken
(notably the House of Lords disapproval of Mr Shore's second
guidance insofar as it withdrew sanction for Laker's
'Skytrain').[141] Replacing governmental with self-administered
guidance,removed the opportunity for such parliamentary discussion.

Apart from debates on the guidance, a review of parliamentary debates, questions and statements in the period 1972–80
shows that Secretaries of State have not accepted responsibility
for CAA licensing decisions or regulatory activity. A typical
parliamentary answer was that of the Under Secretary of State
for Trade and Industry (Mr Onslow) when asked a series of
questions on types of licence and control in 1972. He replied
simply that this was 'a matter for the Civil Aviation
Authority'.[142] When issuing new policy guidance in 1976 the
government refused to publish the detailed advice upon which
changes in policy were based,[143] and consequently the political
spotlight tended to fall not on the CAA but on the Government.

The other means of scrutiny of significance is that of the House of Commons select committee. Under the departmental committees system, review of the CAA's activity depends on the area chosen for study. Formerly the Select Committee on Nationalized Industries took evidence from the CAA when looking at British Airways[144] but the focus of their attention was on the airlines rather than the regulating body and no recommendations were made concerning CAA functions. More recently, evidence has been taken from the CAA by the Expenditure Committee (Trade and Industry Sub-Committee) when investigating 'United Kingdom Domestic Air Fares'[145] in 1979 and by the House of Lords Select Committee on the European Communities in its investigation of 'European Air Fares'.[146]

In addition, the CAA reports annually to the Secretary of State who lays the report before Parliament. It should be noted, however, that the CAA is not a body under the purview of the Ombudsman in terms of Schedule 1 of the Parliamentary Commissioner Act 1967. Though the above contacts are made with Parliament, it cannot be said that either the observers of the CAA or its staff are aware of anything more than the most indirect control by Parliament.

(vi) Conclusions: the CAA and Government

Though the debate on abolishing governmental guidance is deferred pending consideration of the effect of guidance on the CAA's licence allocation and policy-making functions, certain conclusions may be drawn on the CAA's relationship with government during the era of such guidance.

It is clear that policy guidance replaced those other forms of political control that had been used to ill effect in the 1960s. Appeals and traffic rights in the period to 1980 were not used disruptively. The policy guidance system put flesh on the CAA's statutory objectives by means of an open process allowing extensive consultation between CAA, airlines and government. Moreover, guidance and its required publication supplied the main forum for parliamentary debates of civil aviation policy. In the seventies the guidance encouraged a viable division of functions between the CAA and government. Co-operation on traffic rights and the foreign relations implications of licensing was achieved in a manner unexperienced by the ATLB.

Although the policy guidance system was challenged when it

was used with excessive zeal by the Labour Government in 1976, we may conclude provisionally that, in the CAA's early years, guidance was a useful device in the governmental machine. Whether or not the policy guidance system remained useful or even viable in the years after the CAA had found its feet and after the Court of Appeal had restricted its scope is a matter to be returned to below.

10
Regulatory Issues and CAA Procedures

In this and the following chapter we deal with what many lawyers may see as the kernel of the problem: how the CAA has sought to reconcile the use of trial-type procedures with its policy-making, managerial and regulatory functions. The difficulties faced are not small: when Louis J. Hector resigned from the US Civil Aeronautics Board in 1959 he informed President Eisenhower:

> . . . my experience on the Civil Aeronautics Board has convinced me that an independent regulatory commission is not competent in these days to regulate a vital national industry in the public interest. . . . The Members of the CAB, like those of other regulatory commissions, have duties and responsibilities of policy-making, adjudication, administration and investigation which are by their very nature incompatible.[1]

The tribunalistic ATLB, we saw, was troubled by both the political and the procedural horns of the justiciability dilemma. With a commission-style body like the CAA there is a more even balance of policy-making power between agency and government but to combine trial-type procedures with a well-developed expertise gives rise to the more acute questions of compatibility to which Louis J. Hector refers. In analyzing CAA case law four particular problems should be born in mind.

(a) Polycentricity

Civil aviation licensing issues may be typified as 'polycentric' (multi-centred): each is like a spider's web:

> Pull a strand here and a complex pattern of adjustment runs through the whole web. Pull another strand from a different angle and another complex pattern results.[2]

In this respect the polycentricity problem is more specific than the procedural limb of the justiciability question: polycentricity looks to the interrelated complexity of issues rather than the appropriateness of trial-type procedure for answering a particular (often specialist rather than multi-centred) kind of question. From this point of view licensing has been said to present almost insuperable problems for the trial-type process: as Lon Fuller has argued:

> Generally speaking, it may be said that problems in the allocation of economic resources present too strong a polycentric aspect to be suitable for adjudication.[3]

He added:

> . . . courts move too slowly to keep up with a rapidly changing economic scene . . . the forms of adjudication cannot encompass and take into account the complex repercussions . . . it is simply impossible to afford each affected party a meaningful participation through proof and argument.[4]

In the case of the CAA, however, we will see, how, by a combination of trial-type and rule-making procedures, and by the application of an extensive expertise, some effort has been made to render genuinely polycentric issues amenable to a process involving public hearings, but one not restricted to the court model of adjudication. We will see how polycentricity may not necessarily rule out adjudication by means of the trial-type process—provided that the right package of procedures is adopted.

(b) Case Law or Rule-making?

It has been argued, notably by Kenneth Culp Davis,[5] that trial-type procedures are useful for resolving questions of *adjudicative fact* (such as 'who did what, where and when?') rather than matters of *legislative fact* that relate to wider issues of law, policy and discretion and which can best be resolved by written submissions or informal arguments—the primary procedural techniques of rule-making. Like Louis J. Hector, Davis argued that over-reliance on trial-type adjudication leads to a neglect of standards and broader policies. Hector's solution was to transfer policy-making functions from agency to government[6] but Davis has argued for increased judicial requirements that agencies indulge in rule-making.[7]

When looking at the CAA, the strengths and weaknesses of case-by-case adjudication versus other procedures for policy-making can be assessed in the light of American experience. Many, of course, would value the legislative/adjudicative facts distinction less highly than Davis,[8] but such commentators also question the extent to which trial-type hearings are suitable either for making policy[9] or resolving economic issues.[10] Although the problems of distinguishing between rule-making and adjudication have to be acknowledged,[11] analysis of CAA policy-making is helped by bearing in mind a classic account of the advantages and disadvantages of rule-making as opposed to trial-type adjudication of particular issues.

David L. Shapiro has said of rule-making:[12]

(i) It aids the articulation and elaboration of statutory standards.

(ii) It leads to fair and effective administration—it allows general participation in the deliberative process by all those who may be affected by a rule. Such opportunities are not usually offered in adjudications.

(iii) It is conducive to planning—the agency is not dependent on sporadic litiagion but may choose where to direct policy.

(iv) It is prospective rather than reactive.

(v) It caters for uniformity of application—all regulated parties are affected, not merely those affected by a particular adjudication.

(vi) It is a flexible procedure—agency policymakers may consult more freely in rulemaking than in adjudication.

(vii) It can deal with broader issues than particularised adjudication.

(viii) It allows easy access to the information upon which policies are based and it gives clearer elaboration of strategic policies than adjudication.

(ix) It exposes policies more openly to criticism and judicial review.

Whether or not Shapiro's arguments were meant to be applicable to agencies outside the USA, we will see that CAA policy-making, when successful, has very much depended on supplementing case decisions with forms of rule-making of various degrees of formality so as to achieve some of the above advantages.

(c) 'Managerial' or 'Regulatory' Decision-making?

K.C. Davis has repeatedly advocated that discretions be subjected to controls[13] but others, such as Daniel Gifford,[14] have
gone further towards the development of criteria for judging the
optimal levels of control over discretion. Gifford suggests that the
caseloads of regulatory agencies vary widely and take in very
different kinds of issue. Some cases dealt with are very important
(for example to the achievement of regulatory goals or to the
development of standards or rules) others are less so: some types
of issue involve frequently recurring factual patterns, in others
there is far less factual repetition. These variations in issue-type,
it is argued, have a bearing on the suitability of certain forms of
control over discretionary power.

The range of issue-types also explains, says Gifford, why there
are differences of view among certain commentators. Those who
advocate the setting of standards such as Davis and Judge Henry
Friendly[15] assume that issues are recurrent and so they advocate
a *'regulatory'* mode of decision-making in which discretions can be
structured by rules, policies and standards. I.L. Sharfman,[16] on
the other hand, is said to describe a *'managerial'* mode of agency
decision-making in which non-recurring issues are dealt with *ad
hoc* and in which the agency balances competing considerations
with reference to particular cases rather than looks to broader
policies.

The way forward, for Gifford, is for agencies to improve their
matching of processes to issue-types and to build up a sufficiently
broad base of information to be able to do this intelligently. This
approach can be contrasted with the method of 'muddling
through'[17] in which agencies adhere to existing policies and
procedures, only to adopt them in incremental fashion as circumstances change. There are, indeed, strong arguments against
incrementalism in regulation:[18] where industrial changes are
rapid, reliance on past experience may be misleading—a total
're-think' of both procedures and policies might be preferable.
Similarly, where repetitions do not occur, experience with one
regulatory issue may be irrelevant to another—incrementalism
may obstruct the accumulation of regulatory expertise.[19] Here
we see once more the implications of regulation by commission
as opposed to tribunal —for this is what Gifford says must be
done to counter 'muddling-through':

... adequate regulation requires an agency to collect and to evaluate significant amounts of information about the regulatory setting in which it must act beyond the information of the particular facts of the case before it and the information it has collected from deciding past cases. Indeed in the situations described, the agency must collect information extensively, in the manner in which it would proceed were it to be engaged in rulemaking.[20]

The CAA employs five times more staff on economic regulation than the ATLB did. The extent to which it is able to employ those resources in a manner that matches processes to issues and avoids 'muddling -through' is a matter of keen interest not only to administrative lawyers but to those looking for value for money from the agency.

(d) Politics and the Regulatory Process

The multi-powered agency that uses trial-type procedures must do so in a way that both preserves political legitimacy and allows the development of effective regulatory strategies. The ATLB fell down on both these counts, Louis Hector despaired of combining functions and James M. Landis, another former CAB Chairman, suggested that the CAB had been charged with what was essentially a managerial job unsuited to either adjudicative determination or to judicial review.[21] The CAA, for its part, has survived for over a decade, its trial-type procedures have so far been accepted as legitimate but the innovatory policy guidance system has already been abolished and there are signs that the future may be more strewn with political difficulties than the past.

The following review of policy-developments concentrates on CAA case-law but does so against the background of parallel developments in rule-making and policy-disclosing procedures of differing degrees of formality. It should be stressed: in comparing the CAA and the ATLB what is important is to see how a body on the commission, as opposed to the tribunal, model has been able to put trial-type procedures to use in a complex, contentious and fluid area of regulation. First, however, a description of the licensing process.

Procedure

Not all civil aviation route licences are issued after a hearing.

Where a routine application has been made by an operator whose fitness is not in question and where there is no objection lodged with the CAA, it has been usual for a licence to be granted without a hearing, provided that it may be issued in the terms applied for. In such cases the applications made and decisions taken are published in Series 2 of the Official Record of the Authority (Air Transport Licensing Notices (ATLN)).

The provisions for granting unopposed applications were designed to reduce the number of formal hearings and, coupled with the CAA's 1974 reclassification of licences,[22] did so. Only about ten per cent of applications were the subject of public hearings in 1980 but before 1974 (when inclusive tours were licensed individually) the ratio was less. In 1973–74, 101 applications out of over 4,500 considered went to a hearing.

Of the seven basic classes of CAA air transport licence most public hearings concern scheduled services (class 1 licences), charters (class 4), cargo charters (class 6), and sole-use helicopters (class 7). 'Blanket' authorization has massively reduced hearings on inclusive tours issues and substitute charter operations (class 5) are rarely contentious. Having cautioned that only a small proportion of applications lead to a public hearing, it must be added that most of the important policy decisions made concerning route allocations involve objections and hence hearings. Hearings, therefore, have an importance in policy-making terms that goes far beyond anything suggested numerically.

The standard procedure adopted in applying for an air transport licence is as follows. The operator sends in a written application to the Authority. This must contain such information as the CAA has specified[23] in its Official Record Series 1, such as the nationalities of the controllers of a company, details of financial resources and arrangements, the number and types of aircraft to be used, organization and staffing arrangements, provisions for liability, the class of licence applied for, the proposed period of duration, an indication of existing potential need or demand for the service, commercial agreements relevant, destinations proposed and the proposed tariff. Details of the financial position of an operator and of organizational arrangements[24] need not be given on each application since this is done routinely; they must merely be kept up to date.

The Authority publishes particulars of the application in its

Official Record and it keeps a copy for public inspection.[25] Many applications are uncontroversial and if these are not objected to within 21 days of publication then they are processed internally. The CAA's licensing branch staff pass them on to the policy section who consider any implications involved. If deemed uncontentious in terms of the CAA's policies then the applications will be approved automatically without reference to a board member. If there is an issue such a reference will be made but, in any event, the vast majority of unopposed applications are approved without a hearing—which could be demanded were the CAA to propose variation of the application. Only in rare cases does the CAA invite an applicant to a hearing to clarify costings or other arrangements.

If objections are lodged within the 21-day period the licensing branch sets a date for a hearing and, in more important cases, refers to a board member for discussion of such issues as panel membership. CAA staff are forbidden to discuss cases with applicants or other parties once an application has been submitted. The Authority view is that this would undermine the hearing which is the only place to resolve such issues: as one senior policy-maker in the CAA told the author: 'The quasi-judicial system is holy as far as we are concerned'. For this reason the CAA does not formally act as arbitrator between potential objectors and applicants. It is clear, however, that staff will often 'help the parties to understand each others' position' and, so close are relations in the industry, that this often catalyses negotiations between the airlines—by which means an application is perhaps amended so as to placate a potential objector. CAA staff see this as a 'commonsense' or 'pragmatists' approach which has a marginal effect in streamlining the licensing process. It is said to help avoid instances in which 'months of work may lead up to a hearing in which a misunderstanding is cleared up within ten minutes. . .'.

Although the quorum for a decision is one CAA member,[26] formal hearings take place before panels, usually consisting of three persons, at least one of whom is a member of the Authority (normally two are) the rest being officials of the Economic Regulation Group. Certain members of the Authority have, especially in the CAA's early years, tended to specialise, e.g. the first Chairman tended to hear major tariff applications and major competition cases. The CAA (under Regulation 12) has a duty to give those with a right to be heard (or those whom the Authority has chosen to hear) a copy of or summary of:

> ... any information in the possession of the Authority which has been furnished in connection with the case or which the Authority has reason to believe will be referred to at the hearing of the case.

Although parties must be given notice of the date of a hearing[27] the regulations make no provision concerning minimum notice for the submission of written evidence. CAA staff often ask for supplementary material from an operator and sometimes receive statistical evidence of importance in a case only a couple of days before the hearing. The airlines have tended not to 'show their hands' earlier than has been necessary and this did affect the ability of CAA staff to review their submissions until in May 1981 the Authority issued a notice in its Official Record requiring that written submissions be given 25 days in advance of hearings.[28]

Further speed is often required and the regulations[29] allow the CAA to forego the fourteen days notice of hearing in cases of 'compelling urgency'. Thus, when an operator has the chance of a short-notice charter contract which is not permitted under its existing licences the CAA might telephone the other airlines to see whether they will object and may hold a short notice hearing under Regulation 14(5). In Domestic Tariff applications non-parties to the case with no *right* to be heard (e.g. representatives of users' and regional bodies) may similarly be approached for their views so that the CAA may judge whether to exercise its discretion to hear their views in public. By this means, even publication of an application may be avoided in some cases.

Having received the parties' evidence in chief, the CAA may, in a major application, call for a preliminary meeting (under Regulation 13) in order to discuss the conduct of the case. This has not proved a revolutionary procedure however. The Edwards Committee recommended its use[30] to review evidence and dispose of differences of facts and to agree on the issues to be argued before the Authority. Such meetings are infrequently held,[31] they are confined to procedural issues in the main and representatives of the airlines consider them fairly unimportant, although they can help to shorten the hearing proper by cutting out irrelevant issues. The CAA has told operators in pre-hearings what kinds of evidence and argument it believes will be relevant to the hearing proper but the potential of the preliminary meeting is diminished in many cases by the parties having already submitted their evidence in chief in writing and by the CAA's reservation of substantive issues for the hearing. Staff of the CAA have, in addition, largely bypassed the preliminary hearing by writing to the operators and telling them what information they believe will assist the panel's decision.[32]

When a hearing before the Authority is to take place operators are requested (in the Official Record Series 1) to give two days notice of their representative and his status. Before the panels there usually appear either legally trained advocates specializing in civil aviation matters or representatives from the licensing or comercial departments of the operators. B.Cal. uses either their licensing manager, his assistant or more generally in major cases, the company secretary (a solicitor experienced in aviation licensing). British Airways use either representatives from their licensing departments, few of whom are legally trained, or in more important cases specialist counsel. The smaller independent operators tend to use their licensing or commercial staff or else solicitors or counsel specialising in the field.

From the late 1970s onwards legal representation increased. During 1980 there were 35 hearings at only seven of which were lawyers not used. At six, only one of the parties was legally represented but at 14 hearings all of the parties were represented by lawyers. Sir Nigel Foulkes, CAA Chairman from 1977 to 1982, assessed the position since he arrived at the Authority:

> The use of lawyers was small when I came here, and of barristers insignificant. There has been more use of lawyers in my time and the average length of hearings has doubled. It has now reached the point where operators, even small ones, think that they cannot not use legal representation. It is certainly more time consuming and only occasionally does it make a difference to the party.[33]

Hearings procedure is similar in route licensing and in domestic tariff cases. Following submission of the application, the licensing division publishes the application in the earliest practicable issue of the CAA Official Record and consults advisory bodies such as the Channel Islands Air Advisory Council where relevant.[34] Objections again have to be made within 21 days of publication and this includes objections from organisations and individuals other than those having a right to be heard.

In the sixth week a decision without hearing would be given, or in the sixth and seventh weeks evidence from objectors followed by rebutting evidence would be submitted. Formal notice of hearing and the preparation of the panel's brief (if not commenced earlier) occurs in the seventh week also. In the eighth week the panel is briefed, followed shortly by the public hearing. Finally in the tenth week after application, the panel's decision-making begins.[35]

The hearing before the CAA is conducted in a manner described by a CAA official as 'fairly informally and relaxed but within a formal court-like framework'.[36] The applicant argues on the basis of written evidence-in-chief with which the panel and the other parties are familiar. He or she may call witnesses (e.g. representatives from the operator's marketing division or senior management or from regional bodies, tour organizers, business associations, tourist boards etc.). The usual reason for this is to make a case for demand in relation to a potential operation. Witnesses may be cross-examined by opposing parties and the panel often ask them to clarify matters of concern to the Authority. Those making objections or representations may then state their case and produce witnesses. The panel try not to let formal procedures prevent an open discussion of key issues and their own cross-examination of witnesses may be crucial. From panel questioning the operators' advocates attempt to identify those matters on which argument will be most productive.

It has been on the subject of written pleadings that there has been the most pressure (from lawyers appearing before the CAA) to judicialize procedures. In the period November 1980 to March 1981 the CAA responded to this pressure by considering a proposal under which parties would be required to put written evidence to the Authority in advance of a hearing but (and this was the novelty) they would not be permitted to raise new issues at the hearing without the consent of the CAA panel.

Keeping the Council on Tribunals informed, the CAA held joint meetings with all the airlines' legal representatives and, separately, with airline managements. Many of the lawyers advocated the pleadings system on the grounds that it allowed the parties to know precisely where they stood. A conspicuous dissenter from this view was Laker Airways' American lawyer who argued that the CAA's flexible procedures were preferable to those of the US CAB under whose regulations many days were wasted on procedural argument.[37]

In the end, the CAA was of the opinion (one shared by the Council on Tribunals) that introducing such a change would be of dubious value. The Authority's Legal Advisor gave the following reasons to the Council on Tribunals:[38]

(a) The Authority was not a Court of Law. It was assisted in reaching its decision not so much by the presentation of evidence in the normal sense of the term, but by such things as forecasts of traffic on the route and other expressions of expert opinion and by argument on whether the airline's proposal was or was not consistent with the established policies. While much of this could be reduced to writing in advance, other useful and relevant points might emerge when expert reacted to expert during the course of the hearing. A good deal could be lost if parties were constrained within the strait-jacket of their written submission.

(b) If parties were required at the hearing to keep strictly to matters arising from the written statements, there could be protracted legal argument as to whether a point being made by a party did not arise from those submissions. This would not in itself improve the efficiency of hearings and would increase the time spent on them.

(c) There would be pressure on the CAA to exercise its discretion to allow new evidence to be admitted, this would open the way to legal challenge.

(d) Pleadings that attempted to be exhaustive would be excessively long.

(e) The CAA consistently sought to ensure that airlines who do not employ legal representatives are not prejudiced at hearings but managements have admitted that under the proposed system no-one could risk not being legally represented if procedural questions were to assume greater importance.

In the end a compromise was reached[39] in which written submissions were to be delivered to the CAA 25 days in advance of hearings and new evidence might occasion an adjournment or delay of the proceedings. For the time being the CAA had managed to hold the lawyers at bay.

After parties have argued their cases, the panel members retire to consider their decision, which is published at a later date.

Shorthand and taped records·of the hearing are always taken[40] but transcripts are only made if an appeal is lodged or if requested by any person (who must pay for them). The secretary to the panel, who is present throughout the hearing (in public and in camera), provides the main working summary of the case though panel members may have their own notes. The secretary is often a junior staff member in the licensing division. He or she is familiar with the documentation in the case and notes down salient points as the case progresses. Although there have been occasional complaints that points have been missed by the secretary, an opportunity to resolve disputes is offered by the appeals system where reference may be made to a transcript of the hearing.

Briefing

The panel of the Authority hears and decides cases on the evidence adduced at the hearing but with the benefit of background briefing. In international cases such material is supplied by the CAA's international services section and sets out the Department of Trade's views on any traffic rights implications of licensing, e.g. whether mere designation within an existing agreement is required or whether rights will require negotiation; whether foreign reaction of some kind is expected.[41] Observations on the DoT's views will be supplied when appropriate.

A second brief contains analysis by the CAA's own staff. Before 1973 the panel, in continuation of the ATLB system would have been provided with an interpretative and analytical brief[42] of parties' evidence plus additional information from CAA sources. During 1973 however, the panel demanded:

> ... more sophisticated analysis and economic appraisal— particularly of costs and profitability.[43]

An important step in restructuring the briefing system was the establishment in that year of a briefing unit in the Economic Services (ECS) division. This comprised two full time staff with the resources of the whole division to call upon. The unit no longer merely examined operators' figures but, as the CAA noted in its second report:

> ... an interrogative procedure has been developed whereby the briefing unit requests specific data of parties to an application

and this may be followed by detailed consultation with the parties concerned.'[44]

Instead of merely taking a retrospective approach, the Authority, as its expertise developed, turned more to the future, with staff being allocated to a forecasting unit.

The post-1980 system involves the production by different CAA teams of a number of briefs which are co-ordinated by a Briefing Liaison Officer. A licensing brief outlines the application and objections, gives a history of licensing for the past few years on the route and draws out the licensing issues involved. A brief is also prepared on the competitive situation relevant to a route and the implications of licensing for the development of the industry. (Thus questions of diversion, networking and the needs of various operations are discussed.) This is integrated with a policy brief that deals with the wider issues raised by an application. The Airline Economics Branch offers a statistical and economic analysis and, where relevant, there will also be briefs on airports and noise implications.

The above documents all deal with the economics of regulation: a further brief, however, is compiled on financial fitness and may note any safety aspects of an operation. Thus the Economic Services group may consider whether a certain operator has sufficient capital resources to mount an operation and whether airline's general financial situation is such that it can be entrusted with an operation.

The object of all briefs is to present the panel with a distillation of relevant facts and arguments, a commentary on these and an indication of matters that might usefully be pursued at the hearing. The panels of the CAA have always been careful to preserve their discretion by treating the briefs as advice rather than as uncontrovertible analyses of finding of fact.

The Authority adopts the view that its decision is based upon evidence put to it at the hearing or in written evidence and, being subject to the rules of the Council on Tribunals,[45] it will not consider evidence submitted by parties after the hearing. It decides in the light of its own knowledge, which might include clarifying a matter with licensing staff after a hearing ('putting the figures into context') but would not involve further research or collection of facts at that stage.

Where the Authority has calculated figures relevant to an

issue being argued in public (e.g. diversion or growth) it adopts a judicial attitude again: the panel members do not offer the CAA's own figures, as set out in the staff brief, to the operators for dissection but keep such data to themselves and listen to the two competing cases. The panel's own brief thus constitutes not evidence but a stock of knowledge that allows panel members to test the parties' evidence by means of questioning at the hearing.

When a decision is made it is usual for the secretary to the panel to draft the narrative part of the reasons and for a member of the panel to draft the analysis and reasons themselves. There is no committee set up by the Authority to consider particular licensing decisions but an Economic Policy and Licensing Committee was formed by Lord Boyd-Carpenter in 1972. In doing so he announced that since the CAA was not confined to the 'quasi-judicial role' which characterized the ATLB, he had set up the EPL Committee so that:

> ... licence applications could be considered against a policy background as well as against the background of the evidence and arguments presented at a hearing.[46]

It met weekly and was presided over by the Chairman of the Authority. It normally contained the Deputy Chairman, the panel chairman and all the other Members who hear licence applications together with heads of EPL and ECS divisions. Where their areas might be concerned, the Financial Controller, Head of Operational Safety Division and representatives of the DoT attend. The Authority said of the Committee:

> It does not decide individual licensing cases but it may consider particular policy issues arising from them. It also provides a forum in which the members of licensing panels may keep each other informed so as to ensure a homogeneity of decision-making.[47]

The EPL Committee catered for policy discussions between board and staff, as such it was an important policy-making body. The same could not be said of its successor, the Economic Policy Committee (EPC) set up after Lord Boyd-Carpenter left the Authority. Under a more devolved system of management the EPC (which meets only monthly) serves as an advisory rather than policy-making institution.

The Problem of Information

The CAA is almost unique in British regulation in attempting to combine a massive technical knowledge with a system of trial-type public adjudication.[48] A fundamental question, therefore, is whether it can decide issues on the basis of such knowledge without rendering the hearings process meaningless and without undermining its legitimacy.

Apart from the information gathered under section 22(1) of the 1971 Act relating to particular applications, the Authority has extensive powers to gain general information under section 35 of the Act. The Authority uses this power to demand regular financial returns from operators and these serve as the basis for its own researches. On 1 January 1974 it introduced an improved system of collecting statistical data from operators. Airlines were required to submit monthly statistics of two kinds, firstly operating and traffic statistics, giving information route by route on such matters as frequencies operated, passengers carried or sectors flown[49] and, secondly, financial statistics concerning the company and serving as the basis for the CAA's monitoring of the financial health of UK airlines. (In 1974 the Authority began publishing its 'Monthly Bulletin of Statistics' giving details of traffic figures derived from the above results.) In addition to the above monthly returns, all domestic route operators submit six-monthly statements of costs, revenues and traffic, capacity productivity and analyses of operating expenditure giving results of the previous year, forecasts for the current year and estimates for the following year. (These figures are used by the CAA in assessing applications to vary the Domestic Air Tariff.) The Authority asks for these figures to be given in an up-dated form before important hearings, and it often requests supplementary information: e.g. a breakdown into unit costs in pence per available seat kilometer.

The CAA has, since its inception, set out to build up a store of information for use in support of licensing decisions and for policy-making. In addition to the information from monthly returns, it has held private meetings with airlines and tour organizers—not to decide licensing issues but for examining their financial fitness.[50] Thus the CAA in its 1973–74 report stated that it had started:

... monitoring airlines' current results with the intention of identifying potentially dangerous situations before they become critical.[51]

If an operator should become short of capital resources the CAA aim is to discover this from returns and use persuasion[52] or its powers under section 23 of the Act (to revoke, suspend or vary a licence in the event of inadequate financial resources) to produce an improvement in the capitalization of the operator.[53]

In the process of collecting information from operators either routinely or in relation to a hearing, the Authority's staff often consult the airline on a point and they attempt to gain clarification of issues.[54] The situation has arisen (concerning March 1976 Tariff applications) in which the Authority has sent economists to airline headquarters in order to sort out a misunderstanding on statistics but the Authority does not conduct negotiations into particular licensing matters—it adheres to the position of an examining body.

Disclosure

Given that the Authority has the above information as well as data from its own researches, how can it incorporate this knowledge into decisions? A principal problem is confidentiality. The Regulation 12 duty to supply parties to a case with a summary of information is tempered by a provision that the Authority should not furnish any information relating to the commercial or financial affairs of the person who provided it (and which could not be disclosed without disadvantage to the provider) unless that disadvantage was warranted by the advantage to the public or to the prospective recipient of the information.

Furthermore, section 36 of the 1971 Act provided that no information relating to a person and given to the Authority under the Act, should be disclosed[55] unless the provider of the information had consented in writing, or the Secretary of State, after considering representations, had determined that the information be disclosed.[56] This was not, however, to prevent disclosure under Regulation 12 or for the purposes of giving reasons for decisions under section 24(3) or (5) of the Act.

The position, therefore, was that, unless the operator consented,[57] the Authority had to decide for itself on the balance of advantage, whether to disclose information to parties in a case or in its reasons for decision. Until the late 1970s the airlines routinely put in their information to the Authority before a hearing and claimed confidentiality. Thus a number of situations could occur: the CAA might have the figures of each party and decide not to disclose parts of them to respective parties, it might disclose the figures to parties only or it could publish the full figures.[58]

In cases where parties have been willing to disclose information to other parties but not to the public, the Authority has held part of the hearing 'in camera' to consider arguments relating to confidential documents or figures (generally the airlines are concerned to keep details of costings secret). The question of whether to disclose information has been considered frequently. When the CAA has decided not to disclose these costings to the other parties this has made the objector's case more difficult and it has also deprived the Authority of hearing argument on the matter. Such difficulties arose but were resolved in a 'Wanderer' tours case[59] in 1975. Both BA and Britannia Airways had submitted information which the Authority was asked to treat as confidential. Since the issue of diversion from BA was crucial, the Authority discussed the matter of disclosure with the parties and ruled that BA tables setting out actual costs and estimated passenger traffic on services to Athens, Corfu, Hiraklion and Rhodes should be disclosed to Britannia and Thompsons on their undertaking that these would not be divulged to any third party.

On many occasions where the disclosure of information to competitors would obviously be harmful, the CAA has attempted to gain unanimous agreement on the disclosure of information. This has not always been forthcoming and, in one such hearing the CAA warned:

> ... it would be difficult to proceed in a meaningful way other than by using the statistical exhibits presented by the parties.[60]

Matters only improved when, by 1980, the CAA had secured agreements amongst airlines that all data would be disclosed unless positive requests for confidentiality were made and that such requests would be minimized.

In applications to change the Domestic Air Tariff the disclosure of information may involve confidential information relating to an operator's costs, revenue, traffic, operating expenditure, financial results on all services, efficiency, future plans etc. The CAA has, however, consistently ordered that all statistical information including cost and revenue data be disclosed to the parties and objectors 'in order that the case may be properly argued'.[61] (This sometimes involves holding proceedings in camera). On some occasions[62] the CAA has ordered disclosures to be restricted to individual routes. In the early seventies it was again routine for airlines to claim confidentiality for all submissions but by 1980 the administrative presumption favoured full disclosure unless an exceptional claim was made.

The airlines' licensing representatives have expressed some concern about the lack of information concerning other operators' activities but they appear more troubled by their inability to understand what information they are given. On matters of diversion the problem is not acute and those involved are confident that they can fairly accurately work out from available figures the effect that one service will have on another. The real difficulty concerns other airlines' costings.[63] Generally an operator will give a degree of information concerning a proposed route to the CAA and to other parties to a case but this will not always be sufficient to allow detailed cross-examination. With smaller operators the problem is that accounting procedures have not been standardized and so one airline might not know, for example, the basis of amortization of another's aircraft, the sum allowed for writing aircraft off or the price paid for them—airline users' representatives are in an even weaker position. With larger operators, the problem for their opponents is to calculate the indirect costings and cross-subsidisations occurring. Thus in the 'Shuttle' hearing of August 1975 when B.Cal. was arguing that BA's Glasgow to London shuttle service constituted operation at uneconomic fares and hence unfair competition, B.Cal. submitted costings for BA's shuttle based not on BA's figures but on B.Cal's own calculations of what the shuttle should cost.[64] This case involved an enormous amount of work analyzing costings and yet, because of the size of the organizations involved, there was little agreement on the assumptions being made. The CAA was left to choose between two different sets of calculations that did not meet head on.

CAA Calculations

A March 1975 freight charter hearing introduced the question of the Authority's duty to disclose its own statistics. Before that case the Authority had conducted a review of freight charter operations and had issued a document to the airlines explaining a proposed new policy. British Caledonian's representative Mr David Beety argued that Regulation 12 demanded CAA disclosure of its own figures and information, not merely the information submitted to it by airlines. The Authority did not give B.Cal. detailed statistics concerning their new policy but explained that the Authority's policy statement was intended to provide 'guidance and assistance'[65] and that confidential statistics could not be disclosed. As noted already, the CAA's unwillingness to make its own figures known stemmed in part from its judicial approach but it has also been clear that the CAA has consistently sought to avoid the embarrassment of having either its own figures subjected to scrutiny or its own staff submitted to cross-examination in public hearings.

In the freight charter case Mr Beety was worried that the Authority had, in using their policy statement, (which advocated relaxing the restrictions on freight licences) placed a heavy onus on B.Cal. to argue against the 'new policy', an onus which they found difficult to discharge since they did not have access to the statistical data serving as the foundations of the new policy.

Another airline lawyer later described how CAA decision-making by reference to policy statements had been combined with a movement towards greater use of CAA officials (as opposed to 'amateur' board members) on CAA panels:

> The result of all this is that the character of the licensing panel has changed from a tribunal judging on evidence to an in-house panel of staff members hearing argument on a regulatory policy that the CAA is proposing—that may be a slight exaggeration, but it's going in that direction.[66]

Use of the public hearing to argue the pros and cons of a new policy can thus be seen by critics as a device capable of justifying less involvement by airlines at the policy planning stage without giving, by means of useful discussion, any compensating involvement at the hearing.[67]

Publication

Disclosure (to parties) must be distinguished from publication in general. The CAA, under Regulation 12, may order the publication of statistics if it feels that that advantage to the public would outweigh any harm to an operator. The ATLB repeatedly argued[68] for the public disclosure of financial information upon which it based its tariff decisions and for the power to publish such information. Edwards stated that such financial data 'must be made public in order to ensure that the arguments for fare increases can be fully tested'.[69] In an October 1972 tariff hearing the CAA ruled that the balance of public interest was best served by keeping secret the financial and other data provided by airlines.[70] Since then the CAA has introduced the publication of 'Monthly Statistics' which give information about carryings, the financial results of operations etc. It has not ordered full publication of documents in domestic tariff hearings but has restricted the use of 'in camera' hearings to the most confidential arguments; consequently substantial details of costings etc. do emerge in the course of oral debates.

Conclusions

Procedurally the CAA licensing hearing is necessarily imperfect: the exercise of judgment by an expert body in an area involving complex and sometimes confidential material does not lend itself readily to adjudicative procedures of the classical court-room type involving decision making according to legal rules principles and standards and based on evidence presented in adversary fashion before a court that considers, at one point in time, past wrongs, actions and rights. In terms of Abram Chayes' distinction between 'traditional' and 'public law' models of adjudication,[71] the CAA comes within the 'public law' camp insofar as it is concerned not only with past fact but with prediction; it looks to future relations, not past wrongs alone; its relationship with the parties is continuing, not determinate; the decision-maker is closely involved in fact finding and in organizing the result of the case, and the contest involves public policy as much as private rights. Parties to CAA hearings do have certain difficulties in obtaining information about, and in understanding, an opponent's case, but, on the other hand, staff of the airlines do accept a degree of vagueness as necessary in the system. As far as disclosure of CAA calculations is concerned, there has been worry in the exceptional case, such as cargo charters in 1975, when it has been felt that, because of lack of access to the CAA panel brief or staff calculations, the onus of controverting a 'CAA line' has been too heavy. Where an existing policy has been applied to particular facts rather than where a new policy is being developed, there may be similar concern that the panel brief has not been questioned in detail. Thus an airline representative who is told that his figures for diversion or traffic are 'too high' might find it difficult to challenge CAA assumptions except by resort to an appeal. At this stage it can be said that, for all its departures from the court paradigm, the public licensing hearing was one virtue perceived by all: even if tainted with vagueness it provides an opportunity for the applicants to air their case in public and it thereby increases confidence in the fairness, if not the efficiency, of the licensing system.[72]

11
Discretionary Justice and the Development of Policy

Some lawyers tend to conceive of justice in terms of sure precedents and precise rules. Thus Judge Henry Friendly's major criticism of the American CAB in 1962 was its lack of defined standards in adjudication.[1] On the other hand, some have seen reliance on a system of case law or precedent as a sign of stagnation, debility and decline[2] and an indication that the efficiency element in justice has been neglected.[3] On both sides of the Atlantic commentators have for some time questioned whether a movement away from judicial procedures in regulatory decision-making must always involve injustice and they have offered alternative systems ranging from hybrid schemes to administrative decision-making subject to various checks.[4]

From the point of view of administrators, however, criticisms that their decisions are unpredictable may be viewed sceptically. CAA Chairman, Sir Nigel Foulkes, has given the pragmatist's response:

> Complaints of lack of predictability from an airline usually mean that we didn't find for them. It is necessarily difficult to predict a result if there are, say, four competent applicants for a route. We are meticulous and listen to days of boring information so as to give a fair decision 'on a whisker'. Often it is very finely balanced and anyone could have got the licence.[5]

Whether or not legalistic rigidity in case decisions is desirable or possible,[6] it is clear that where hearings procedures are used, some sort of credible balance has to be found between consistency and fairness on the one side and efficiency and flexibility on the other. As Jeffrey Jowell has put it:

> Decisions may be made in an adjudicative setting without the elements of participation or reference to rule, principle or standard that Fuller requires. It is suggested, however, that the

integrity of the process of adjudication will be eroded or destroyed if the reality often veers too far from the ideal.[7]

The role of case law in the CAA licensing process is described here not by selecting decisions, rules and policy-statements that are consistent but by looking at all the major decisions relevant to certain topics. An exhaustive review of CAA policy will not be attempted, instead we look at developments in three key areas: (1) scheduled service competition; (2) passenger charters; (3) cargo charters.

A preliminary assessment should be made of the CAA's attitude to decision-making, and, in particular, to the doctrine of precedent. This was set out in condensed form in a 1977 decision. The Authority said:

> It was argued that in any case the CAA is not bound by precedent; this is true, although the Authority attaches great importance to the consistency and continuity of its decisions.[8]

In an interview with the author in October 1980, a board member of the CAA qualified this statement saying: '"coherence" rather than "consistency" is the right word; it should "hang together": if a decision differs from others then reasons have to be given.'[9]

A review of all CAA decisions up to 1980 reveals a concern to reconcile flexibility with these elements of consistency and continuity. To this end, the CAA panel considers each case on its merits but in the light of the CAA's legal and policy frameworks, the staff briefs and their discussion of relevant past decisions. Argument at hearings involves frequent reference to prior cases. The extent to which precedent operates may be seen in the prevalence of four practices: openly exempting a particular case from the system of precedence; distinguishing previous cases; acknowledging the creation of precedent and applying established policies.

To deny the setting of a precedent in a specific case is to imply the relevance of precedent to others. This the CAA has done. In response to a number of applications it has granted licences on an exceptional basis stating that a particular decision creates no precedent for similar cases and it has reminded operators that 'every application is considered on its merits'.[11] Similarly, in one case on domestic charter services the Authority made it clear that, since relevant policy was only at the stage of development, no precedent was to be implied.[12]

Previous cases have also been distinguished by the CAA when avoiding a precedent[13] and the belief that one licence may open the door for similar applications is clearly held by airlines. On numerous occasions operators have objected 'to the principle' involved in a licensing decision or in fear that 'a precedent might be set' and further diversion from their own services allowed.[14] It is usual for the CAA to remind such objectors that cases will be treated on their merits and that objection may be taken to any application as it arises in the future.

It is, however, the CAA's own linking together of cases that best demonstrates a concern to establish continuous policy. Where a case involves discussion of a policy matter in a detail that goes beyond that found in the Act or guidance, both airline advocates and the CAA panel will be concerned in any future case to relate back to the 'fleshed-out' policy. There are many instances of cases being decided on the basis of principles or arguments adopted previously. Thus, in a Dan-Air Services' application A15946 of 18 September 1973 for a Gatwick to Newcastle service, the operator's representative quoted at length from a previous Heathrow to Newcastle decision and its assertion of separate passenger catchment areas for Gatwick and Heathrow.[15] The CAA accepted this argument. In other instances the CAA, on citation of a similar case, has 'not been persuaded to take a different view' on the application in hand[16] and has often referred to its own prior reasoning in justifying or explaining a decision.[17]

As the CAA's experience has grown it has used its reasons for decisions to set down in greater detail its interpretation of certain elements of policy. Thus, when considering applications for a number of short-haul services from Gatwick in August 1979,[18] it said:

> The Authority's policies on the licensing of new short-haul services from Gatwick . . . were set out in its decision of 26 October 1977.[19]

The extent to which reasons for decision in major cases could be used to set down detailed policy as well as explain CAA philosophy was best indicated when in November 1979 the CAA issued a draft statement of its licensing policies for consideration in relation to the Civil Aviation Bill 1979/80.[20] That document set out policies in relation to Gatwick services by reference to two other cases,[21] stating that it had: 'tried to build up over the last few years a policy framework within which individual decisions may stand coherently'.

The above review only shows the CAA's *willingness* to develop policies by means of the hearings process. It does not indicate whether the CAA *has* successfully developed principles, standards and rules in a way that might satisfy such commentators as Friendly, Davis, Sharfman or Gifford, nor does it describe the role of trial-type procedures and case law in this process. An attempt must therefore be made to examine policy developments in specific areas.

(i) Scheduled Service Competition

The CAA started licensing in 1972 with reference both to the objectives in the 1971 Act and to the first guidance. Its policy-making faced two main challenges: to improve the effectiveness and potential of the industry and to produce policies of sufficient coherence to guide licence applicants and airline planners. Consideration will be given to three issues: the role of the two main operators, BA and B.Cal.; entry to a route, and airports policy. The first topic gives an indication of how broad strategy was developed, the last two indicate how more detailed policies emerged.

The Two Main Operators and Competition Policy

In accordance with section 3(1)(b) of the Act the first guidance stated that BA were to remain the 'principal providers of scheduled services' and B.Cal. the 'principal independent airline'. The two operators were to be given 'adequate opportunities to compete effectively' and, to this end, licences to other independent airlines for international scheduled routes were to be restricted. Paragraph 16 of that guidance advocated competition internationally where this would increase the total British share of traffic on a route and paragraph 17 gave B.Cal., for the sake of development, 'a measure of preference' over other airlines in allocating licences for new scheduled service routes.

A limited 'spheres of interest' policy had emerged from the ATLB and through the creation of B.Cal. The Civil Aviation

(Declaratory Provisions) Act 1971 had, as we have seen, given B.Cal. a number of West African routes formerly belonging to BOAC but, in accordance with the guidance, the CAA sought to strengthen the B.Cal. network. When that airline and Dan-Air both sought a London-Brussels licence in 1973, B.Cal. were licensed. The CAA said:

> We have found the guidance to be explicit. Paragraphs 15 and 17 ... require us to give preference to the second force airline; B.Cal. ... Dan-Air have not adduced sufficient evidence to enable us to disregard the clear words of paragraphs 15 and 17.[22]

In accordance also with paragraphs 16 and 17, B.Cal. were licensed on a further set of ('Cannonball') routes to Boston, Singapore, Toronto, and Montreal[23] and, in August 1973, B.Cal. replaced BEA on the London to Algiers service. (Though the above licences were given in order to encourage B.Cal's development, in fact traffic rights were never gained for the 'Cannonball' routes which remained unoperated.)

B.Cal. considered that their preference under paragraph 17 was limited to building up their sphere of interest and viability as a world force. They judged the preference to be 'used up' after the Brussels licence (A15922) was granted in December 1973 and their representatives no longer relied heavily upon it. In the spring of 1975 when Dan-Air and International Aviation Services (IAS) sought a number of advance booking charters (ABCs) to Ghana in competition with B.Cal.,[24] the latter invoked paragraph 17 only to be told by the CAA that the preference was 'neither automatic nor complete'. The charter services were shared.

If B.Cal. looked to paragraph 17 then BA's assurance lay in paragraph 15 which provided that they were to be the principal providers of scheduled services. Occasionally BA would oppose the licensing of a private operator on the basis of this paragraph but such arguments were seldom conclusive. Thus the BA subsidiary Cambrian Airways unsuccessfully opposed the licensing of Dan-Air for a Lyons service in October 1972 when the CAA stated that paragraph 15 had to be applied 'judiciously to individual cases'.[25] Nor would the privileged position of BA protect them where a superior service was offered. On 11 July 1974, British Midland Airways (BMA) were granted a licence (1B/

24252) to operate from East Midlands to Copenhagen and gained the revocation of BA's parallel service. The principal reason for this decision was passenger advantage. A subsequent appeal by BA based on paragraph 15 failed.

Clearly paragraphs 15 and 17 were treated by the CAA as strongly persuasive though they did not dictate a decision or take away the Authority's discretion to consider a case on its merits. The policy guidance secured spheres of interest for B.Cal. and BA but the two major operators enjoyed something short of complete protection and this was most strongly emphasised when Laker's 'Skytrain' was licensed for the London to New York route on 26 September 1972.[26] The CAA, in the first 'Skytrain' decision,[27] admitted some concern about possible diversion from the major carriers but granted the licence in order to cater for an unsatisfied market. Over two years later the CAA refused to revoke the licence after BA had produced evidence of a sharp decline in North Atlantic profits in the period after 1972[28]: Laker was merely advised to defer commencing 'Skytrain' until recovery of the market.

Case law as such played no large part in shaping policy for the industry in the period 1972–76. After route exchanges setting up B.Cal. had been arranged, adjustments were made in the decisions noted above but the profitable long-haul scheduled services posed few problems for the hearings process since there were too few cases to build up expectations of any case law. Operators knew the B.Cal. and BA spheres of interest and realized that they would have to have an exceptional case to be licensed. Any problems for operators lay in political considerations rather than with the absence of standards in case law. Issues in this area were, in Gifford's terms, important but non-recurring.

It was political action that produced the next major decision on long-haul competition policy. The Shore review of 1975–76 resulted, as we have seen, in the second guidance, and its restriction of competition on long-haul routes. It might have been thought that such guidance produced stability at the price of the CAA's option to licence competitively but stable guidance it was not. Laker Airways' successful challenge to the *vires* of paragraphs 7 and 8 of the guidance resulted in the vague state of affairs already described in Chapter 9. After the 'Skytrain' decision, the CAA was left to decide whether paragraphs 7 and 8 were *ultra vires* for all purposes and whether it had complete freedom to licence competitively on long-haul routes. Case law finally set out the CAA's position. In the three decisions noted above[29] it described its adherence to the general policy of spheres of interest but felt 'able to depart from this if a sufficiently compelling and acceptable case was made'.[30] It would not regard itself as committed to absolutely defined spheres of interest or to the total exclusion of competition on long-haul routes.[31]

Retention of the discretion to licence competitively in exceptional cases allowed the CAA to make some licensing decisions of key importance. To add to the New York 'Skytrain' Laker was given permission for a similar service to Los Angeles in May 1978.[32] Likewise neither the guidance nor the spheres of interest policy prevented the licensing of B.Cal. to compete with BA on the London to Hong-Kong route on 17 March 1980.[33] By the time the Conservative government came to consider abolishing policy guidance in 1980 it was clear that in dealing with the international routes that have a major influence on the shape of the industry neither case law nor guidance offered much help to operators in setting down recurring principles or standards. It is arguable that this was not a regulatory sector amenable to detailed structuring of discretion in the Davis or Friendly manner: each case might be considered exceptional and dealt with *ad hoc*; political considerations loomed large and, in many instances, what might be achieved by way of the negotiation of traffic rights proved to be the determining factor in any licensing issue.

Route Entry

The most contentious issue in civil aviation licensing arises when one airline seeks to compete with or to replace the existing operator on a route. This is an area, therefore, in which more factual repetition and more structuring of discretion might be expected than would be the case with long-haul competition policy. Two central questions are commonly at issue. What protection will be given to the existing operator? What standard of service has to be offered in order to merit that protection?

On competitive licensing, the 1971 Act directed the CAA to secure the satisfaction of public demand for services consistent with high safety and an economic return to efficient operators (section 3(1)(a)) and to 'further the reasonable interests of users of air transport services' (section 3(1)(d)). The first guidance gave more help, stating that more than one airline should be licensed for the same route or traffic points *wherever* the CAA was satisfied that: (a) traffic was likely to be sufficient to support competing services profitably within a reasonable time, or (b) the choice and standard of services available to the public was likely to be improved (paragraph 16).

In cases involving B.Cal. in its formative years the paragraph 17 'preference' applied and some protection for existing operators was also implied in the CAA's duty to further 'the maintenance and development of a viable network of scheduled services' under paragraph 14. More general guidance demanded consideration of an airline's skills and resources (paragraph 11), its suitability for an operation (paragraph 12) and the desirability of both avoiding monopoly over types of operation and avoiding fragmentation of effort.

The CAA sought to apply to particular cases the sometimes contradictory advice contained in the Act and the guidance. Soon, however, there began to emerge an approach to competitive licensing that was based on more detailed considerations. One principle was rapidly formed. An operator's investment in a route would enjoy some protection during the initial period of development. Thus in September 1973 BEA's application for a Glasgow to Dublin licence was refused in order to protect British Island Airways' (BIA) investment of £500,000 in new aircraft. Similarly British Air Ferries (BAF) were refused a licence on the Southend to Lyons route[34] in March 1974 when Cambrian Airways pleaded that they had only operated for twelve months and would not make a profit until the third year.

It was clear, nevertheless, that competition would be allowed if an established service was inadequate, if traffic on a route could support a second operator without undue diversion or if a proposed operation brought a significant improvement in service. B.Cal. were given a London to Brussels licence in December 1973[35] because the CAA accepted that the existing BA service was inadequate and Cambrian Airway's service from London to the Isle of Man was similarly found lacking in 1974.[36] In both cases an additional operator was licensed in spite of allegations of diversion. The principle was extended by the CAA in 1974 so that failure to use a licence was also deemed to remove from an airline the protection that would have been enjoyed by an efficient operator.[37]

Later in that year, the CAA developed its position on the

weight to be attached to *promises* of services from non-operating licence holders. Severn Airways applied for a scheduled service licence from Bristol to Leeds/Bradford. Dan Air Services, who held a licence objected and said that the 'time was not ripe' for operation but that they were interested in developing the route at a later date. Granting the licence, the CAA noted the premise of Dan Air's case—that they should have a protected option on the route—but called this 'unacceptable'.[38]

During the processing of BMA's Copenhagen application, BA suffered another blow when BMA were licensed from Heathrow to Sumburgh and from Gatwick to Aberdeen.[39] BA's Gatwick to Aberdeen licence was withdrawn after the CAA had stated:

> We are concerned that the development of the oil industry . . . justifies additional services, which do not appear to be forthcoming from BA. As BA have not utilised, and do not intend to utilise their traffic rights between London (Gatwick) and Aberdeen, we think it right to transfer this route to another operator with plans for early operation.[40]

This case contrasted with an earlier decision: in February 1974 Air Anglia's application for the Aberdeen to Sumburgh route had been refused in consideration of BA's investment in new aircraft and because subsidies might have been required.[41] The Authority had at that time accepted that BA would improve existing services and that competition was unnecessary.

These were issues in Gifford's middle range: there was some recurrence but new factors intruded intermittently. Even given distinctions between those cases in which the licence holder did not operate and those concerning deficient operation, the underlying principles on protecting operators emerged only vaguely from case law. In any particular application it was uncertain whether an investment would be protected since, in a high proportion of instances, new or exceptional factors might sway the decision. Additional considerations played a part, for example, in Peters Aviation Ltd's application in 1974 for a Norwich to London licence. Peters argued that Air Anglia's existing Norwich to Amsterdam operation allowed international interlining via Amsterdam and so drained the UK balance of payments in contravention of paragraph 10 of the policy guidance. In spite of this point, however, the CAA decided to protect the existing operation to Amsterdam 'because of the importance of the local traffic it carries and because of the interlining facilities'.[42] A further factor in the decision was implied by the CAA's statement that it would not award scheduled service licences to Peters until the company had more firmly established itself through charter operations. Reasoning in the case was brief and a precise ground for decision difficult to extract.

Another qualifying principle was that of resisting the 'creaming off' of peak period traffic from the regular operator. This factor came into play in 16 March 1973 when Invicta International Airlines applied for licences to operate weekend tours from Cardiff to Paris to cater for rugby spectators.[43] Cambrian Airways objected that their scheduled service could not survive such skimming of peak traffic. The licence was granted only because refusal would have considerably inconvenienced passengers.

Even protection from skimming had to be earned. When Invicta International Airlines applied for six charter flights to cater for Jersey's 'Battle of Flowers' in 1974 the scheduled operator, Dan Air, objected. The CAA found that Dan Air's response to the market had been too slow and granted the licence.[44]

Against those cases allowing competition with the existing deficient service, there have to be balanced instances in which the cost of competition was found excessive. Scottish Airways successfully opposed Air Anglia's application for an Aberdeen to Shetlands licence in February 1974, on the basis that that diversion would cost them £200,000. In another case the argument of inadequacy of service was defeated when BA justified high load factors on their London to Channel Islands service and convinced the CAA that the route could not support an additional operator.

In further contrast, competition has, at other times, been allowed at great cost. BMA were given a Belfast to Gatwick licence on 29 January 1975 in order to offer competition for BA's Heathrow operation.[45] The CAA licensed BMA for the sake of consumer choice in Northern Ireland in spite of accepting that the presence of a second operator would raise fares on all Belfast services and would cost BA £1 million per year in diverted revenue.

Yet another qualification affected the broad rule. Although the deficient operator would rarely be protected, credit would be given for either developing a route or for sustaining it in a difficult period: furthermore, a temporary cessation of service might not be considered too great a public disservice if economically justifiable. In May 1975 B.Cal. and Gibraltar Airways Ltd. lodged applications to compete with BA on their London to Gibraltar service.[46] B.Cal. argued that they had flown the route for years; that they had suspended operations following a £79,000 loss on the route in 1974 but that they did intend to re-start with higher tariffs. The CAA provided 'an equitable result': Gibraltar Airways were allowed to fly—but only seven flights a week. It was felt both that B.Cal's former efforts and subsequent losses merited further opportunities to profit from the work they had done but also that their withdrawal from the route had imposed a burden on BA. A licence was therefore given to B.Cal. for only three flights a week and was made subject to cancellation for non-use.

Nor would the holder of an unused licence be allowed to reap the benefits of another's development. Thus B.Cal. successfully removed rights between Glasgow and Amsterdam from a BA licence in February 1975.[47] B.Cal. had commenced their service ignorant of the existence of BA's unoperated licence but then BA had introduced a similar service whose flights departed shortly in advance of the private operator's.

These cases give an indication of how in a complex and changing environment neither rigid nor precise case law emerged in the CAA's early years.[48] Although cases supplemented the guidance to some extent and principles emerged on some issues, on very few matters did these determine an application's result. Exceptions to each principle, standard or rule were common and either particular circumstances or subordinate principles, standards or rules intruded to prevail over more general considerations. Reasons for decision did not go into great detail and failed to define reliable standards. No specific period was designated during which new investment would be protected, nor was there any definition of the period within which an operator had to achieve viability on a new service: acceptable diversion was not quantified nor were particulars supplied on what constituted failure to satisfy demand.

In terms of the theoretical questions posed at the start of the chapter, the early cases on route entry display a set of issues that could to some extent be dealt with *ad hoc* through particular case-decisions but which increasingly required a 'regulatory' as opposed to 'managerial' style of decision-making—one in which longer-term strategies would lend coherence to individual decisions. By 1974 the CAA had not developed its own knowledge sufficiently to move from 'muddling-through' to a more rational and more prospective strategy—but such a change was to be expected following the accumulation of agency expertise.

More detailed provision of standards was indeed to come as the CAA's licensing experience developed. In 1974 the Authority undertook a long-term study of short-haul services, especially European scheduled services and fares. A number of routes from London were studied in detail after consultation with the airlines and, when the Shore committee reviewed policy in 1975, it received a detailed statement of CAA findings and strategy. By this time, the CAA was able to set down in detail the conditions under which it would licence new short-haul domestic and European routes.

The second policy guidance of 1976 owed, as has been noted, a great deal to CAA submissions. Although the general considerations of the second guidance remained largely the same as in the first one, paragraph 9 set down new principles for scheduled short-haul competition. The former presumption in favour of competition had shifted. The Authority was to take 'full account' of the effect that a new service might have on existing ones. Competition was to be allowed on satisfaction of the same conditions as formerly (sufficiency of traffic within a reasonable time and improvement of service to the public) but, instead of allowing this *wherever* such conditions were satisfied, the instruction changed to '*only if* satisfied . . .'. Added to paragraph 9 was an important new instruction that reflected a transition from *ad-hoccery* to the structuring of discretion by an expert agency; the Authority was to 'make public the factors it will take into account in applying this paragraph'.

In accordance with this instruction, the CAA's Official Record Series 2 announced on 23 March 1976 'Criteria for Licensing Competing Airlines on Short-Haul Routes'.[49] These related both to European short-haul and to domestic routes and gave a more precise indication of policy than had been formerly available. Thus new short-haul scheduled services would not normally be licensed:

> . . . unless they can reasonably be expected as a minimum to cover direct operating costs in the first full year of operations and

to yield a fully remunerative rate of return in and after the third year, assuming in all cases efficient operation. . . .[50]

Full allowance would be made for 'quantifiable network effects' including diversion to or from long-haul services provided these effects did not 'imply structural cross-subsidization of a kind that would be inconsistent with paragraph 16 of the guidance' (which stated that each charge should be related to costs).

According to paragraph 3 of the criteria, short-haul services would not be licensed if they would 'impair the progress of existing efficiently operated services (directly or indirectly competing) towards profitability' on the above timescale, or if they would bring profitable services below break-even, or for more than one year make them less than fully remunerative (assuming efficient operation). A 'rare exception' would be made if it could be shown convincingly that the new service would represent a major improvement over existing services in terms of service to the public or the national interest.

Subject to the above provisions, the CAA stated that new competition between airlines on a route between the same city pair would normally be licensed only where a choice of airports was thus provided and the benefits to the public were clearly identifiable. Where such a route catered for business and interline traffic the Authority 'would normally expect the second operator to be able to sustain a minimum frequency of two round trips a day, five days a week' (paragraph 5). Nothing in this was, however, to preclude the licensing of one operator in place of another in order to secure higher quality or greater efficiency of service to the public (paragraph 6). On the role of the criteria, paragraph 7 concluded that they would 'guide licensing panels within the framework of the guidance' and cautioned: 'It is always possible that exceptions will need to be made in particular cases in the light of the evidence and the arguments adduced. However, if exceptions need to be made at all frequently this will point to a need to re-examine the criteria'.

This statement at last offered real guidance to potential applicants. They were told fairly precisely what they had to show in order to gain a licence and some structuring of discretion had occurred both at the general and more particular levels.[51] In the period 1976–79 the criteria remained unchanged apart from the addition of a new paragraph on airports policy in May 1978.[52]

The status of the criteria was soon commented upon. In July 1976, British Island Airways Ltd. (BIA) applied for a Manchester to Isle of Man service, and argued that paragraph 3 of the criteria merited granting a licence as an exception to the general prohibition on competition contained in the guidance. The CAA, however, refused the licence, saying that even exceptional cases in terms of the criteria had to come within the limits set by the guidance, which prevailed in cases of conflict.

It was, however, possible to gain an exceptional licence because of improvements offered to the public in accordance with paragraph 3 of the criteria. Air Anglia were given rights on the Aberdeen-Edinburgh sector of their Norwich service on 22 November 1976[53] in spite of the existing operator, BA, not being in a profitable position on the route. The CAA commented that it had to 'have particular regard to the interests of the public'. Less success was enjoyed by Peters Aviation Ltd. when they applied for a Norwich to London licence in 1977. The proposed service would not have been remunerative within three years and the CAA refused to make an exception to paragraph 2 of the criteria.[54]

A flexibility of approach was demonstrated in another case. Air Westward were awarded a number of services from the West Country on 31 January 1978.[55] The CAA thought that on a network basis the proposals satisfied the criteria but that the Exeter to Glasgow route would fail to be remunerative in the third year of operation, nevertheless, in view of the Authority's confidence in the operator and the provincial contribution of the service, a licence was granted. Similarly, Air Westward were licensed on the Exeter to London route some nine weeks later in spite of the CAA's finding 'a degree of uncertainty as to whether the proposed . . . service would fully comply with its criteria'.[56]

As far as protecting the existing operator was concerned, paragraph 3 of the criteria provided comfort only to 'efficient', 'adequate' or 'profitable' services. When Dan-Air Services and Air Wales applied for licences to compete with BA on routes from Wales to Germany, the CAA decided that BA's single frequency per week running at a loss was 'hardly a service . . . which merits the protection of paragraph 3'.[57]

As the criteria were applied more frequently an effect was to focus arguments.[58] Operators would lead evidence to show satisfaction of matters set out in paragraphs 2 and 3 and the

CAA, when granting licenses, tended to draft reasons for decisions in terms of compliance with those criteria. Apart from such exceptional cases as are cited above, failure to comply with the criteria resulted in refusal of a licence. Thus, when Air Anglia were refused a Belfast to Amsterdam service on 21 February 1979[59] (on failing to show that they could satisfy paragraph 2 in terms of profitability) the CAA refused to allow the operator to take a financial risk saying:

> If the Authority were to abandon paragraph 2 ... , the way would be open to pre-emptive licensing bids, designed purely to obtain route rights'.[60]

By this time, then, the CAA had managed to structure its discretion in a difficult area of regulation where cases, to some extent, repeated but where new factors intruded. Although some flexibility was allowed in the system, real limits were imposed. In some cases it was, for instance, pointed out to operators that, whilst they would be protected from competition on a route for three years in terms of paragraph 3, after that time it was in the public interest to expose them to competition.[61]

In assessing the effect of the criteria from 1976 to 1979 there are two factors to be emphasised. Firstly, standards were set out publicly and (as Davis and Friendly would have argued) this led to more precise argument in applications. Secondly, the CAA's reasons for decision improved vastly during this period. Generally from three to six pages in length, they dealt with the points raised by the criteria, interpretations of the criteria in previous cases and any distinctions to be drawn between similar applications.[62] As was the case before 1976, exceptions were possible; the important difference was that they would be justified in relation to defined standards that lasted over a number of years.

In February 1979 the Authority supplied further information of guidance to applicants in the shape of a report entitled 'Domestic Air Services: A Review of Regulatory Policy'.[63] This thirty-page booklet did not offer more 'criteria' for licensing but set out the CAA's findings following an internal review of policy conducted by EPL staff. Describing itself as a 'consultative document', it aimed to 'stimulate discussion' on how the regulatory system might be used to improve the climate for air services. The Authority hoped that, following subsequent consultation, it would be able 'to put forward definitive proposals for change'.[64] Comments in the form of written submissions were invited.

In substance the document constituted a discussion of the CAA's regulatory philosophy. As such it provided a background for the 'short-haul criteria', describing the regulatory framework and considering the arguments for and against regulation: it placed existing standards in context rather than added to their number. It concluded that 'complete de-regulation of domestic services is simply not feasible',[65] but the CAA did favour allowing the market to work 'to the maximum feasible extent' and keeping regulatory intervention to the 'unavoidable minimum'.[66] An approach more favourable to competition emerged. In relation to route entry the CAA said: 'the general principle is to allow new entry except where it can clearly be demonstrated that entry would raise, not reduce, the average cost per passenger carried or would have the effect . . . in the longer term, of reducing the range of services offered'.[67]

The CAA position in 1979 thus resembled that set out in the first guidance rather than the second but it was described in far greater detail and at a number of levels. The protection to be afforded to an existing operator was further explained in discussing the scope for change on routes. Since few city pairs could support two operators, the CAA said: 'direct competition cannot be the sole tool of regulatory policy. A more effective tool may be the possibility of substituting one operator for another where standards of service have been allowed to decline or costs have been allowed to get out of control'.[68] This statement went further in the direction of competition than had those statements in previous cases[69] that 'a most powerful case' would be required before an operator would be deprived of his licence.

In the use of such statements and in passages describing the CAA's view of the industrial position, the Domestic Air Services' booklet added another layer to the stack of material available for operators. Reference to the document was soon made in hearings but in early 1979 one airline advocate disputed another airline's right to quote from the booklet saying that it was only an undiscussed consultative paper of 'no legal status'.[70] The CAA indicated in a later decision that the document was 'designed to stimulate thought' but did not reflect any change in Authority policies.[71] It was clear, however, that it served as a basis for policies and argument. The CAA has more than once noted the compliance of a decision with the document[72] and airlines have continued to quote its terms.[73] When a further statement on 'Air Transport Licensing Policies' was published in November 1979 the Authority stated that 'policy for domestic services will be determined in the light of . . . current consultations with airlines and others on the basis of the consultative document. . . .'

As far as the development of CAA policies on competitive licensing is concerned, it can be concluded that by reference to the objectives of the 1971 Act, the guidance, the criteria, case decisions and the 1979 consultative document, operators by 1979 were given a wide range of principles and standards to guide their applications. CAA policy-making in this area had been founded in the first instance upon trial-type adjudication but had moved from the 'managerial' to the 'regulatory' model because of two factors: the recurrence of issues in decisions and the development of an expertise that allowed prospective formulation of regulatory strategy. The CAA experience also indicated that the structuring of discretion might operate best not on a single plane but when used on a number of interlocking levels of generality.

Airports Policy and Competition

Airports policy impinges on competitive licensing in a number of respects. The CAA must consider whether services from one airport will divert traffic from other airports. It must, when given a choice of services from different airports, decide which is the most useful service. Furthermore, the Authority has to co-ordinate its licensing strategies with a duty to have regard for those airports policies adopted by the government.[74]

In the early seventies a major question was the extent to which Gatwick services would divert from Heathrow. A number of cases established that, at least domestically, the two London airports enjoyed separate catchment areas.[75] (CAA research confirmed this finding when the report 'Origins and Destinations of Passengers at UK Airports' (CAP 363, 1974) showed that only 16 per cent of Heathrow passengers came from the Gatwick area.) As far as provincial airports were concerned, the CAA's policy was developed in a number of reports which took the form of advice (under paragraph 20 of the first guidance) to the Secretary of State.[76] In deciding route applications the Authority's reasons referred to the policies (for example of protecting the 'hub' airports, Manchester and Birmingham) set out in those papers.[77] For its part, the Government joined the consultative process in 1975–76 with a two part document 'Airport Strategy for Great Britain'. After the second guidance was produced in February 1976, the CAA's functions with respect to airports' policy changed. Added to the Authority's role of advising the Government it was given a duty under paragraph 14 to 'act in pursuit of such Government policy on airports as may from time to time apply'. With this governmental policy in mind, it was advised under paragraph 12, to examine the scope for reallocating routes so as to widen public choice. It was also 'to seek to promote the development of scheduled services to and from Gatwick' (paragraph 14).

The Secretary of State for Trade, Mr Dell made the next major statement of airports policy in the House of Commons on 5 April 1977.[78] He stated that if congestion at Heathrow was to be avoided, more extensive use of Gatwick would be required. Government policy aimed to bring this about by prohibiting whole-plane charters at Heathrow after 1 April 1978 and by transferring some scheduled services to Gatwick. Mr Dell concluded that proposals by airlines to start new operations or to increase capacity at Heathrow would be considered by the CAA and DoT in the light of this policy.

The April statement had rapid licensing repercussions. In September 1977 three independent operators applied for a number of short-haul scheduled services from Gatwick to various European destinations.[79] These airlines sought to delete Gatwick from the equivalent licences held by BA. The designed effect was to offer competition to BA's Heathrow services, to develop Gatwick and to offer consumer choice. In deciding the case the CAA considered the competitive aspects of each route and its viability against paragraph 9 of the criteria. In accordance with the second guidance the matter was said to turn on the Government's policies for developing Gatwick. These were taken to be set out in the Secretary of State's April statement to Parliament as amplified in a letter of 15 July 1977 to the British Airports Authority. Such policies were said to be 'entirely consistent with the Authority's own advice given in the course of many consultations in recent years'.[80]

The CAA then took the opportunity to set down a full statement of its policies on new Gatwick services. It said (paragraphs 118–21) that it was vital to build up a network of scheduled services from Gatwick to new destinations that would yield a high level of interline traffic and that such a network could not be built up without some diminution of growth at Heathrow. The CAA, in considering applications had attached weight to diversion 'only to the extent that Heathrow services might become uneconomic within the terms of the Authority's criteria of 23 March 1976'. Though there would be scope for smaller operators in the supply of feeder services, it was essential, if Gatwick was to avoid typecasting as a second-division airport, that services to principal destinations be provided by first-division airlines. To this end it was 'inconceivable that Gatwick could develop without the substantial involvement of both BA and B.Cal'.

A further statement (paragraph 123) was made on the issues raised by BA's having (by historical accident) formal permission in its London licences to operate from Gatwick as well as Heathrow. The CAA indicated that in future applications for competing Gatwick services operators should apply to delete BA rights. If BA responded with proposals for Gatwick services, both applications would be treated on their merits. The CAA implied that if BA merely defended their Heathrow operations, they might be liable to competition under the 1976 criteria. As for the airlines involved in that particular application, neither BIA nor Dan Air was said to be of 'first-division capability' as far as major international connecting routes were concerned. All their applications were refused but those of B.Cal. were granted.

The above case exemplifies detailed CAA reason-giving. Regulatory strategy was set out, not this time by policy-statement or rule-making, but through the hearings process. The case was to serve as a basis for later decisions,[81] not merely on the significance of Gatwick operations but also on general competition philosophy.

Governmental airports policy made a further advance with the publication of a White Paper in February 1978.[82] For air transport licensing the White Paper was important in providing a framework for development and dividing airports into four categories: gateway international, regional, local and general aviation. The Government's aim was to achieve greater use of airports outside the South East, to rationalize principal air services and to concentrate on a limited number of regional airports.

Manchester would be the principal gateway airport outside the South East and main regional centres would be Birmingham, East Midlands and Leeds/Bradford airports.

Three major cases on the development of Gatwick were heard in 1979. On 20 April the CAA, as ordered on appeal, re-heard an application by B.Cal. to operate from Gatwick to Stockholm in preference to BA.[83] The CAA affirmed the policy of developing Gatwick as set out in the original hearing (the 26 October hearing on European routes described above) and, once more, chose to use its reasons for decision to set out its principles for Gatwick operations and to give a clear warning to BA:[84]

> The Authority . . . sees a continuing role for B.Cal., as the principal resident Gatwick operator of scheduled services, in the development of services from Gatwick to the continent either alongside the services of British Airways from Gatwick or in place of British Airways from Gatwick where the quality of British Airways service including especially the interlining opportunities offered and the levels of fares charged are inferior to those which the resident airline was ready to offer.[85]

A second case emphasized the advantages of residence at Gatwick: in August 1979 Dan Air Services were given a licence to operate Gatwick to Aberdeen services in competition with BA from Heathrow.[86] BA's rights from Gatwick were revoked. The CAA stated that it had monitored Gatwick operations since the 26 October 1977 European decision and had concluded:

> . . . that the development of services from Gatwick is in many instances more easily pursued with determination and more likely to succeed where the operator is resident at Gatwick . . . although it must remain inconceivable that Gatwick could be fully developed without the active and enthusiastic participation of British Airways, a route like Gatwick-Aberdeen is more likely to receive high priority and close management attention if served by a Gatwick-based operator, leaving British Airways free to concentrate on developing the Heathrow-Aberdeen route.'[87]

So firmly established in case decisions[88] were the principles on this point that they prevailed over the published criteria:

> . . . the importance of developing services from Gatwick should in this case take precedence over paragraph two of its criteria for licensing short-haul services. . . .[89]

After the change of government in 1979, the Conservative Secretary of State for Trade, Mr Nott, made a statement on 9 October reasserting the need to continue diverting traffic from Heathrow to Gatwick. When the CAA produced its 'Statement on Air Transport Licensing Policies' in November 1979 it paraphrased the above statements taken from the Stockholm and Aberdeen cases[90] and 'welcomed' Mr Nott's October statement.

Airports policy was a potentially difficult area for the CAA because of its guidance obligation to pursue the policies espoused by government. Examination of policy on Gatwick services indicates, however, that a strategy did emerge and that close consultation between the CAA and the DoT (and some agreement in this area) did facilitate matters. What is notable for our purposes is the role of case law here. Whereas entry to a route was largely governed by statements of rules and policies (the guidance and short-haul criteria), strategy here has in recent years been largely set out by the very different means of reasons for decision. Leaving aside the fact that to some extent policies were set out by the Government as opposed to the CAA, a number of factors can explain the CAA's reliance on case law: (i) this was not an area of first importance in terms of its own long-term technical research, (ii) the issues related closely to particular airlines needs, (iii) the development of Gatwick involved a very rapidly changing set of regulatory issues and, (iv) the CAA had to react to individual applications as they arose. Looking to David Shapiro's reasons for rule-making we see that this was not an area in which highest priority was placed on such factors as general participation, long-term planning, wide consultation or disseminating information to all regulatees. The aims were more modest and regulation in this field was more reactive and *ad hoc* than in others. Case law served two principal purposes: to update policy in rapid response to events and to reconcile, or set out priorities amongst, the many relevant licensing considerations applicable to the particular case.

(ii) Passenger Charter Policy

When the CAA began regulation in 1972 the rules on affinity group charters were being abused to offer ultra-low fares. Scheduled services were unable to offer competing promotional fares because the International Air Transport Association (IATA) price-fixing machinery was unresponsive and inclusive tours were subject to price controls.

The CAA set out to introduce cheaper, cost-related fares on scheduled routes and workable rules for charter services.[91] Because most scheduled passengers, especially on the North Atlantic, were travelling at reduced and often uneconomic rates, the CAA supported BOAC's attempts to gain approval in IATA for Advanced Purchase Excursion (APEX) fares on North Atlantic scheduled services. After initial failure, IATA agreement followed CAA discussions with the American CAB in February 1973.

At the same time as APEX fares were being negotiated, the CAA, with the co-operation of the DoT, took the lead internationally in proposing new rules based on the advanced booking concept[92] so as to replace affinity with advanced booking charters (ABCs).

The initiative for ABC's came from the CAA and was an example of positive ('pro-active') regulation by the Authority. The ABC was available to anyone, its advanced booking requirement offered some protection to scheduled operators and it did not present the same problems of enforcement as the affinity charter. The UK government negotiated the ABC's introduction with the United States, Canada and the member countries of the European Civil Aviation Conference. The end-product was the Ottawa declaration of agreement to ABC terms in November 1972.

Innovations in this area were introduced by a procedure very different from that used in relation to airports policy. The public hearing was deliberately avoided. The CAA said: 'The Authority has instead sought to place greater emphasis on consultation with the industry as a way of reaching its decisions. This process is facilitated by its power to publish proposals and establish schedules of conditions. Thus the introduction of ABC's and the granting of Class 2 licences to six airlines for the carriage of ABC traffic were accomplished by consultation and without a formal hearing.'[93] Only two hearings were called on ABC licences in 1973 and on both occasions[94] Donaldson Hire (Air Services) Ltd. were refused ABC licences because of under-capitalization.

Where consultative procedures did not produce agreement between scheduled and charter operations then public hearings were held[95] but nothing that could be called a 'case law' developed. CAA staff took the view that the hearings process could be avoided on this kind of question which was relatively uncontentious. The central regulatory issue was seen, not as deciding which of a number of competing operators was to receive ABC licences, but of gaining governmental agreement to the introduction of ABCs. Thus, the CAA sent staff on a government team to Ghana in 1975 and secured an agreement to ABC's, during the negotiation of which the hearing of applications for the services was delayed.[96] Again it was the regulatory body that instituted change when in 1976, as part of its programme of liberalizing charter services, the Authority proposed, and then adopted, a reduction in booking periods from 60 to 45 days for travel to the USA, Canada and the Caribbean. Dialogue continued with ECAC on the introduction of ABCs to Europe.

As far as inclusive tours (ITs) were concerned, these were allocated under a different (Class 3) licence from ABCs but the CAA adopted a similarly liberal approach. Whereas the ATLB had become embroiled in the price control of ITs, the CAA heeded Edwards' proposal[97] that IT charters should be free to charge their own tariffs (subject to filing these with the Authority) and that a system of bonding be introduced. Both guidances stated on this point that the Authority 'should aim always to impose the least restraint upon the industry'.[98]

From the start, the CAA deregulated. In November 1972 it announced that control of IT prices would be suspended as from 16 October 1973 in order to allow flexible pricing; operators were to file their rates and, again, the public hearing procedure had retreated in favour of less formal administrative controls. Increased protection for the public was provided when Air Transport Organizer's Licensing (ATOL) commenced in April 1973.

The CAA, in dropping price control, avoided many public hearings formerly occasioned by the objections of scheduled carriers. When it re-classified licences on 1 January 1974 the Authority introduced the new 'blanket' inclusive tour licence for European tours. These (Class 3A) licences were issued to the major charter airlines for periods up to 5 years and permitted ITs between any place in the UK and any place in Europe. They accordingly did away with the licensing of individual routes. They were issued after a lengthy hearing in which the major concern was the financial fitness of the applicant and, after licensing, the CAA merely monitored financial progress.

In the years preceding the blanket IT licence, a limited case law had developed on whether a scheduled operator would be protected from charter competition. The CAA had required that a case be made on demand and viability (in the latter case even if no objection had been made). Decisions indicated that by 1974 the Authority was distinguishing between 'scheduled' and 'charter' types of traffic and would not allow charterers to 'cream-off' peak-time passengers and so impoverish the normal scheduled service.[99]

If demand was strong or aimed at a market different from that served by scheduled traffic then the Authority was liable to grant a licence, especially in the case of a small series of flights.[100] On the other hand, scheduled services serving as 'lifelines' to communities or of importance in business or political terms would be sustained: the Berlin route was thus considered a special case for protection[101] as were services to the Channel Islands.[102] As with the question of route entry, this was a contentious area involving a mixture of recurrent issues, rapid change and frequently intruding new factors. It was at a public hearing that liberalization was challenged in September 1975 when BA applied to vary Britannia Airway's Class 3A licence.[103] Britannia were operating 'Wanderer' holidays, which BA argued abused the IT concept since accommodation was supplied on a 'throwaway' basis. BA demanded that accommodation should be pre-booked and be of certain price and standard. In spite of Britannia openly attracting passengers from scheduled services, the CAA refused BA's application because such control would have necessitated reimposition of price control. In February 1976 the Secretary of State upheld this decision on appeal.[104]

On long-haul routes, where applications meet few objections, the CAA has generally allocated IT licences without hearings. In cases that have been contested the issue has usually been diversion and this has been assessed in the particular case.

The development of charter policy has thus largely taken the form of re-drafting the distinction between charter and scheduled services: to balance the liberal licensing of charter servicing the CAA has encouraged the introduction of promotional services and fares by scheduled operators. The original decision to allow scheduled operators to carry a proportion of charter passengers exemplified the prominent role of the public hearing in early CAA policy-making. Thus, after the Authority reclassified its licences in January 1974, the former Class A scheduled service licence became the Class 1B licence which, by definition allowed the operator to reserve 50 per cent of seats for charter passengers. CAA strategy was explained at a hearing in March 1974 when five operators applied for 117 Class 1B licences with the 'part-charter' facility: 'The purpose in adopting the present definition of a Class 1 licence was in large part to facilitate the examination and testing of such issues by way of formal hearing'.[105] This policy, unlike others of a less contentious nature (such as the introduction of ABCs), was thus to be challengeable through the trial-type process rather than allowed to emerge as the product of private or public consultations. Following argument and objections by charter carriers, the 50 per cent facility was granted and the CAA set down its views on the role of part-charter services.

By 1976, scheduled operators had been given a flexibility that allowed them to respond to charterers with a range of services and fares including: special group inclusive tours (SGIT); inclusive tour excursions (ITX); advanced purchase excursions (APEX); youth and spouse excursions and instant purchase excursions (IPEX).

Early in that year, the CAA took more positive steps to control the charter/scheduled service balance and did so by a new procedure. Until that time the Authority had approved scheduled service fares without great debate. When, however, BA sought approval for very low scheduled service fares to the Iberian peninsula for groups of three people ('Group 3' fares) the possibility of diversion from charter operations arose. For the first time the CAA arranged a 'public consultation'. It set out the proposed fare in a press notice, invited written comments and arranged a meeting. This process was less formal than a public hearing and more inquisitorial. The CAA panel questioned airline representatives for two and a half days and later announced that the 'Group 3' fares were set too low to be properly remunerative. It ordered that prices be increased by 15 per cent.

The device of proposing changes in licence conditions and holding subsequent hearings[106] was used on other occasions, notably in proposals to require the pre-listing of passengers on inclusive tour charters[107] in 1976–77. After publication of the proposal in letters to licence holders and in the CAA's Official Record, hearings would be held and the plans would later be either implemented or withdrawn. As also happened in the case of cargo charter policy announcements, it was not unknown for representatives at the hearings to object that the CAA had produced no evidence to support its proposals.

What the 'Group 3' case did more than anything else was to spur the CAA's attempts to find a way of permitting viable competition between charter and scheduled services. It did so by indicating how high *normal* scheduled service fares in Europe were set; the CAA stressed:

> . . . on some routes the normal economy class fare on scheduled services is as much as five times the fully economic seat rate on a charter flight . . . a major effort is needed to secure that fares bear a closer relation to the costs.[108]

It was during the period 1975–76 that the CAA began to move rapidly towards a more expert, less *ad hoc* method of regulation. Part of this process was the accumulation of information. In 1976 two studies were commissioned, to be carried out jointly by staff of the CAA and BA. The 'Cascade Study' compared the costs of scheduled and charter services on a number of representative European routes. The 'Fare-Type Analysis' broke down the costs of scheduled services on a sample of European routes according to the different types of fare and service. In January 1977 another 'public consultation' was held at the CAA premises:

> . . . the meeting was a consultation or kind of seminar; it was not an inquiry nor a formal public hearing. . . . It was intended to be a frank and relatively informal discussion.[109]

Its aim was to work out an economic basis and rationale on which European air fares were derived; it was intended to 'strengthen the foundation' for the CAA's future decisions.[110]

The findings of the subsequent seventy-page report are too lengthy to detail here.[111] What was important for operators was the document's analysis of the principles underlying CAA policies on fares and the implications of these for the charter/scheduled balance. Detailed consideration was given to such crucial issues in the Act, guidance and criteria as the 'relationship of fares to costs', 'efficiency', 'rate of return', 'rational tariff conditions', 'satisfaction of all substantial categories of public demand' and 'minimum regulation'. A chapter was devoted to 'the role of scheduled airlines in European leisure markets' and further joint research was announced with B.Cal. and charter airlines on the roles of different kinds of operator. Conclusions were put forward tentatively as the CAA 'viewpoint'. The Authority aimed to move from a reactive procedure on fares to a planned approach and a rational fares system. It would try to relate fares more directly to costs and, by research into routes and fare types, it hoped for better decision-making on the basis of clearly understood concepts.

As was the case with the 'Domestic Air Services' report, that on 'European Air Fares' was to provide the foundation for future CAA policies, including those on the charter/scheduled service balance. The CAA's licensing policy statement of November 1979 referred to its 'present policies' as set out in the 'European Air Fares' booklet, thereby giving the discussion document new importance.

To summarize, the CAA started developing charter policy by deciding in individual cases and at public trial-type hearings whether diversion from scheduled services was acceptable. As its researches continued it adopted new procedures. Proposals were developed and either consultations or seminars were conducted after their announcement. In Shapiro's terms the public consultation procedure is explicable with reference to the CAA's increased ability to look to longer term policy and its perceiving the advantages of 'public consultation' for the rapid collection of views and the smoothing down of potential areas of conflict.[112] Finally, a process of *continuing* research and consultation was instituted. Crucial licensing problems were argued out in detail in either consultations, hearings or applications following the publication of reports. A trend towards liberalization changed issues from the particular to the general so that, as areas were 'hived-off' to the regulation of the market, there was less need to rely on licensing applications. The formal hearing began to be used more for applying general policy to problem cases than for developing policy itself and trial-type procedures shrank further in importance as the CAA's expertise increased. One CAA official described the process:

> As you cut the undergrowth away the clearer things become and the policy issues that remain become more 'macro': they are therefore less liable to be decided at a single licensing hearing.

(iii) Cargo Charter Policy

The CAA played a major part in reducing anti-competitive

restrictions in scheduled versus charter competition in transporting freight. It is perhaps in this area that we see most clearly how the CAA moved away from policy-making via trial-type adjudication to a mixed system of hearings and informal policy statements.

After 1945, 'split' cargo charters (i.e. those allowing more than one consignor to use an aircraft) were not allowed under IATA rules. Britain, however, allowed splitting on the cabotage routes of the Empire. In the late 1960s, air freight grew rapidly with charter development and, after 1966, the ATLB's Class EJ licence allowed split charters for up to four journeys between named places. No more than four consignors were to share the aircraft and no consignment might be less than 1000 kgs weight: these conditions were designed to protect scheduled operators' markets. By 1969 such limitations were found to be 'unduly restrictive' by the Edwards Committee which advocated that scheduled and charter operators should compete for large consignments, that the consignors limitation should be dropped and that the weight limit should be retained or increased from 1000 kg.[113]

In spite of Edwards, the ATLB retained the consignor limitation on its standard licence but it liberalized by granting 'specific' licences of a more generous nature where demand on individual routes was shown.[114] The ATLB would licence a cargo charter operation even if this affected the scheduled service—provided that demand was growing rapidly.

When the CAA took over, it continued to licence on proof of demand. Scheduled operators became increasingly concerned that their position was being eroded by the provision of regular services by charterers and by the evasion of regulations on consolidation. In 1972 BOAC claimed that over half of its cargo weight came in consignments over 1000 kg and that its traffic was imperilled.[115] The CAA undertook to make a general study of the problem. Pressure from the charterers mounted in 1973 and, at a hearing on 26 and 27 February 1974, five major operators applied for the relaxation of cargo charter conditions.[116] They stressed their need to be allowed more consignors and more journeys in order to compete with foreign opposition and, in response, the CAA announced that it was to undertake a comprehensive review of cargo chartering.[117]

The Economics and Statistics (ECS) and Economic Policy

and Licensing (EPL) divisions of the Authority conducted an extensive investigation into the whole cargo charter process in 1974, consulting users and providers of services, airline agents, wholesalers, shippers and their customers. Memoranda and forecasts were submitted to the CAA and discussions were held on these. CAA officials met airline staff on a number of occasions to discuss the study, the aim of which was to find ways of decreasing restrictions on charters without unduly prejudicing scheduled operators.

When airline representatives went to a private meeting with the CAA in early 1975 they were given a three-page document entitled 'International Air Freight Charter Services' which stated that, although the Authority had not completed its review of cargo policy, it had reached some conclusions which 'would guide its licensing decisions for the coming year'. It saw no further justification for restricting the numbers of consignors under the Class 6A licence and stated that, from 1 March to 31 December 1975, the standard 6A licence would only be subject to a minimum consignment weight (1000 kg) and a maximum number of journeys (10) between two places. The prohibition on consolidating consignments under 1000 kg was to be retained but after the end of 1975 the CAA said that it would:

> ... expect any airline wishing this condition to be retained ... to put forward convincing arguments. ...

The CAA gave notice that, in 1976, it would consider applications for Class 6 licences of up to five years duration, it would discuss with scheduled freight carriers the possibility of their adopting more competitive rates, it would consider whether capacity restrictions should be placed on charterers and it would produce a further consultative document based on its reviews.

The 1975 document gave a clear indication of the CAA's change of policy on the consignors restriction. It was clear to operators that those opposing this change at public hearings would be placed in a difficult position. On 10 and 12 March 1975 all major freight charterers applied for 'standard' class 6A licences and BA and B.Cal. objected to all applications involving relaxation of the consignors limitation.

At these hearings not all parties agreed to disclose confidential information[118] and so this was restricted by the CAA. The Chairman of the panel explained that the CAA policy statement was 'intended to provide guidance and assistance' but that the panel 'would be prepared to hear arguments on the proposals'.[119] Mr David Beety of B.Cal. asked the CAA to disclose the detailed figures behind the Authority's policy statement and the CAA circulated some information following this request. The panel admitted that the figures given were sparse and, for reasons of confidentiality, less informative than they might have been. B.Cal were worried that the CAA had adopted a policy in advance of the case and had not disclosed figures sufficient for examination of this policy at the hearing. B.Cal and BA considered that the CAA had chosen to experiment in this area and that the public hearing would make little difference to a policy already adopted. All applications considered at the hearings were granted without limitation on numbers of consignors. The scheduled operators felt that between public hearing and private consultation the CAA had somewhere avoided the need to justify its policies. They did, however, see the hearing as having some value as an opportunity of publicly expressing their views.

In September 1975, as promised, the CAA published a 'consultative document', 'International Air Freight Services'.[120] This thirty-eight page booklet went into far greater detail than the earlier policy statement and was meant to assist 'in the further discussion of . . . options and of . . . policy issues facing the air freight industry'.[121] The CAA rejected complete liberalization in favour of allowing further competition. It proposed to end the 1000 kg consignment limit, saying that belly capacity on scheduled flights, when costed in relation to charters, did not merit protection but that schedule services were to be protected during the initial development of a route since belly capacity provided the most efficient method of transporting small amounts of freight. The airlines welcomed the discussion document as an exposition of the CAA view and as an analysis of the regulatory issues. The editor of the magazine *Airtrade* commented that it was the most concise, lucid and logical review of airfreight that he had ever read.[122]

To follow up this document, the CAA held 'a programme of consultations and discussions' with users and providers of air freight and continued its researches. In February 1976 it used its 'Official Record' to make an announcement on 'Freight Regulatory Policy'[123] and set out a new set of principles which were to 'guide' it in freight cases in the near future.

The new policy entailed reducing the minimum consignment size for both 'standard' and 'specific' 6A licences to 500 kg but consolidation of loads below this size was still to be prohibited. An experiment was proposed for the Hong Kong route: there would be no minimum consignment size or prohibition on consolidation and results would be monitored in order to test the effect on scheduled service freight tariffs. (Being a cabotage route, and so free from IATA controls, scheduled operators could compete freely.) No new limitations on flight numbers were to be imposed and 'specific' licences would continue to be allocated on the basis of shown demand. The Authority promised that the policy would not preclude arguments for or against liberalization in particular cases.

Applications by charter operators for three Class 6A (Standard) and eighteen 6D (Specific) licences were heard on 13 and 14 May 1976. All applications had been amended in accordance with the CAA's proposals. Class 6A licences were granted for five years but the CAA considered that no case had been made for extending Class 6D licences (for specific routes) beyond one year since the policy review and the Hong Kong experiment were to continue. As for the number of flights asked for on specific routes, the Authority commented on BA's failure to produce evidence of diversion and saw no reason to limit these except where the scheduled service appeared vulnerable.

Further intensive studies and consultations resulted in another statement on freight regulatory policy, published in the CAA's 'Official Record' on 1 March 1977.[124] This proposed to allow consolidation of loads to make up the minimum of 500 kg weight and to modify licence conditions so as to replace capacity control defined in terms of specific destinations with aggregate control defined by the number of pairs of points served.

Following the above statement, a freight hearing originally planned for May 1977 was postponed until November of that year. A further statement reiterated the above policy on 28 June 1977.[125] A number of operators requested that a fuller explanation of CAA policy be supplied, and, in response, the CAA produced and circulated to parties a paper setting out the reasoning behind the latest proposals. This paper, together with a parallel statement on scheduled air freight policy was published in August 1977 as 'Air Freight Policy—a Consultation

Document'.[126] This sixteen-page 'brown book' dealt with regulatory options and philosophy in great detail and the CAA's proposals were argued for rather than merely set down. On scheduled air freight policy the Authority proposed that where demand did not justify the operation of a scheduled freighter the use of bellyhold capacity on passenger planes should be encouraged. To this end, freight rates, it said, should be allowed to find their own level, and the use of bellyhold capacity maximized. With respect to charter freight operations, it proposed to replace capacity control in terms of specific destinations by aggregate control defined by the pairs of points served. This was to leave the achievement of balance between supply and demand on individual services to commercial rather than regulatory factors. Control of consignment size was to be retained at 500 kg but consolidation would be allowed.

When operators applied for freight licences in November 1977 they did so not so much with regard to prior case law but on the basis of 'the brown book'. The CAA decided those applications collectively in four pages of reasoning and stressed the need for a precise regulatory framework where control was to be applied. Though accepting the need to distinguish scheduled from charter traffic on long-haul routes, the CAA accepted that this would not be so necessary if scheduled operators could adopt a competitive rate structure and it urged them to do this. In accordance with the discussion document, it retained the 500 kg minimum consignment size but discontinued the prohibition of consolidation within that limit. It said that it would control charter capacity on longer routes for the time being but would do so in terms of weight carried rather than numbers of flights. Since the Authority had decided to issue 'standard' 6A freight licences for five year periods, it envisaged a change in licensing procedure:

> ... large annual freight hearings will no longer be needed; instead it should be possible to consider applications for 6D licences for particular markets together as need arises.[127]

After November 1977, the hearing, as was intended, further diminished in importance in charter freight licensing[128] as a liberal regime was applied.[129] A further indication that cargo charters did not include the most contentious issues in licensing came with the publication in November 1979 of the CAA's 'Statement on Air Transport Licensing Policies': no outline of cargo policy was given.

Although this area has rarely occupied the spotlight in air transport regulation it did prove significant in the 1970s. It was concerning cargo charter policy that the CAA developed most rapidly a combination of different regulatory procedures. In the 1960s, policy had emerged case by case, it lacked continuity and a consistent strategy. The first detailed process of consultation followed by administrative rule-making took place in 1975 and resulted in the document *International Air Freight Services*. That publication signalled the start of a new way of developing regulatory policy. Instead of argument at public hearings, there came debate via research and consultation. This was followed by publication of 'proposals' or 'discussion documents' which were to serve as the bases for licensing decisions that dealt with large numbers of applications collectively. With liberalization of licensing and the use of longer term 'blanket' licences, the public hearing further diminished in importance. The adjudicative process had, with the development of regulatory expertise, been replaced with a system in which administrators, in the main, made decisions, policies and rules by informal and more flexible means.

Conclusions: The Role of Public Hearings in Policy Development

Unlike the Restrictive Practices Court[130] or the ATLB, the CAA was equipped to supplement policy-making via the trial-type process with other procedures. It has done so and what has been striking has been the variety of procedures used in the different regulatory areas. Although the CAA started off life relying very much on public hearings as the ATLB had done, there were soon changes. In the field of competition policy it published its own criteria to supplement the Act and the guidance; charter policy involved 'policy announcements' and 'public consultations'. Combined research work such as the 'Cascade' study and the 'Fare-Type' analysis were conducted with the airlines and a series of 'brown books' were produced across the regulatory arena. On some topics, such as ABC charters, the public hearing was shunned, on others, such as part-charters, it was deliberately employed. Hearings played a prominent role in airports policy development but in the cargo-charter area they were secondary to policy-announcements. More recently the CAA has taken major steps towards the structuring of its own discretion and the description of its strategy following the general statement of licensing policies of November 1979: what had formerly been set out in discussion or consultative documents had concretized as policy. How then has the CAA coped with the problems highlighted at the start of Chapter 10?

(a) Polycentricity

CAA experience indicates that polycentricity may not threaten the integrity of the decision-making process provided that agency expertise is sufficient to lay bare the context within which discretion operates[131] and provided that undue emphasis is not placed on the trial-type process. Jeffrey Jowell has argued that urban planning decisions are so polycentric as to 'threaten the integrity of decision by adjudication'[132] but in aviation licensing meaningful arguments can be made at public hearings on a range of issues[133] in spite of the CAA having to exercise a considerable degree of judgment and having to balance a host of different considerations in taking most of its decisions. The commission type of agency can juggle with a far greater number of inter-related issues than the tribunal—this is a function of expertise and is achieved by applying that expertise in a number of ways that Davis would call the 'structuring' of discretion.[134] As Gifford puts it:

> ... the guiding, structuring or confinement of discretionary decision-making is ultimately a function of the process of information collection and evaluation.[135]

What danger there is comes from the experts and professionals using the hearings process as 'something to hide behind'. One staff member commented on this point:

> The quasi-judicial procedure means that in finely balanced cases where the issue turns on professional judgement you can use the discretion to exercise expertise that is built into the system. Wearing a more legalistic hat you might say we shouldn't strictly do that but what we're talking about here is marginal cases or cases where the evidence doesn't give a clear-cut pointer in any direction. You have to make the quasi-judicial procedure fit the system.[136]

Since the evidence indicates that decisions are 'glossed' in comparatively few cases this may be accepted as a price that has to be paid in a system that seeks to combine disparate functions to achieve the best of a number of worlds. CAA decisions indicate that whether the best of those allegedly incompatible worlds can be achieved and whether polycentric issues can be dealt with acceptably depends largely on two things: the balance that is effected between the public hearing and other procedures and the success of the agency in making decisions that are perceived to be coherent and legitimate. To these we turn.

(b) Case Law or Rulemaking?

It is clear that many of Shapiro's advantages of rule-making have been sought by means of various formal and informal CAA procedures. Standards have been articulated in the 'short-haul criteria', participation has been provided in seminars and consultations, the planning of longer-term strategies has gone ahead by means of the 'brown books' and this has allowed not merely wide consultation to take place but has disseminated information to the industry and has led to open discussion of policy. Except in limited areas, the CAA has not waited for applications to be submitted so that it can formulate policies but has used its resources to look forward to what it sees as potential regulatory problems—as in its analysis of the European fares market.

It might be questioned whether the Authority has always taken positive decisions to develop certain procedures rather than others. In fact, the determining factor here has been the development of the CAA's regulatory expertise. Thus the short-haul criteria and new cargo charter policies arose out of the period 1974–75 when the CAA's economics branch were perceived as having developed their ability to apply economic theory to regulatory issues.[137] At the same time, following the fuel crisis of 1973–74, the CAA board and senior staff were concerned especially with low domestic profitability and were determined to strengthen the airlines' economic position. One CAA executive told the author how in 1975, and leading up to the publication of the short-haul criteria, there was 'a coming together of a developed theory and a pragmatic recognition that we ought to do something about the industry'. When asked whether the application of more rigorous standards to case-decisions had been a motive for producing the criteria, he stated that the criteria 'did serve to supplement the guidance', but that 'the need for consistency was definitely a second-order factor'. Legalistic values were clearly placed lower on the scale than economic and pragmatic considerations.

One factor, however, that did directly influence the choice of whether to consult, publish policies or adjudicate by public hearing was the anticipated degree of airline or other resistance to proposals. Thus, the three year profitability rule set out in the short-haul criteria was considered uncontroversial and so was not the subject of prolonged consultation or a special hearing. In contrast, when the 'part-charter' facility was introduced in 1974, CAA staff arranged to hold a public hearing specifically because they envisaged a dispute between charter operators and the larger scheduled airlines. In the case of the 1979 review of regulatory policy entitled 'Domestic Air Services', both economic and organizational motivations played their part. By that time the airlines' financial position had improved and the CAA had reached 'a new stage in the evolution of CAA thinking' in which the Authority took a step backwards to examine in depth what the policy guidance stood to achieve. By this time also, departmental specializations in the CAA had blurred to produce a more co-ordinated approach. The economists had gained a greater appreciation of, and a greater involvement in, policy issues and the policy makers were more able to suggest avenues of economic investigation to their colleagues. One person closely involved contrasted the operation of a 'multi-disciplinary team' to procedures in the CAA's earlier days when some administrators would isolate a problem and immediately 'find out what the economists say about it' rather than work on the policy issues themselves and then turn to the specialists. By 1979, under the more co-ordinated system that had been encouraged by the hiring of both policy and specialist staff from industry rather than the Civil Service, there were three main influences behind the policy review: the CAA's desire to look more closely at its objectives; the fact that less severe economic conditions encouraged a less restrictive approach to regulation and the advent of a new CAA chairman with a wish to see 'regulation with a light touch'. Revisions in the use of the public hearings system were by-products of such changes rather than objectives. On the aims of rule-making and policy-statements another senior CAA staff member said:

> We aim to create a policy framework based on the best knowledge
> available and on the Act, one that allows us to put proposals to
> the airlines which can be challenged but a framework that also
> allows the airlines to put new proposals back to us: you always
> have the fall-back of the quasi-judicial hearing.[138]

Of published research and policy documents, Sir Nigel Foulkes,
commented:

> The CAA aims to simplify and minimize regulation. The brown
> books look at dark areas, at underlying policies. I think the CAA
> can't just lurch from one decision to another. The statistical,
> research and consultation work is part of a process of seeing if we
> can understand the industry, regulation and the airlines. They
> constitute the raw material for reassessing policies.[139]

If Gifford's test is applied and it is asked whether the CAA has
matched its structuring devices to the different types of regulatory issue, the answer is that, whether the perfect balance has
been achieved or not, the agency has been sensitive to variations
in issue-type and has been highly adaptable in dealing with
these.

(c) 'Managerial' or 'Regulatory' Decision-making? Muddling-Through or Coherence?

In looking at how an agency can make coherent decisions it is
helpful to move from K.C. Davis's focussing on the need to
structure discretion to an examination of the amenability of
decision-types to structuring. Examination of the CAA shows,
moreover, the folly of dealing with the discretion of any body as a
single, constant factor. To assume that all the decisions of a
particular agency such as the Supplementary Benefits Commission (SBC), the CAA or the IBA are of the same kind, is rash. It
makes little sense to question whether the decisions of an agency
are 'justiciable' or 'polycentric' or anything else without first
examining what varieties of decision the body makes. The kinds
of control that may usefully be applied to discretions may in
practice only be assessed in relation to quite particular circumstances. That is not to say that we should ignore general analyses
of the advantages and disadvantages of 'legalizing' (imposing
substantive rules on) or 'judicializing' (applying adjudicative
procedures to) agency activities: this will aid consideration of

individual discretionary powers but it is no substitute for analysis on the ground. As Jeffrey Jowell has stated:

> ... an understanding of the limits as well as the merits of legal techniques will allow us to provide for the control of administrative discretion in a manner that is sensitive to the nature of the administrative process and the constraints operating upon decision-makers, and is hence more likely to prove successful.[140]

Davis himself has stressed that 'almost every proposal (must) be examined in each of the thousands of specific contexts of particular discretionary powers'.[141]

Within one agency there can be, as Gifford has pointed out, a massive array of issues that have to be decided in the course of regulation. In the case of the CAA some hearings are concerned with complex non-recurring test cases and new policies (e.g. should 'part-charters' be allowed on scheduled passenger services?). Others deal with one case within a larger policy framework (e.g. Skytrain applications) and yet more are routine issues being decided not in terms of new policy lines but of relatively well established and recurring standards (e.g. simple questions of diversion). Some policy issues are politically contentious, others give less cause for concern. There are cases involving just two parties and others that entail debates between a multitude of operators. Even the concept of the public hearing is indefinite: many important policy decisions are made not at formal licensing hearings but on the basis of informal consultations and semi-formal consultative hearings that may resemble public inquiries or even academic seminars. The CAA employs a wide variety of procedures both to decide a multitude of issue-types and to 'structure its discretion by openness'.[142]

Appreciation of the range of discretionary activity within each agency should discourage unqualified generalizations of the kind 'the CAA should adopt more precise standards' or 'the SBC should operate on a "rights" basis', since it is plain that such prescriptions cannot apply to all the decisions of such agencies.[143] Similarly, another temptation may be resisted. Bodies such as the IBA, CAA and SBC are all independent and specialist and so there is a tendency to overplay parallels between authorities of similar institutional status. When details are taken into account, however, we may be dealing with very different forms of decision and contrasting decision-making contexts. The CAA's regulatory clients are an expert few enjoying considerable resources: they are interested in a small number of decisions involving substantial economic values. Such a position contrasts with the SBC whose clients are on the whole inexpert, huge in number and, by definition, lacking resources.[144] The SBC is concerned with a plethora of decisions which, taken individually, tend to involve small amounts of money. If, therefore, we are examining the advantages of rule-making as a method of structuring in relation to the powers of the CAA and SBC, there is a limit to useful generalization. Legalization in the one field may be based on perceived needs to focus planning and to increase political legitimacy. In the other, it is more likely that rules are used to regulate clients' demands and to increase the speed with which cases are processed.[145]

If an attempt is made to break down agency functions into different classes of decision-making it becomes clear that in evaluating agency rule-making and procedures it is unhelpful to apply tests of 'predictability', 'efficiency' etc. across the board.[146] Apart from espousing what might be called 'the fallacy of homogeneous decision-making', it implies that there exists some sort of consensus on the optimal levels of predictability or efficiency in the regulatory scheme. It would be mistaken, however, to assume that even the airlines all want predictable and formally rational decisions: their interests vary. The large operators, who are concerned to preserve their existing routes, to rationalize investment decisions and to plan safely for the future, may advocate such a system even at the cost of delay, but (as was indicated to the author) certain private operators of an aggressive disposition would prefer CAA decisions that place more emphasis on speed and responsiveness to economic change than to any dictates of consistency or precedence: they hope to benefit from any degree of chaos that results from changing existing route structures. The fact that a wide spectrum of such demands is made of the CAA does not, however, indicate that 'anything goes' in CAA decision-making. In the end, credibility still has to be preserved and the Authority has to justify decisions not merely to the operators but to the public and to the Secretary of State as appeal authority.

The implication of this account of the CAA is that it may be a misapplication of emphasis generally to favour certain models of decision-making and particular forms of control over discretions.

Within an agency there may be something more important than a willingness, say, to create standards across the board or to decide issues openly or to give the appearance of rationality: administrative justice may, more than anything, depend on the skill of the agency in adjusting its procedures to fit the kinds of decision-making it is required to indulge in.[147] The more a body is involved in 'polycentric' issues, and the greater the number of constituents to be satisfied, the more that the choice of procedures and rule-making devices becomes a political art rather than an administrative or judicial science. The test of success in such issues may be public confidence—whether politicians, regulatees and consumers have faith in an agency's control. To this extent the regulatory agency's tendency to direct its activities towards self-justification is understandable. For those studying the agency, the lesson is to limit the premium attached to general analyses of procedures and to consider the match between procedures or issues and the processes used in adapting those procedures to ends. Not only academics such as Gifford have stressed the importance of the adaptive process: it was no other body that the American Bar Association that said:

> . . . administrative procedures, initially developed as a safeguard against the threat of regulatory abuse, have come to mimic the judicial process, with inadequate regard for the flexibility available under existing statutes. Regulatory procedure requires a new flexibility which respects traditional concerns for accuracy, fairness and acceptability, but meets the need for more efficient administration.[148]

There is a difference, however, between advocating that formal licencing procedures should be more responsive (in the sense of less time-wasting and rigid) and appreciating the stronger sense of 'flexibility' that involves a preparedness to consider all the varieties of agency decision-making and the need to adapt these to changing circumstances. A body's 'discretionary power' is a package containing disparate elements that interact (as we have seen public consultations and public hearings do in CAA procedures). This rules out the divorcing of discretionary activity from policy-making and demands that the relationship between the two is explored. Thus we could not account for CAA decisions on major route applications without looking at relevant CAA research and policy development through the 'brown books'. K.C. Davis would advocate neither the separation of policymaking from discretion nor the abolition of discretion[149] but his argument is open to narrow interpretation, especially at the hands of lawyers. He says that we should eliminate all unnecessary discretion and control what remains by confining, structuring and checking it. He inserts qualifications (e.g. that we should aim for the 'optimum breadth' of discretionary power and that discretions be looked at in context) but the thrust of Davis's argument is towards an unexplored concept of justice. His central concern is:

> How can we reduce injustice to individual parties from the exercise of discretionary power.[150]

It should be repeated: focussing concern in this way biases any analysis of discretion in favour of legalistic values. The broader the responsibilities of a government agency, the less useful it is to treat discretion as an issue of justice rather than of judgement, administrative art or politics. The real questions are sidestepped when Davis states:

> Whenever any agency or officer has discretionary power, rulemaking is appropriate. The general objective should be to go as far as is feasible in making rules that will confine and guide discretion in individual cases.[151]

He adds, however, a footnote:

> Unfortunately how far is feasible is a question that must be determined for each discretionary power in each particular context.

We may agree that the particular context must be looked at but the point underemphasized by Davis is that, when we do examine the exercise of discretion in individual cases, we find that not only is it unhelpful to prescribe techniques of structuring and confining across the board but that we cannot ignore the political dimensions of discretionary activity. The heart of the matter lies in his footnote: the real question is not about *justice* but about *feasibility* and the balances that have to be established between predictability, efficiency, openness, political self-justification and many other factors. To concentrate on justice to the individual in any case fails to take on board the public's interest in regulatory activity[152] and, from the agency's point of view, justice to the individual must be a secondary consideration when put next to political survival.

Here again Gifford proves helpful. Soon after Davis had published *Discretionary Justice*, Gifford argued that those involved with agency decision-making should concentrate their attention not on the development of standards but on 'decisional referents'.[153] Most theorists had 'avoided asking why one standard is employed rather than another',[154] but decisional referents were 'whatever a decision-maker deems significant in deciding'[155] and they included and went beyond rules, criteria factors, considerations, principles, policies, goals and reasons. They thus allowed a broader and more policy-oriented approach to decision-making. The notion of decisional referents could, for instance, explain the taking into account of potential states of affairs —matters of special concern to regulatory bodies with their vague mandates and prospective orientation.

Decisional referents, for Gifford, had to 'possess more content' than generally-stated goals or directives and he gave as examples: studies and analyses; specialized disciplines and programme plans. Davis might stretch 'rule-making' to cover the consideration of hypothetical instances but Gifford looked further. CAA regulation suggests that Gifford was right: 'rules' do merge with non-rule decisional factors, there is a continuum of tentative through to firm considerations operating in agency decisions, factors taken into account by individuals do blur into those handed down by organizations, informal relationships are of relevance in decisions and decisional referents are in a constant state of flux. What might be added to Gifford is this statement: in areas of complex economic decision-making the attempt should be made not merely to develop standards and a range of decisional referents but to express the latter *in a layered fashion so that each layer is reinforced and made intelligible by others*. These layers should extend from the most general to the particular and cover not merely legal and policy but political considerations.

In the case of the CAA, the development of a 'layered' discretion was made possible because the Authority did not restrict itself to the trial-type process. A range of procedures had emerged by 1980 with the effect of both substituting for hearings and of harnessing them to the regulatory process. This allowed legislative and trial-type adjudicative methods to be applied to a wider range of activities than would otherwise have been possible and meant that public hearings could be used both to adjudicate on particular issues and to promulgate major rules.

In addition, the mixed system allowed hearings to be used in relation to comparatively rarely-recurring cases and to regulatory areas subject to rapid change.[156] Whereas in the ATLB's days policy only existed at two levels, the most general (the Act) and the specfic (the case decision), there emerged under the CAA a wide-ranging system of policy-making and accountability. A licensing representative could look not only to the 1971 Act but also to the policy guidance and this provided a crucial link between statutory and administrative principles, standards and rules. The guidance attempted, with limited success, to describe policy in terms of some precision but of sufficient breadth to allow the CAA operational flexibility. It influenced CAA rule-making without compelling any one approach. The system that emerged by 1980 was one in which the absence of a rule or policy on any one point or level might be balanced against the existence of a broader policy or principle[157] and all policies of detail might be interpreted against a background of published CAA statements of regulatory philosophy. As a final reference, representatives, in preparing cases, were also able to consider relevant case law against their background knowledge of the views or attitudes of CAA members and staff as expressed at the various forms of consultative or public meetings.

On the question whether the CAA simply 'muddles through' in an *ad hoc* or incrementalist fashion, it is useful to refer to Charles Lindblom's contrast between rational-comprehensive (root) and successive limited comparison (branch) styles of developing policy in relation to complex issues.[158] The former is said to rely on the clarification of values and objectives, policy-formulation is approached by selecting the means to achieve defined ends, analysis is comprehensive, all values are considered, all relevant factors are taken into account and theory is relied on. The branch method, on the other hand, links the selection of value goals with empirical analysis: it relies very little on means end analysis; policies are based on short-term choices; a high degree of selectivity ignores important alternatives and values and policy-making by a succession of comparisons reduces reliance on theory.

Lindblom's point is that the more complex a problem, the less useful the 'root' method becomes and the more appropriate 'branch' policy-making will be: one could take into account all the relevant factors involved in directing traffic on a bridge but to suppose that this could be done in making national foreign policy would be misleading. Branch policy-making is therefore said to be flawed but 'it is not a failure of method for which administrators ought to apologise': it often makes sense to simplify choices, to rely heavily on past policies and only to change these incrementally.

Taken to its extreme, the argument for 'muddling through' would seem to rule out the need for truly expert agencies that differ from tribunals in taking a more comprehensive view of 'the factors attending a decision or policy'. Quick and cheap decision-making, it could be said, is therefore preferable to expertise. The contrary view, however, is supported by this review of the CAA. Lindblom's arguments are at their strongest in relation to the 'one-off' (e.g. foreign policy) decisions of individual administrators: they are weaker where, as in the case of civil aviation licensing, mere 'muddling through' would fail to yield the longer-term policies that are needed to render particular decisions coherent. Incrementalism is also incapable of responding to rapid economic and technological changes with radical new policies.[159] The Lindblom thesis, furthermore, minimizes the role of expertise (in his view it is impossible and so misleading to attempt to priorize values): in aviation licensing, however, the contrast between the CAA and the ATLB shows how an approach that is more ambitious than mere pragmatism can avoid many pitfalls.

The CAA, for its part, falls between the Lindblom models: it acts incrementally in some areas (e.g. airports policy) but in others its staff have attempted to take a 'new look' at a whole problem (e.g. at ABC's, 'blanket' charter licenses, cargo charter liberalization) and it has both relied on theory and a priorizing of values. Lindblom points out that the objectives of many agencies are limited by statute. This is so in the CAA's case and, to some extent, this restricts the breadth of approach that the CAA can take. A developing expertise, has nevertheless, played an important role and the ATLB's ad-hoccery has been avoided. What counts in aviation licensing is, as we have seen, the potential to make policies that are intelligible and responsive, lasting and politically secure.

(d) Politics and the Regulatory Process

The political legitimacy of the CAA is closely dependent on its policy-making and its case decisions being seen as coherent expert and efficient. In so far as the CAA has succeeded where the ATLB failed it has avoided gross confusion of policies and has established a framework to render most of its decisions intelligible within the real world of political contention. Trial-type procedures have been combined with other devices without turning the public hearing into a charade and lawyers have been used in hearings without causing undue rigidity. Arguably because of the policy guidance and the resulting relationship between CAA and the Department, the CAA has managed to develop its own policies without suffering the kind of interference via ministerial *ad hoc* and political inconsistency that was seen in the ATLB era. The benefits of 'layered' policy-making have been clear. Those seeking in the CAA a source of both longer-term and day-to-day policies, have, if necessarily imperfectly, been offered both. The extent to which the CAA's achievements in combining powers might have been (and will in future be) possible in the absence of the written policy guidance system, is, however, a matter to be returned to in Chapter 13.

12
Regulatory Performance and the CAA

Whether or not the CAA's policy framework stems from guidance, its own policy statements or a system of case law, its *raison d'être* remains the efficient control of an industry in accordance with a set of statutory objectives.[1] In pursuance of these aims it has furthermore been clear that regulation has to be minimal, thus the first paragraph of each guidance urged the Authority 'always to impose the least restraint upon the industry or upon the users of its service'.[2]

Control by the CAA with these aims in mind may be considered in the light of the principal criticisms that commentators make in relation to the regulatory agency. It is said (notably in the American literature) that regulatory agencies are: (i) unnecessary; (ii) slow and inefficient; (iii) unfair and unpredictable; (iv) prone to industry-orientation; and (v) politically anomalous.

(i) Regulation is Unnecessary?

A common response to regulation was summarized in the conclusions of the House of Commons Industry and Trade Committee of 1981:

> ... it is our firm opinion that no regulatory body—however enlightened its policies or however good its intentions—will produce a more satisfactory service for the air passenger than will fair competition in the market place.[3]

Whether fair competition actually exists or not, it has been clear in recent years that the political and (at least in America) academic tides have been running against the agencies and in favour of deregulation. 'Sunset' legislation has been enacted to wind down bodies such as the CAA's United States equivalent, the Civil Aeronautics Board (CAB).[4] Economists of the Chicago school as well as others have argued not that agencies are 'captured' but that they are designed for the industry's benefit and they would do away with them.[5] The American Bar Association has recommended that:

> In lieu of governmental intervention in the economy reliance should be placed when feasible upon the competitive market as regulator supported by antitrust laws.[6]

The latest anti-agency wave started as long ago as 1970 when Paul MacAvoy published *The Crisis of the Regulatory Agencies* and advocated both massive deregulation and a movement away from control of industry by independent regulatory bodies.[7] Democratic and Republican administrations in the USA have continued to call for an end to anti-competitive regulations[8] and academics have recommended a change from control by regulatory bureaucracies towards the manipulation of economic incentives. This strategy, it is said, would be easier to administer, less disruptive to business and more effective in achieving regulatory goals.[9]

This is not an economic treatise setting out to compare models of a regulated and an unregulated industry and will not therefore engage at length in the above debate.[10] This book accepts that at least some degree of regulation is necessary in British civil aviation and examines the role of trial-type procedures and political controls in the system of regulation. The Industry and Trade Committee report of 1981 and the American literature does, however, impose some obligation to consider the way in which the CAA has acted to select the *degree* of regulation appropriate to different sectors of industrial activity. As has been seen in previous chapters, the level of regulation imposed may be crucial in judging whether appropriate procedures have been adopted by the regulating body and an indication of the CAA's response to this problem may be obtained by examining its approach to deregulation.

The most concise analysis of arguments for and against regulation in internal British civil aviation is contained in the CAA's own book *Domestic Air Services*[11] and this is perhaps worth reviewing. The agency's main arguments in favour of intervention may be summarized:

(a) without regulation, network benefits may be lost; competition may not produce a reasonable balance between concentration and dispersal;

(b) free competition may not produce a regular scheduled service available for off-peak as well as peak periods;

(c) given the absence of price competition, the scarcity of traffic on UK routes and, given conditions favouring the larger operators, it may be difficult for new carriers to enter markets. Lack of regulation might therefore produce, at best, imperfect competition, at worst, monopoly;

(d) there is some evidence, particularly on North Atlantic scheduled services, that where competition does exist it tends to be wasteful or destructive. A tendency exists for the over-provision of capacity at peak periods. The scope for predatory pricing or over-stressing short-run revenue maximization is considerable;

(e) experience suggests serious grounds for expecting excess capacity in a competitive environment.

The principal arguments against regulation were given as:

(a) civil aviation is a naturally competitive industry: there are minimal economies of scale and airlines cannot derive significant advantages over competitors by virtue of size; aviation technology is freely available; entry into the industry is easy; there is flexibility in operating aircraft capacity; neither the broad network operator nor the specialist has a preponderant advantage over the other;

(b) free competition is preferable to regulation: competition would produce regular services in order to attract traffic; off-peak periods would be utilized and, given pricing freedom, off-peak traffic would be generated; networking would be in the interests of the carrier;

(c) regulation is inherently undesirable: it purchases stability at the cost of inefficiency; a quasi-judicial system favours the easily-justified status quo; it blunts innovation and responsiveness to consumer needs; price regulation limits competition, innovation and new entry; it blunts the incentive to efficiency and cost-consciousness.

The CAA report applied the above arguments to the UK industry and concluded that, whilst the relaxation of regulation should be examined, there existed several features of the UK industry that might limit the effectiveness of such relaxation. These were: the small scale of the domestic industry and the limited number of routes able to support more than one airline; the limited effectiveness of competition from surface transport on longer routes; the fact that one airline, BA, accounted for about three-quarters of total seat-kilometres on domestic services, and airports policy, which restrained growth at Heathrow in favour of Gatwick.

The CAA considered that, because of the thinness of most UK routes, competition would tend to sacrifice any economies of volume. On many routes, existing operators would not be challenged effectively and, even if this happened, price reductions would be unlikely. In the absence of effective rail competition, BA would dominate routes in a manner allowing predatory pricing and new entrants might be deterred. There must, said the CAA, be considerable doubt whether price competition would occur on higher scheduled service fares. Lower prices would be matched and so yields would be reduced. The Authority concluded:

> All these considerations suggest that complete de-regulation of domestic services is simply not feasible. It should, however, be possible to move significantly further to meet some of the objections to a highly regulated system while taking advantage of the positive aspects of relaxation. This policy would aim to let the market work to the maximum feasible extent consistent with the limitations which have been described. Such an approach might look slightly untidy; slightly different solutions might be appropriate to the different types of route.[12]

The CAA, therefore, looked for alternative strategies:

> In a market where few city pairs can support the services of the two airlines, direct competition cannot be the sole tool of regulatory policy. A more effective tool may be the possibility of substituting one operator for another where standards of service have been allowed to decline or costs have been allowed to get out of control . . . it may be more important to ensure that more than one operator is available than to insist that two operators compete.[13]

It proposed to keep regulatory intervention to a 'necessary and unavoidable minimum'[14] and saw some scope for more liberal policies on pricing and on small-scale entries to provincial routes.

These principles of regulation were described in 1979, but, well founded or not, can it be said that the CAA has put them into practice? Examination of the period 1972–80 indicates an increasing philosophy of regulation 'with a light touch', a phrase coined by the CAA's second chairman, Sir Nigel Foulkes in 1977[15] and explained thus:

> Very low-key regulation . . . we don't let regulation become a way of life, a good in itself. It is a burden, it may be essential but you can have too much—it becomes like glue sniffing, it grows on you.[16]

An attempt has accordingly been made to limit regulation in the light of those circumstances relevant to each regulatory sector as perceived by the CAA. On charter operations, (both freight and passenger) long-term blanket licences have deregulated to a large extent. Long-haul international scheduled services that were open to competition in the 1960s were largely divided into 'spheres of interest' for BA and B.Cal. in the 1970s but, in spite of this policy, competition (e.g. 'Skytrain') was allowed on prestigious routes such as the North Atlantic. Here, of course, the degree of regulation was to depend not merely on CAA policies but on governmental strategies as formulated in air service agreements such as 'Bermuda II'. On domestic routes free competition, for the reasons outlined above, was deemed to be of limited value. In response to the argument that a quasi-judicial procedure favours the status quo it can be pointed out that competition has been allowed on major trunk routes and between certain airports (notably Gatwick and Heathrow). The threat of replacement became a useful tool of control given the availability of competing airlines and it has been used in some notable instances (e.g. the Gatwick to Aberdeen route in 1974 and 1979).

Little has been said thus far on air fares. On domestic routes, the major regulatory concern of the CAA in the 1970s was to see that services would make a return covering fully allocated costs, capital costs and the costs of replacement. Economic conditions largely ruled out price competition as a way of securing consumer benefits.[17] Furthermore, the CAA acted in place of the Price Commission in applying government pricing policies to air fares, a duty incompatible with deregulation. In spite of this function, the CAA has allowed experiments in the late 1970s with 'differential' fares (e.g. on the Belfast route) and, in its 1979 review, it encouraged discussion of proposals to regulate fares by creating 'zones of reasonableness' and by the adoption of a policy of discretionary intervention rather than approval of all fares. This started a movement towards a process similar to that already adopted on international routes in which fares are filed with the Authority rather than subjected to the full licensing process.

Different considerations have applied to international fares. At the January 1977 public hearing on European fares B.Cal. argued that the CAA should review rather than fix prices; the CAA, on the other hand, considered that it had to take a 'positive role in fares policy'.[18] It was prepared merely to 'monitor' charter operations and those scheduled services where relatively free competition did apply, but on other scheduled service routes considered that the Act and guidance demanded regulation of prices since market forces could not be relied upon to ensure that prices related to the costs of the efficient operator.[19]

Although the high level of fares and low level of competition on European routes have been criticized, most notably by the House of Lords Select Committee on the European Communities and the House of Commons Industry and Trade Committee in their reports on 'European Air Fares'[20] the responsibility for this state of affairs rests with the Governments of the European countries and their (counter-competitive) desires to protect 'flag-carrying' airlines, rather than the policies of the CAA.

What the 1977 public consultation and the 'European Air Fares' document sought to do was to work out rational principles to govern the assessment of fares. It emerged with five 'fundamental principles'.[21] The Authority also instituted in the mid-1970s a programme of research into the economic methods of assessing fares proposals of different kinds and on different routes. The aim was to regulate with a light touch, and on the basis of agreed principles, fares on those routes where conditions of free competition did not apply.

Critics of the CAA's regulatory activities would argue the merits of a free market. If, however, we accept that there is at least some truth in the CAA's outline of imperfections in the British aviation market (conditions very different from those obtaining in the USA) and, if the artificiality of European competition is acknowledged, certain conclusions may be drawn on the kind of regulation imposed. By 1980 it seems that the CAA had genuinely moved towards a philosophy of minimal regulation. It had conducted researches attempting to isolate those areas most in need of control and it had either deregulated or allowed increased competition in several sectors of the market (e.g. passenger charters, cargo charters, North Atlantic services). Its proposals of the late 1970s showed a willingness to investigate further areas of liberalization (e.g. on small scale entry to domestic routes) and, as far as the principles governing the control of competition were concerned, steps had been taken to discuss these at length in hearings, reports and consultations. It might be concluded therefore, that, whether or not the arguments for complete deregulation are convincing, the CAA has, procedurally at least, adopted a flexible approach in setting levels of regulation and in developing principles to govern that regulation.

(ii) Regulation is Slow and Inefficient?

Criticisms of agencies for being slow, for creating mountains of paper and for failing to react to industrial needs are not new.[22] Perhaps a more recent concern, especially in the USA, has been the desire to look for ways of regulating industries by methods that would be less restrictive to the industries concerned than resort to bureaucracies.[23] Even if we were prepared to write off the views of the extreme deregulators as the statements of those with an exaggerated trust in market forces, and even if we assume once again that complete deregulation is not feasible, the question remains whether the CAA's system of regulation has proved unduly burdensome to the civil aviation industry.

By the year 1980–1 economic regulation by the CAA was costing airlines an annual £3,020,000 (£2,020,000 in 1979–80); such income gave the CAA an operating profit of £310,000 (£164,000 in 1979–80) on economic regulation. For each flight across the North Atlantic, operators were wont to say, the cost of one seat was devoted purely to keeping the CAA in existence.

The cost of CAA regulation must be matched against the consumer benefits that result from the Authority's substituting other factors for absent market forces. By optimizing capacity levels and through its monitoring strategies (such as threatening to replace inefficient operators) the CAA has aimed to create the best balance of conditions for both consumers and industry. Advocates of the free market have at consultations and hearings, in submissions and elsewhere, criticized the CAA principally on the grounds that it is too protective of existing operators; it is too consumer-oriented; it favours the status quo; it offers no incentive towards cost-consciousness; it impedes innovation because the licensing process is slow and it creates planning difficulties for the airlines in their attempt to build efficient networks or services.

As far as protecting existing operations is concerned, analysis of CAA decisions and policy statements reveals that a 'most powerful case'[24] has to be made by an operator who seeks to replace another on a route but that this has been by no means an impossible burden to discharge. The licensing of Dan Air from Gatwick to Aberdeen in 1979 together with the revocation of BA's licence[25] was an example of successful challenge by a new entrant. Further examples exist of unoperated licences being revoked.[26] On the other hand, the licensing procedure has to some extent favoured the existing operator: that airline may base its case on concrete operating statistics as opposed to the challenger's mere forecasts. Nevertheless, the CAA is increasingly able to judge for itself whether performance on a route is satisfactory. With regard to quality of service, the Authority may look to evidence received from witnesses, from the Air Transport Users Committee or from other organizations at both hearings and in the course of regulation. On the matter of costs, major questions for the CAA are whether an operator, perhaps one enjoying a degree of protection from competition, is being sufficiently successful in keeping costs down and whether prices are related to costs. The CAA has to judge, on figures supplied by the operators, whether efficiency and prices are acceptable.

The area in which most detailed work on this problem has been carried out has been European air fares and was described in the 'brown book' of that name.[27] The CAA, by 1977, had commenced a study of costs and fare levels on a number of key international routes which were to be 'regarded as representative of the related network . . .' in order 'to examine the long term fare levels appropriate to the route'.[28] In order to conduct such studies the CAA demanded from the airlines detailed information on (i) traffic and revenue, (ii) capacity offered, and (iii) the cost of providing that capacity. As the total sum of information on key routes increased, so the CAA's expertise in assessing fares proposals against models of costs grew. In addition, a classification of the principles underlying fares policy was encouraged. It is expected that in the mid-1980s such principles will be applied by further studies to other regulatory areas (e.g. domestic routes) as the need to consider the relationship of prices to costs increases, for example with increasing pressures towards domestic price competition. For the present, CAA staff are quite confident that they can calculate European costs quite precisely and, allowing a 'margin for argument', can come quite close to allocating those costs accurately to the various classes of passenger.[29]

Against charges that CAA regulation impedes networking and planning, staff of the Authority point out that the dominance of the huge BA might, on deregulation, give private operators greater cause for concern that the CAA does at present. The CAA has shown in its decisions[30] that a factor to be considered in allocating routes is the advantage or disadvantage to operators' particular schemes of operation, and the 'short-haul' criteria of 23 May 1978 stated: 'Full allowance will be made for quantifiable network effects.' The CAA has not, on the other hand, structured networks by inviting particular applications nor will it grant licences merely to utilize aircraft or fill 'empty legs'.[31] It has, however, dropped hints in its decisions as to applications that would be viewed favourably[32] and, with the CAA willing to consider network arguments in such instances, the operators may be relied upon to submit the appropriate applications. On long-haul routes that serve to impose an overall structure on the industry it could hardly be said that the CAA, with its support for 'spheres of influence', has created an unstable environment for airline planning or networking. On domestic and short-haul routes it has gone some way in a similar direction by publishing its licensing criteria and its philosophy; so much so that the Authority is perhaps more prone to accusations of conservatism in this sector than of rendering operators insecure. As already noted, however, any evaluation of CAA performance in this area may depend on a particular interest: the small independent airlines may have very different ideas of the level of stability desirable for the industry. What can be said is that the CAA of the late 1970s and early 1980s certainly sees itself as licensing more liberally than in former years.

Returning to international matters, the CAA has clearly

imposed certain restrictions on innovation in opposing complete deregulation of the industry. It did not, for example, give carte blanche to 'Skytrain' worldwide, nor has it been within its power to throw European routes open to free competition. On the other hand, the CAA has increasingly relaxed its grip on the reins by liberalizing in the passenger and cargo charter areas; by allowing 'Skytrain' both to operate to further destinations (e.g. Los Angeles) and to use provincial airports (1981) and by moving in the direction of greater pricing freedom on scheduled services. Whereas the ATLB failed to regulate positively, the CAA has taken a stronger hand in securing the development of the industry. Thus in its first year the CAA proudly announced that it had 'taken a leading part in securing international agreement on the introduction of . . . the ABC':[33] it had introduced its own fare concept, not that of the airlines, in negotiations with US and Canadian authorities. In the same year, the CAA took up and promoted the new advanced purchase excursion (APEX) fare[34] on the North Atlantic after BOAC had proposed it. The introduction of 'part-charter' facilities on scheduled service flights, although resulting from BA initiatives in IATA, led to the CAA's reclassification of the class 1B licence in 1974. The 'fly-drive' tour and the £2 Gatwick discount fare[35] were catalysed by the Authority after consultations with the airlines.

In the longer term, the CAA's programmes of research, resulting in publication of structural plans for various markets, clearly have had and will have great significance for operators in terms of planning and innovation. It is for economists to judge whether particular market strategies are likely to achieve CAA objectives; for those concerned with the administrative process, the form that such planning has taken is significant in showing how an agency has, by a mixture of devices, attempted to transcend the *ad hoccery* of individual case-decisions in favour of a policy programme.

In so far as the requirement to obtain a licence may impede innovation in terms of simple delay, the average time taken by the CAA to decide a case involving a hearing (between 120 and 180 days) should be compared to the American CAB's 550 days;[37] it should be remembered, moreover, that in cases of urgency provision may be made for short-circuit procedure under regulation 7(3) of the CAA's 1972 regulations. More concern has been expressed with the time taken to decide CAA appeals. Between April 1980 and October 1982 there were 26 appeals that took between 56 and 259 days to decide with an average time of 170 days from the date of the CAA decision. Considering the rule against submitting new evidence on appeal, it seems difficult to justify taking roughly the same time to decide an appeal as to rule on the decision at first instance.

(iii) Regulation is Unfair and Unpredictable?

An agency has to tread a narrow path between accusations of capriciousness and complaints that it is inflexible or short-sighted. The ATLB, we saw, was heavily criticized for lack of consistency but the American agencies have been condemned both for their failure to develop standards[38] and for rigid adherence to rapidly out-dating rules.[39] What Judge Henry Friendly wanted was the development of:

> ... standards sufficiently definite to permit decisions to be fairly predictable and the reasons for them understood.[40]

He did not equate administrative with judicial adjudication but, like John Dickinson before him, considered that administrators could learn from lawyers.[41] Friendly wanted standards to ensure like treatment, to allow planning and prediction, to limit discretion, to maintain agency independence (he argued that the CAB and FCC were the agencies most subject to political pressure and those most lacking in standards) and to aid policy formulation.

Implicit in Friendly's argument was the belief that agencies could formulate policies by the case-law system, an opinion that contrasted with Lon Fuller's view that the FCC and CAB had failed to develop standards because they had *over-emphasized* case law. Fuller believed:

> The reason for this failure lies ... in the nature of the tasks assigned to these agencies: they are trying to do through adjudicative form something that does not lend itself to accomplishment through these forms.
> ... tasks of economic allocation cannot be effectively performed within the limits set by the internal morality of law. The attempt to accomplish such tasks through adjudicative forms is certain to result in inefficiency, hypocracy, moral confusion and frustration.[43]

Unlike Fuller, Friendly did not advocate abandoning the case-by-case method and was not unhappy 'that the quest for better definition of standards must lead to what is opprobriously called the judicialization of the administrative process'.[44] This was an extreme thesis later to be revised by K.C. Davis who, though agreeing with 'the thrust' of Friendly's book, rejected any 'extravagant' version of the rule of law that catered for no discretionary power within government.[45] Davis's answer was not to eliminate discretion but, as has been noted, to confine it within boundaries, to structure it with plans, policy statements and rules and to check it with various forms of review. As for standards, the hope, for Davis, lay not in legislative or judicial but in administrative action: he suggested that courts should order agencies to strive as much as possible 'to develop and to make known the needed confinements of discretionary power through principles, standards and rules'.[46] He concluded:

> The procedure of administrative rule-making is in my opinion one of the greatest inventions of modern government.[47]

Considering the CAA in the light of these arguments, what is clear is the difference between its approach and that of the ATLB. The CAA, as we saw in Chapter 11, has not relied exclusively on a case-by-case method of policy-making but, depending on the sphere of regulatory activity, has used public hearings as one device amongst many. In this respect, Friendly's arguments, calling for more policy-making by lawyers, miss an important point: policy that emerges from a variety of sources may be more useful to lawyers, operators and the public than confining decision-making to the one forum of the public hearing. For one thing a diversity of sources gives expertise a higher priority. As Barry Boyer has said:

> Trial-type proceedings tend to give the lawyers the whip hand and to place scientists in the decidedly secondary role of witness rather than decision-maker.[48]

From the arguments made in the last chapter it should be clear that to condemn the CAA for unfairness and unpredictability would be to adopt a narrow view of administrative justice. At the risk of repetition, the point should be stressed: instead of a system in which decisions are made formally on the basis of administratively-issued rules, it may be better to have a hybrid system which relates procedures to particular issues. Such a system, we have seen, may involve not one system of rule-making but a continuum varying not merely in generality but in policy-orientation and content. Thus, with the CAA the range extends through statutory aims and considerations to policy guidance, administratively issued policy statements, agency proposals, discussion documents, formal researches, informal joint researches, formal policy discussions/hearings, informal policy discussions/ hearings, informal policy statements, contested case-hearings and uncontested case-hearings.

It has already been stressed in Chapter 11 that, in the regulatory sphere especially, attention must be given not only to particular questions of justice but also to general issues of policy. Policy-oriented procedures allow a more effective and predictable way of limiting discretionary powers especially where the judgments of specialists are involved. It is the virtue of the multi-faceted agency that, unlike the traditional tribunal, it possesses the resources and ability to set its discretion within such a context.

Having rejected the criticism of 'failure to adopt standards' we may deal more briefly with the obverse attack: that agencies through their lives come increasingly to rely on case law, to adopt rigid stances and to adhere to out-dated rules.

In his account of the California Industrial Accident Commission (IAC), Philippe Nonet[49] has described how an agency changed from an administrative authority into a court of law. Legal argument replaced administrative policy-making, policies changed into rules and informality gave way to formal procedure in a general process of ossification at the hands of lawyers. The key, Nonet said, was 'the growth of adversariness' whereby political confrontation was transposed into legal controversy. A first sign of this was the changing of policies into rules:

> A policy becomes a rule when it is charged with such authoritativeness as to warrant holding the decision-maker accountable to it; it is then withdrawn from the realm of adoptive problem-solving, or of unexamined routine, and made a governing standard by which conduct and decisions are systematically and consciously assessed.[50]

In Britain an agency may at law make policy so long as it imposes no fetter on its discretion[51] but the issue is not so much legality as the effective application of resources. On this issue it is arguable that the CAA has so far avoided both caprice and blind rule adherence. This is not surprising given the CAA's youth and early stage in any regulatory life-cycle;[52] Nonet's IAC, after all, took some forty years to decline into a court. The signs of change must, however, be monitored. The scenario for a CAA deteriorating into a tribunal-like ATLB would be a retreat from flexible rule-making via consultation and an increasing emphasis on precedence rather than coherence in case decisions. The airlines' interests would be converted into due process rights (at the expense of other interests) and these rights would be extended into areas of regulation now governed by less formal procedures such as proposals, consultations and joint researches. At present there are no rule-making demands placed on the CAA akin to those encountered by the American agencies in the Administrative Procedure Act and its requirements for notice, comment and hearing.[53] Were the CAA to change over to a system of rule-making or consultation via lawyers and the adversary process then a considerable loss in responsiveness would follow. As part of this process of increased legal scrutiny, the CAA could be expected to retreat into a defensive posture and into policy-making by either case law or formalized rule-making. It would devote correspondingly fewer resources to researching longer-term policies and, in deciding cases, would strive to make them as far as possible immune from attack via the appeal or judicial review.[54]

The CAA is relatively healthy now but already there are signs that hearings, though used to decide fewer cases, are taking up more of the CAA's resources. The Air Transport Users Committee (AUC) now appears at selected hearings to argue the consumers case and thus an extra dimension has been added to the trial-type setting. In 1980–81 the CAA devoted 73 days to public hearings compared to 51 in 1978–79 and staff of the Authority have indicated (for example, in relation to domestic tariff issues) that more longer-term research into industry problems would be undertaken if resources could be released. If it were to become the case that the CAA decided issues with reference to the possibility of legal challenge rather than to regulatory objectives then decline would have set in.[55] Resistance to the process of rigidification may depend on a number of factors: resources are important as are the personalities involved; if there is strong leadership in the agency then defensiveness and legalism may be staved off. Political support (to which we will return below) is another important issue: if an agency is criticized on all sides and is given little encouragement from within government then retreat into the judicial shell is more likely. For the present, the CAA has established a balance in the shape of its 'light touch' regulation. It is when the lawyers and politicians respond more aggressively to the CAA that its regulatory strategy will be tested.

(iv) The Regulatory Agency is Industry-Orientated

Perhaps the most common criticism of American agencies is that they serve not the public interest but the interests of the regulated industries.[56] The terms 'clientelism', 'agency capture' and 'producer protection' are readily used to denote this process[57] but judging whether an agency serves industry interests or not is a difficult matter. Paul Quirk puts it thus:

> . . . an allegation of industry influence usually rests on an (often unstated) assumption about what the agency *would have* done in the absence of industry influence—an assumption that tends to derive from what the critic thinks *should have* been done.[58]

Objective tests, therefore, are hard to find: there are many studies of the costs of regulatory activity[59] but few take into account the alternative costs of deregulation and ensuing competitive inefficiencies. There is often no direct conflict between, say, airline traveller and airline because each have not single, but multiple interests (e.g. higher fares may suit the operator but the consumer may be offered a more frequent service). Without comprehensive analysis we cannot calculate the trade-offs between the various factors that are affected by regulatory action, and, in order to make a judgment on agency activity, we would require a similar analysis of the deregulated state of the industry.

Different analyses have been offered. Bernstein's notion of 'capture' was of a process whereby agencies were created to benefit the public interest but became subverted to industry interests.[60] As we have noted, both Kolko and Stigler revised this approach in their different ways to argue that industry input into the design of regulatory legislation and into the continuing politics of regulation means that regulation is organized so as to benefit existing industrial interests in the first place. Such accounts, however, are at their weakest in explaining regulatory regimes that are designed to counter wasteful competition so as to benefit the public interest.[62] In the case of agencies like the CAA with duties both to encourage a healthy industry and to further the interests of consumers,[63] it is particularly rash to assume that industrial and consumer interests are diametrically opposed.

We will return in the next section to the issue of the continuing political balance between industry and agency. In terms of assessing 'capture', however, the 'political' theories present problems similar to those already discussed: they operate at a general level. In examining individual bodies it is more productive to concentrate on particular aspects of their structure and operation. This is the strategy adopted by Quirk in asking whether capture has occurred in the Federal Trade Commission, the Civil Aeronautics Board, the Food and Drug Administration and the National Highway Traffic Safety Administration. His approach is to examine whether there are factors that act as 'policy incentives' for agencies to favour industry as opposed to public interests. A number of such factors are abstracted from prior studies by Quirk and, with minor amendment, will be borrowed here for the purposes of examining CAA orientation.[64] There are three main lines of argument to be dealt with.

(a) *Agency Decisions are Based on Information Supplied by the Industry and Only Industrial Interests are Represented at Formal Proceedings*

We have seen above that CAA decisions are not made only at formal hearings but emerge from a variety of procedures. It is true that the statistics used in these processes come largely from the industry but this is not wholly the case, nor is the CAA powerless to review those figures. In the case of licensing hearings the Authority works from its own collected statistics but also from the figures that an airline supplies in support of a particular application. In assessing, for example, costs or traffic forecasts the CAA has a number of computer models based on route-types which it has built up for the purpose of obtaining figures to compare with those of the operator. The CAA's resources are such that the balance of expertise does not unduly favour the airline (some airlines have even come to CAA House to run their figures through the Authority's computer). It has, furthermore, been argued to the author (thought by a senior CAA staff member) that by 1981 the greater experience of CAA staffing as compared to that of the airlines had resulted in CAA personnel often being more familiar with the economic and regulatory issues raised on a particular route application than the airline representative concerned. Such comments must be taken with a pinch of salt but indicate to the observer that, at least within the CAA, there is little fear that airline control of raw economic data causes a regulatory 'lag' such as would deserve the name 'capture'.

On public consultations and CAA rule-making the case against capture is stronger since, as we have seen above, proposals for regulatory reform tend to come from the CAA by way of publishing the results of research produced by the CAA's economics or policy branch. When, therefore, the CAA publishes an analysis of, e.g. costs on European routes or the scheduled/charter balance in an area, this work derives either from joint researches with the airlines or from the CAA's own work. Although in the case of joint research there is room to argue that the Authority has become too closely associated with the operator concerned, there is less reason to hold that control of the research lies with the industry rather than the CAA. Few airlines would argue, for example, that it was anyone other than the CAA that devised the proposals on freight regulation reform in the period after 1975.

As far as the representation of non-airline interests in CAA decision-making is concerned, the regulatory process has been subjected to a major change in recent years. Consumer interests were first catered for in CAA licensing when the CAA set up the Airline Users Committee (AUC) in the summer of 1973. This was chaired by the CAA's own Chairman, Lord Boyd-Carpenter, in accordance with his view that the AUC:

> . . . is not set up to supervise the Authority, which itself does not operate air services. It is set up to act in co-ordination with the Authority to assist in protecting the customers of British Airlines . . . the Committee and the body which appoints it are basically working for the same purpose.[65]

This non-statutory body comprised a wide range of user interests, from business travellers to holiday makers and freight consigners. Initially it was by no means independent; even its secretariat was made up of CAA staff who also served as the CAA's own Consumer Affairs section. The idea was that, instead of a slow-acting formal relationship with the CAA, the AUC could achieve more rapid responses from the Authority via its joint chairmanship, and could, by staff sharing, enjoy the advantages of proximity to the most extensive information available on airline costs and operational matters. When this adjacency was criticized, the AUC stressed its common objectives with the CAA saying:

> It was suggested during the year that a Consumer Advocate might be appointed to represent the consumer view at public hearings, following the example in the United States. It seemed, however, that this function would have to be separated from the Committee because the pursuance of such a formal role would have made it very much more difficult for the Authority to maintain a close relationship with the Committee, since the Committee would, in these circumstances, have to be treated in the same restricted way as a party to a hearing.[66]

The AUC thus adopted the role of advisory body to the CAA and the kind of adversary consumer representation favoured, for example, by many American lawyers was rejected in favour of British informality. As for the AUC's work, it undertook a number of visits to operators and airports and negotiated with both airlines and the BAA on such matters as overbooking and baggage facilities at terminals; it established a committee system and worked on a submission to Mr Peter Shore's policy review in 1975–76. Complaints were dealt with only after referral to the airline concerned and the AUC considered so few of these (e.g. 181 in 1973–74 and 237 in 1979–80) that it was prepared to admit the insignificance of its role in this respect when compared to the US Civil Aeronautics Board.[67]

That some tension might arise out of the AUC's relationship to the CAA, was seen in 1976 when the AUC published a report on European Air Fares. Although the consumer body was in agreement with the CAA in calling the then European fares structure 'a jungle', it exhorted governments and regulatory bodies to work towards fares reform. It clearly would have made such calls more authoritatively from a position of greater independence.

When Mr (later Sir) Nigel Foulkes took over as head of the CAA in March 1977, he decided that the AUC needed greater freedom of action and, accordingly, he gave up his AUC chairmanship in favour of an independent person, Sir Archibald Hope. The AUC continued its visits and researches into such topics as European travel and passenger tariff structures, but it did not appear at public meetings to argue individual cases. What gave the AUC more influence, however, were the CAA's new methods of consultative policy-making: thus the AUC report on European Air Fares was an item considered at the CAA's public consultation on that subject in January 1977. If this was an improvement on the status quo, the complaints role still declined: in 1977 the AUC claimed to have become better known to travellers via its numerous publications but, for the second year running, the number of complaints received had gone down and, since the AUC had failed to persuade operators to give it worthwhile data on the complaints the airlines themselves had received, it was 'unable to reach any conclusion' on the reasons behind its own declining response rate.

In April 1978 the AUC gained more complete independence from the CAA by taking its offices from Space (now CAA) House and moving up Kingsway to the Authority's old premises at Aviation House. It changed its name to the Air Transport Users Committee (still AUC) and no longer used CAA staff, though it remained funded by a CAA grant. Quoting the CAA Chairman's own words, the AUC announced that it fully intended 'to take advantage of its freedom to say and do what it thinks best in the interests of the air traveller—including freedom to criticize the CAA'.[68]

Where AUC independence made a difference was in its freedom to appear at CAA licensing hearings.[69] In the spring of 1979 it claimed 'substantial credit'[70] for opposing increases in domestic fares asked for by British Airways. The AUC argued to the CAA in public hearing that there were such inadequacies and inefficiencies in BA operations that fares increases were not justified. The CAA accepted much of the AUC submission on BA's overmanning and inefficiency and rejected a number of proposed increases. The AUC continued to make this case before the Industry and Trade Committee of the House of Commons whilst also pressing for reductions in European fares.

The AUC has appeared before the CAA at numerous public hearings dealing with both fares and route entry applications. Its staff prepare detailed briefs but it may be argued that independence from the CAA has removed the AUC a stage further from the information it needs to argue the consumer's case at the highest level of expertise.

What then of the AUC's role as protector of consumer interests? The traveller, it may be taken, is principally concerned with two factors: the overall regulatory policies being pursued by the CAA and the procedures for remedying particular complaints. On the former the evidence is that the AUC does serve as a mouthpiece but one that is limited in scope by the quality of information available to it. Mr Ashton Hill of the AUC told the House of Lords European Committee in 1980 that at the CAA's consultative hearing on European air fares in 1977, 'the CAA's viewpoint was very substantially affected by the evidence which we gave at that hearing'. He continued, however:

> You will appreciate that, because of section 36 we cannot get all the information we would like about operational costs of airlines and one of our very strong suggestions has been that section 36 should be amended and that, as happens in America, the airlines should publish their figures, meaningful figures, because without figures it is a matter of needles in haystacks.[71]

The Civil Aviation Act 1980 amended section 36 to allow the CAA (not as formerly the Secretary of State) to order the disclosure of information received. If this power is used by the CAA this may help the AUC since to counteract the operators interests it must either enjoy preferential access to CAA-held data or must receive the maximum information available for use at public hearings.

In dealing with individual cases of complaint as opposed to general policy, the AUC's effectiveness might be improved by a heightening of profile via further advertising and by co-ordinating all complaints in one body (instead of separating airport from air travel complaints as at present). Although initial reference of complaints to airlines is often a useful device for obtaining swift remedies, the AUC may have to consider whether it would enjoy greater public confidence if it were to deal directly with all complaints. Such a system would do much to set the AUC apart from the airlines in the public mind and encourage the belief that a complaint will result in positive action rather than a vague and unresponsive process of consultation between airports, airlines, AUC and CAA.

To summarize the first argument for capture, we may say that although raw data comes from the airline industry, there is considerable self-generation of information by the CAA and that this acts to counter any dependence: this is especially the case outside the formal public hearing. As far as the representation of non-airline interests is concerned, there have been grounds for criticism in the past, but, given improved access to information, the AUC system does offer limited consumer input into both licensing hearings and the wider consultative process.

(b) Individuals Appointed to High Regulatory Office Identify with Industry Interests with a View to Past or Future Employment[72]

In order to show that individuals in an agency are prone to capture one might point either to their incentives to sympathize with the industry or else their performance. Thus appointment of one of the airlines' heads to chair the CAA would indicate potential industry bias of the former kind whereas a CAA Chairman who publicly emphasized only the need for secure profits for airlines would demonstrate a bias in performance. Of course there are rarely such easy cases to analyse. Dealing with incentives first, there are few grounds for concluding that the two Chairmen of the CAA have been appointed from the ranks of those inclined to identify with the industry; a more prominent factor in each case was some prior knowledge of a field (Lord Boyd-Carpenter had been a Minister of Civil Aviation before going to the CAA and Sir Nigel Foulkes had chaired the British Airports Authority). For his part, Lord Boyd- Carpenter was an outspoken critic of the IATA cartel[73] and, although Sir Nigel has advocated regulation with a light touch, he has, in doing so, espoused competitive policies. The member of the CAA with perhaps the most influence on CAA activity throughout the period of this study, Mr Raymond Colegate, (now Board Member and Group Director of Economic Regulation) came to the CAA, as we have noted, from the Department of Trade and, where competitive policies have been concerned, has been more aggressive than his erstwhile Department. Thus it was the CAA that licensed 'Skytrain' in 1972 and 1975 when, within the Labour administration, there was strong resistance to the idea of allowing increased competition for BA on the North Atlantic. As far as prospective inducements are concerned, there is little evidence that exchanges of staff between the CAA and airlines have unduly influenced Authority policy. Between 1975 and 1982 only one member of the CAA Economic Regulation Group staff resigned to join an airline and only one was recruited from the airlines. CAA staff assert that they are paid at least as well as, if not better than, their counterparts in industry and that this reduces any risk of capture by expectation of future reward.

If substantive policies are examined, it is difficult to conclude that the airlines have been protected by the CAA to the detriment of the consumer. Clearly those to the right of the political spectrum might advocate more freedom of competition than the CAA allows and those on the left would demand more strict regulation. It is not the place here to decide between such political judgments and those who attempt such a task should bear in mind the extent to which the CAA has not developed its own broadest policies but has applied those set down in statute or guidance. Until 1980, the CAA acted under a statute and a policy guidance that instructed it to 'maximize the opportunities for the industry profitably to increase its share of the world civil air transport . . .' and to this end to impose the 'least restraint' on the industry.[74] Clearly then its function was to encourage the development of the industry as well as to satisfy public demand. Those who would point to any lack of competitive licensing after 1976 might be referred to the 'spheres of interest' policy and the restrictions on competition imposed by the second guidance. What can be asked more objectively is whether, in pursuance of its own policy lines, the CAA has been diverted by pressures from the industry. On this issue, examples perhaps balance out; thus Laker was licensed for 'Skytrain' in 1975 against strong political opposition, but was refused the 660 routes to Europe in 1980 when dominant political opinion favoured the application; BA has enjoyed protection in terms of its sphere of interest as defined in the 1976 guidance, but, in 1979, was refused domestic fares increases on the basis of inefficiency.

If a political judgment has to be made on whether CAA policies evidence capture, then it is perhaps wiser to look to the findings of parliamentary bodies rather than to offer a personal opinion. In recent years Select Committees of the Lords and Commons have shown particular interest in the levels of European air fares and in doing so have considered the role of the CAA. The House of Lords European Communities Committee's study[75] concluded that there should be more fares competition in

Europe and a lowering of the normal economy fare: it was well aware that the CAA favoured a similar policy but admitted that the Authority was limited in what it could accomplish because of the requirement that licensed operators should obtain traffic rights permission from European governments before operating any service and that these governments were, in general, reluctant to expose their state airlines to increased competition. The House of Lords' report was published in April 1980 shortly after the CAA had considered a number of pioneering applications for European routes from independent operators.[76] Only six of a number of B.Cal.'s proposed low fare mini-prix services had been licensed and the applications of Air UK, Britannia and Laker (for 660 routes) had been refused. Laker had argued not in terms of the 1971 Act and guidance, but had stated that the free competition rules of the Treaty of Rome applied to air transport and that access to routes should be unrestricted.

The Lords Committee noted that the CAA's refusal to grant these licences had led to its being criticized for excessive caution and said:

> ... had the CAA always been so cautious, it is unlikely that the existing independent airlines could ever have been established in the United Kingdom.[77]

The CAA's answer to this criticism was that it is necessary to promote and develop a receptive international environment through inter-governmental discussion before such applications can be granted and that, in the case of Laker, the terms of the Act and guidance had not been satisfied in a manner required for licensing under the 1971 Act. In its memorandum to the Committee, the CAA said:

> As a matter of policy the CAA would prefer not to intervene in the determination of air fares. It believes that where competitive conditions exist regulatory intervention should be minimal, if it exists at all ... the regulatory climate is not yet right for such a solution. CAA present policy assumes that current international attitudes will cause the present near monopoly on scheduled air services to persist and therefore that regulatory intervention is necessary. This intervention is designed to achieve as far as possible the effects of competition.[78]

In the final analysis, then, the Committee did not disagree with the policy aims of the CAA and it endorsed the CAA's

objective of relating prices to long-run costs via minimal regulation. It was recognized that to license without traffic rights
would serve no purpose, and, although it urged the CAA and the
British Government to press European governments strongly for
reform, the Committee was well aware that this was where most
of the problems lay:

> There are, however, difficulties in introducing any rapid pro-
> gramme of liberalization in Europe, largely associated with the
> prestige of national airlines, and in some cases their commercial
> weakness. . . . Most European governments have yet to be per-
> suaded that the benefits of more competition would not be more
> than offset by the disruption of the existing regulatory system it
> would cause.[79]

In terms of capture then, the report, with its conclusion that
the CAA and government should 'press on with their present
policy regarding lower fares' (para. 70), cannot be taken as a
finding that industry interests had forced the CAA into protec-
tionism. Even if high European fares might have suited British
Airways, the regime was the making of other governments, and
smaller operators such as Laker supported CAA/DoT attempts
to sell liberalization to other countries. When, indeed, Laker
commenced a High Court case in 1981 seeking to apply the
competition rules of the Treaty of Rome (Articles 85 to 90) to air
transport, the CAA and DoT treated this as a friendly action
since they also sought a ruling on this matter so as to spur the
European Commission to act on liberalizing air transport in
Europe.[80]

The House of Commons Industry and Trade Committee
reported on the same topic a year later and did so against a
background of deepening recession. Deregulation on the American and North Atlantic routes in adverse circumstances had led
to low prices, excess capacity and huge losses whilst the Association of European Airlines (AEA), a group of 19 major European
scheduled carriers, including BA and B.Cal., reported combined losses of almost £200 million in 1980 compared to profits of
£200 million in 1979. Whereas the House of Lords Committee
had readily suggested that deregulation might benefit European
air fares as it had done in America, the Commons Committee
was less sure, warning that the 'jury was still out on deregulation'[81] and stating that in America it was difficult to disentangle
the effects of deregulation from those of recession. It concluded:

None . . . condemn outright what happened in the USA but few appear to support the idea of overnight deregulation in Europe.[82]

Having said that, however, the Commons Committee clearly favoured increased fares competition in Europe and advocated measures similar to those proposed by the Lords. It was on the role of the CAA that it made the statement quoted at the start of this chapter:

> . . . it is our firm opinion that no regulatory body—however enlightened its policies or however good its intentions—will produce a more satisfactory service from the air passenger than will fair competition in the market place. . . . We should like to see the conversion of the CAA to a much stronger belief in the virtues of fair competition.[83]

As a critique of CAA regulation of entry and fares in European licensing this conclusion does not offer a great deal. One confusion was that committee members advocated competition (as found in the perfect market) yet focused on a CAA statement that it did not 'believe in competition for its own sake'[84] without appreciating the CAA assumption behind this: that in Europe the market is necessarily distorted, and so simply to allow more carriers to compete is not necessarily a solution to current problems. The CAA's Raymond Colegate told the Commons committee in June 1981:

> We have given a good deal of support and encouragement to existing British operators to secure lower fares, which, as I say, does require international agreement, and we have licensed new operators to introduce new services very often at lower fares, so we are thoroughly committed in that direction.[85]

As it had indicated in evidence to the Lords Committee, the CAA, at a theoretical level, saw its regulatory role as reproducing the benefits that would be achieved in a truly competitive market but which are unobtainable in practice.[86] Such misunderstandings apart, the thrust of the Commons Committee was similar to the Lords': an exhortation to the CAA and the Government to press harder for cheaper fares in Europe. Given the CAA's duty to act in pursuance of its statutory ends and not simply to encourage competition and, given strong Conservative representation on the Commons Committee, such recommendations were modest and predictable. As for capture, no implication was made that the CAA's failure to endorse competition as a value in itself (over and above its statutory objectives) was due to its having given way to industry interests. Once more it has to be concluded that the argument for capture—this time by the assimilation of airline interests via key CAA personnel—has yet to be made in terms either of the career interests of those persons or of the policies they have pursued.

(c) *Industry Control Over Agencies' Policies is Exerted by Threat*
A number of American commentators argue that agencies protect industry interests because they fear the industry resorting to higher authority in terms of appeals, applications for judicial review and political redress.[87] Fear of such action, it is said, leads the agency to decide cases defensively, to ignore the public interest and to make those decisions that are safest from time-consuming and politically-embarrassing challenge.

Leaving political considerations until the next section so as to concentrate here on appeals and challenges in court, it could be argued that the CAA has already adopted a defensive posture, but one of limited proportions. In the light of ATLB experience with appeals, the CAA's staff write reasons for decision in a fashion that (they admit), so far as possible, will ensure immunity from appeal decisions. That is not, however, the same thing as deciding the case itself in such a manner as to avoid review, and therefore constitutes only a minor and procedural form of defensiveness. As one staff member said: 'It is more a test of the robustness of the decision'. The promises of government support in the two guidances have been in the main, honoured, and this has reduced any incentive on the CAA's part to give way to threats from the industry. This platform of general governmental support has allowed the CAA the luxury in contentious cases (such as 'Skytrain' and Laker's 660 European routes) to run the risk of being overturned on appeal. Another factor is the use of written rather than oral submissions on appeal, which, with its consequent time saving, has limited the appeal as an airline sanction against the CAA.

As far as legal challenge is concerned, any public authority and its lawyers must always be concerned to keep within the law. Abnormal difficulty for CAA licencing was, however, caused by the Court of Appeal's ruling in the 'Skytrain' case in 1977. The CAA's staff acted defensively following that case by (literally) ruling-out those parts of the second guidance that they thought might prove challengeable in court (e.g. para. 14 instructing the CAA to give effect to government airports policy in licensing). Once again, the product of such a policy was to be seen not so much in the substance of the decisions of the CAA but in the reasons for decision. CAA panels might have ignored the formal terms of paragraph 14 of the second guidance when *writing* reasons for decisions, but it is doubtful whether this manoeuvre actually changed the *reasoning process* that lay behind the panel's decision. The argument of 'capture by threat' must, for the present, be deemed unconvincing: few CAA decisions have so far been overruled on appeal and no decision of the CAA has been successfully challenged in any court of law.

(v) Regulatory Agencies are Politically Anomalous

In the 1930s the fashion on both sides of the Atlantic was to create apolitical public bodies that would exercise independence of judgment. In Britain, Herbert Morrison championed, in the London Passenger Transport Board, the form of public corporation in which members did not represent vested interests, but instead acted as detached experts,[88] and in the American New Deal, renewed stress was placed on removing industrial policy-making from political influence.[89] It was not long, however, before American critics saw the agencies as constituting a 'headless fourth branch' of government and as paying too great a price for their lack of a secure political power base.[90] E. Pendleton Herring had said as early as 1934:

> . . . the control of business remains too controversial and too vital a political issue to be relegated successfully to a Commission independent of close control by the policy-formulating agencies of government.[91]

In 1956 Louis L. Jaffe[92] stated that an agency would not develop new policy once it had established itself, and that we should look for leadership to the President, to the executive departments or to Congress. At the same time, Marver H. Bernstein[93] was arguing persuasively that regulation was necessarily political and that the fiction that somehow agencies take issues 'out of politics' was largely responsible for their failings. He said:

Strong political leadership is basic to regulatory success. Without the backing of political leaders in the legislative and executive branches of the Government, a regulatory agency will be unable to make significant headway against the opposition of regulated interests. The failure of political leaders to formulate regulatory goals and give support to regulatory policies, paves the way for acceptance by the agency of the philosophy and values as well as specific regulatory proposals of the affected groups.[94]

Bernstein stated that each agency could be expected to pass through different stages of development in a 'life-cycle' that responded to predictable changes in its political environment.[95] The *gestation* period was that in which concern about a problem resulted in creation of the agency; *youth* followed in which the inexperienced agency was out-manoeuvred by the regulatees, but operated with a crusading zeal. Gradually the flush of political support for agency objectives died away and *maturity* was the stage at which devitalization set it. Regulation became more expert and settled but, as the agency moved out of the political mainstream, it began to pay increasing attention to the needs of the industry. As vitality was lost, the agency relied more and more on precedent and it adopted a reactive posture. *Old age* was the final period of debility and decline. Depending on the vigour of leading agency personnel, the agencies took different periods to reach senescence but this happened when the public interest was lost in 'quasi-judicialitis'.[96] The agency became passive and aimed to protect the industry on lines laid down by the regulated group.

A massive array of proposals have been put forward to counter the political isolation of the agencies (for an outline see Chapter 14). Looking at the effects of isolation, we see that in Bernstein's 'life-cycle', the thirteen-year-old CAA occupies a position between youth and maturity: its staff are still enthusiastic but inexperience is giving way to a developed expertize. According to Bernstein, the dangers are of legal ossification, which we have already concluded has not yet set in at the CAA, and of a deterioration in political support that will throw the agency into the arms of the industry. Pessimists would argue that political decline is setting in already: they would point to the abolition of the policy guidance and say that government has taken away the opportunity for parliamentary debate of aviation policy, and in doing so, has cut off a primary source of CAA legitimacy in a way that will allow industrial interests to control regulatory policy. The replacement of the guidance with statutory objectives and an instruction for the CAA to issue its own policy statements, they would say, is an invitation for the Authority to agree a programme with the industry to ensure both CAA survival and risk-free profit-making for the airlines. A finger might be pointed at the CAA's increasingly close relationship to the industry as evidenced, for example, in its conducting joint research into problem areas. The association, it might be said, has become all too cosy and, without overall political direction, the CAA will soon sink into Bernstein's old age.

Although in the next chapter doubts will be cast on the wisdom of abolishing policy guidance, it would be simplistic to argue that abolition has had the effect of depriving the CAA of all political contact. The guidance was one important factor in CAA relationships with the Minister but there are others: similarly there are broader considerations to be taken into account in assessing the danger of the CAA's losing legitimacy. If ministerial support for CAA policies is vital to CAA health, then the most important considerations, at least on international issues, are whether the CAA is supported on appeal and whether the Department co-ordinates effectively with the CAA in securing traffic rights that will complement CAA licencing. In these matters, the prime determinants are those least able to be measured: expertise and personalites. As was noted in Chapter 9, the CAA has so far occupied a secure position because it has possessed high level staff of ability and determination—they have also been expert in working within the civil service machine and are aware of the need to preserve close contacts with governments. As for the dangers awaiting a CAA lacking dynamism, Lord Boyd-Carpenter, for one, might have agreed readily with the Bernstein thesis, or a variant of this in which attacks on the agency come as much from fellow bureaucrats as from industrialists. After he had given up chairing the CAA he warned:

> ... the CAA will only be able to continue to operate successfully if it continues to have, as it has at present in Nigel Foulkes, a Chairman who is able and willing to fight his corner. For Whitehall would like to reduce its role, its status and its independence.[97]

Without denying that the abolition of policy guidance puts additional strains on the CAA's relationship with government, it can thus be argued that the agency will continue, via the departments, to derive the governmental support it needs—provided that it continues to attract personnel of a calibre equal to that of the civil servants and politicians with whom they deal and provided that the CAA continues to be seen as the prime depository of licencing expertise.

As far as wider legitimacy is concerned, James O. Freedman in his study of 'Crisis and Legitimacy' in American agencies suggested that four matters be taken into account: public recognition of the agency's place in government; public perceptions of its political accountability; public appreciation of the agency's effectiveness; and general acceptance of the fairness of decision-making.[98] American agencies, in Freedman's view had been unfairly undermined by misconceptions about the separation of powers.[99] In the case of the CAA however, its innovatory status makes it difficult to assess public reaction to its governmental role. We have seen that the agency does not wholly conform to judicial norms but, if classified in the public mind, then the CAA is probably conceived of as a tribunal. It might not be held in such high opinion, however, if branded a 'quango' in an era when governmental opposition to quangos is made known, as in the Thatcher administration.[100] Since a main plank of recent criticisms of quangos has been their lack of accountability, it may be seen by some as ironic that during the height of the quango's campaign the CAA was 'set free' by abolition of the guidance system. Ironic or not, it may be expected that the new independence of the CAA will bring no improvement in public or parliamentary perceptions of its legitimacy. Similar considerations apply in looking at public impressions of CAA effectiveness: where governmental policies are antipathetic to regulation, public appreciation of regulators is likely to decline. Perhaps what can be said of the CAA, however, is that, though of low profile, its public image is not adverse. It has not been stigmatized as protectionist and the demise of Laker Airways in February 1982 may, if nothing else, have convinced the public that the CAA has been prepared to allow the enterprising operator to run risks. Within a socialist administration, of course, the agency enjoys a more secure position: when Peter Shore was Secretary of State for Trade and opposed 'Skytrain' in 1976 it was clear to the industry and to the public that the CAA, in licensing Laker, had adopted a more enterprising position than the government.

Freedman's final criterion, fairness, is perhaps of less importance to public perceptions of a body like the CAA, which deals with a small number of expert individuals, as compared to an agency that deals with the wider public directly, e.g. the Supplementary Benefits Commission. If unfairness is suspected of the latter, then public confidence will soon decline. In the case of the CAA, however, the public is liable to care less about the fairness of public hearings procedure than about the substance of the CAA's general policies and the price and availability of air travel.

To summarize: the CAA in Bernstein's terms is not yet declining into old age, but is approaching the key years of maturity; it must therefore be prepared for a decline in direct political support (of which there is some evidence in the abolition of guidance, the granting of freedom and the new record of allowing appeals); it must resist the retreat into legalism and its senior staff must strive to sustain vigorous policy-making. Of the American proposals for increasing executive control over agencies, none seems more suited to the needs of the CAA than was the former guidance system. To abolish the guidance was to move against current American trends but, though diminishing direct parliamentary involvement in CAA policies and making the CAA more centrally the object of future contention concerning licencing policies, this need not have the effect of throwing the CAA into the airlines' arms. A crucial period for the CAA will be the time when those staff who joined it in 1972 will move on and take the force of their accumulated expertise with them.

Conclusions on the CAA's Regulatory Performance

Set against the main points of criticism that arise out of long experience with agencies in the United States, the CAA emerges creditably. It has mixed functions in a manner unattempted by the ATLB; political and procedural tasks have been combined with the development of a substantial expertise, and control of the industry has until now not been unduly hampered by this association of functions. The Authority has to a large extent avoided the dangers of over-judicialization that commonly result from systems of precedent and it has also managed to sustain a regulatory strategy within a system of overall political control. It has shown a willingness to lighten the weight of regulation, an ability to develop and publish guiding principles and a capacity to make decisions that are unpopular with the regulated industry. The extent to which CAA success thus far has been dependent on the vigour and zeal of its youth, its present personnel or on the political support so far provided by governmental policy statements will be demonstrated in the forthcoming years when, without such guidance and without its original staff, it faces old age and the dangers of decline.

13
Freeing the Quango

In the years 1972–79 the device of written policy guidance played a crucial role in CAA regulation. The guidance was the 'innovation' in the 'constitutional innovation' mentioned by Mr Michael Noble in introducing the second reading of the 1971 Bill.[1] It was guidance that provided a new way to 'tame the quango'. In November 1979, however, Mr Noble's Conservative successor in office, Mr Nott, presented to Parliament a Bill with the purpose, *inter alia*, of removing from the 1971 Act those provisions allowing him to give guidance to the Civil Aviation Authority (CAA).

Why was it that, having devised a way to achieve seemingly the best of a number of worlds, government chose to abandon the machinery that made this possible? Was it to be concluded on the evidence of nine years experience that written policy guidance did not after all provide a way to enjoy the advantages of the multi-functional agency whilst retaining ministerial and parliamentary control?

The decline of the guidance may be traced to 1977. Until that year it served a useful purpose in three respects. It replaced appeals and traffic rights as the medium of governmental control, it provided a framework upon which the CAA might hang its own system of case law and rule-making and it allowed long-term policy-making on the basis of research and a developing expertise. From that time onwards, developments on two fronts diminished the predominance of guidance in air transport licensing. The first of these was the effect of the 'Skytrain' decision, the second was the increased publication by the CAA of its own guidance.

As seen in Chapter 9, the Court of Appeal's ruling in the 'Skytrain' case put into question the validity of paragraphs 7 and 8 of the guidance and their prohibition of long-haul scheduled

service competition. The CAA responded in three route
decisions[2] by stating that it subscribed to the 'spheres of interest'
policy but felt able to depart from this (and license competitively) if a 'sufficiently compelling' case was made—and, indeed,
such an exceptional case resulted in the licensing of B. Cal. on
the Dallas/Fort Worth route in the face of BA protests that they
should be the preferred operator.

Informally, senior CAA staff began to rely less and less on the
guidance after the 'Skytrain' decision. The Authority's Group
Director of Economic Regulation (chair of more hearings
panels than any other CAA member) began to pencil-out whole
sections of the guidance,[3] not merely paragraphs 7 and 8, for fear
that these provisions might constitute 'direction' rather than
'guidance' and so would prove legally suspect. This course of
action was not unduly burdensome, for, as has been noted, the
1976 guidance did not depart from the CAA's own policies
drastically. The paucity of long-haul routes on which competition was an issue, together with the Authorities' view that it
retained a discretion to allow competition when a case was
made, meant that the CAA was not effectively restrained. The
skeletal guidance that resulted from unofficial 'pruning' thus
proved a convenient device and the need for full policy guidance
seemed less compelling.

By this time, the CAA had also started to set out its licensing
philosophy in far greater detail and with far greater precision
than the guidance was ever able to do. The 'brown books',
'consultative documents', 'discussion documents' and 'reviews of
policy' were to cover, as we have seen, a large area of licensing
activity, from air freight and international freight services to
European air fares, domestic air fares and short-haul competition policy. These documents set out the regulatory framework
adopted by the CAA and its interpretation of the guidance and
1971 Act, so that the Authority has more than once noted the
compliance of one of its decisions with those views expressed in a
discussion document[4] and airlines have continued to quote their
terms.[5] In addition to the 'brown books', the CAA, in the late
seventies, became increasingly willing and able to explain policies in its reasons for decisions. So much so that when the
Authority produced a draft statement on licensing policies in
November 1979,[6] reference was made not only to the discussion
documents but also to the principles set out in major case decisions.[7]

It was against such a background of the judicial restriction of guidance and the increasing importance of agency-issued statements, that, following the installation of a Conservative government in May 1979, senior officials of the CAA and DoT met together to discuss how the new government might deal with the 'Skytrain' decision and its implications for the guidance system. Departmental officials favoured amending the Civil Aviation Act 1971 either to expand the ministerial power of direction or to replace the guidance with expanded statutory objectives. To CAA staff, the abolition of guidance was attractive in reducing the Authority's vulnerability to court action.[8] They considered that the guidance had served its purpose and that, although a new guidance could be produced, it was likely, on past experience, to be close to obsolescence by the time it emerged. They believed that the 1976 guidance had to some extent constituted a 'battening down' after the 1973 oil crisis but, after passing through all the consultative processes, had emerged somewhat inappropriately into a period of expanding markets. They pointed to the 'skeleton' guidance and agreed with the DoT that such condensed provisions might take statutory form. To replace the guidance with expanded objectives would, they considered, free the reins over the Authority. They thought that the guidance had served another purpose: it had convinced those in government that the CAA would act responsibly if released from the shackles of departmental control. They argued that 'the Authority's pupillage' was over and that it deserved greater autonomy.

Proposals to Abolish Guidance: The Civil Aviation Bill 1979–80

After considering civil aviation policy in mid-1979, Mr Nott, the newly appointed Secretary of State for Trade, produced a Civil Aviation Bill. This had two main objectives, the first of which involved changing of BA's status from that of nationalized corporation to private sector company. The second was to change the basis upon which the CAA could issue air transport licences. Implementation of the latter change involved three items: changing the CAA's objectives under the 1971 Act; removing the Secretary of State's power to issue policy guidance and requiring the CAA to publish periodic statements of its licensing policies.

At Second Reading (19 November 1979) Mr Nott argued that

the Court of Appeal's 'Skytrain' decision had made a change in guidelines 'inevitable'.[9] Guidance had been '. . . an innovation, but . . . it has not proved satisfactory'.[10] Explaining the decision to drop the guidance, he said:

> We concluded that it was wrong to place responsibility for an area of policy on an independent organization and then so to hem round its freedom that it was hardly able to pursue an independent line. If we wish to hive-off certain functions of Government . . . we must be ready to take both hands off the wheel . . . [11]

He argued that it would be better for policy to be the expression of Parliament's will rather than the Secretary of State's. This would be done by changing the CAA's statutory objectives so as to give the 'reasonable interests of air transport users' higher priority. One further duty to be imposed on the CAA would be 'to ensure that British airlines compete as effectively as possible with other airlines in providing air transport services on international routes'.[12]

Mr Nott admitted that more than one major airline had expressed concern that abolition of the guidance 'would make it difficult to know the rules of the game',[13] but he said that such points were met by the Bill's provision that the CAA should publish periodic statements of its policies.[14] He added that the CAA would produce a draft policy statement which would be available for consideration at committee stage. The Opposition rejected the proposals and accused the Government of abdicating its policy-making responsibility in favour of the unaccountable CAA.[15] Former Trade Secretary John Smith said that the Bill's conflicting objectives gave the CAA no guidance[16] and Stanley Clinton Davis pointed out that Parliament would be unable to debate the CAA's policy statement.[17] Mr Nott replied that the House of Commons was always concerned about the volume of secondary legislation and that he considered it to be a constitutional improvement 'to contain within an Act of Parliament the basis upon which the CAA should operate'.[18]

Those who had assumed that the 'spheres of interest' policy was common ground between the CAA and government were informed by Mr Tebbit, the Under Secretary of State for Trade, that this had given way to the CAA's new duty to ensure competition.[19] He explained that, though the 'spheres of interest' policy had been useful in stablizing relations between B.Cal. and

BA, 'those days were over'.[20] On division the Bill obtained its second reading by 311 votes to 247.

As Mr Nott promised, the CAA produced a draft statement on 'Air Transport Licensing Policies' in November 1979 which said of the abolition of guidance:

> Some airlines have pointed out that this would leave them uncertain as to future regulatory policies, with important consequences for their corporate plans and investment decisions. This is a legitimate concern on their part and, as a first step therefore, the Authority is making this statement which sets out the main elements of the air transport licensing policies that it expects to continue.

The CAA stated that it was right that policies should 'evolve in the light of changing circumstances'. It would consider cases on their merits but it had 'tried to build up over the last few years a policy framework within which individual decisions may stand coherently' and it would continue to do so. On long-haul international routes it agreed 'with the generality of the "spheres of interest" policy' but did not rule out the exceptional licensing of a second operator if 'consumer's choice of airport or product' would be broadened, nor did it guarantee BA and B.Cal. complete monopoly in precise geographical areas.

On short international and domestic routes, constraints on competition would similarly apply and 'competition would take the form of the threat of substitution'. The CAA would, however, require a 'powerful case' to be made before replacing an incumbent operator who was serving a route well and profitably. As for fares, the Authority said that it would continue to pursue its current policies as set out in its discussion document 'European Air Fares'[21] and its policies on domestic services would be 'determined in the light of its current consultations' with airlines and others on the basis of the consultative document published in January 1979.[22]

Implications of Abolishing Guidance

Looking to the future, the abolition of guidance is of importance in broad constitutional terms as well as to the CAA's method of regulation. Since the guidance system served the twofold purposes of structuring and confining[23] the CAA's discretion, one should ask, firstly, whether the degree of structuring necessary to the fair and efficient exercise of CAA discretion could be achieved as well by self-imposed rules as by external guidance. Secondly, questions of political accountability arise: was it wise to free the CAA from written control?

Could the CAA Structure its Own Discretion?

It is clear from the 'brown booklets' and recent case law that the CAA is capable of giving those affected by its decisions some indication of the policies that it will pursue. Although discussion documents have led to more precise criteria only in limited sectors of activity (such as short-haul competition), there is no reason why criteria should not be produced to cover other areas.[24] It is further arguable that guidance, in the form of discussions of regulatory philosophy together with outlines of matters to be considered in licensing, may be more useful than more concise objectives or criteria in achieving a predictable yet flexible regulatory policy. Study of the various areas of airline activity regulated shows few gaps in the 'brown booklets' coverage, the main omission being a discussion document especially directed to long-haul routes and fares. Even so, operators may, by examination of decided cases and the documents on domestic and European routes, quickly deduce a CAA philosophy on such matters as long-haul competition.

Air transport regulation, by 1979, had arrived at a position in which the guidance had largely been swamped by those criteria developed by the CAA. Perusal of the 24 paragraphs of the 1976 guidance reveals little that, by 1979, had not either been discounted as legally vulnerable or had not been 'internalized' and covered by CAA statements of one sort or another. If the CAA plans in future to continue its practice of working towards the publication of criteria through discussion documents and consultations, then it seems that the Authority can structure its own discretion. Indeed, being the expert, the CAA can do this better than the Government. What is also plain is that those CAA statements of policy that in the past superseded guidance will be liable by the same token to prevail over statutory objectives as indicators of licensing policy. As was pointed out to Mr Nott in debate,[25] the objectives are consequently liable to play a minimal role in the licensing system.

Should the CAA have been Freed from Control by Written Policy?

The main argument for abandoning the guidance system was not that it did not work. It served a useful purpose as the main guide to policy in the early years of the CAA. Rather it might be said that the guidance had served its purpose and had to be dismantled. To those fearing a quango on the loose a number of points might be made. A principal argument for abandoning guidance was that there no longer remained any contentious issues in aviation licensing: the CAA had resolved matters of contention and so there stood to be little lost in taking 'both hands off the wheel'. The introduction to the 1976 guidance stated:

> There is now virtually no major long-haul route on which it would be possible to introduce a second British airline on terms which would leave any scope for the British share of the total earnings from the route to be increased.[26]

Similarly, it might have been argued that deregulation, combined with the CAA's philosophy of 'regulation with a light touch',[27] had minimized areas of contention. Inclusive tours had largely been deregulated by the use of blanket five year licences and the Authority had proposed to move from specific to aggregate capacity control over charter freight.[28]

Against the 'no contentious issues' argument it may be said that politically sensitive decisions will always have to be taken. For a start, certain aspects of civil aviation policy (e.g. the development of regional services) cannot be wholly divorced from issues of national policy. As for choices of carrier, although the opportunities for long-haul scheduled competition are already rare, cases such as the Dallas/Fort Worth application will continue to promote public versus private sector arguments. (Did BA lose a valuable chance to operate Concorde to Dallas/Fort Worth?) It is also clear that a light regulatory touch does not necessarily mean deregulation and the disappearance of licensing issues. In 'Domestic Air Services'[29] the CAA concluded, as we have seen, that with respect to both routes and prices, complete deregulation of domestic services was not feasible.[30] In a market where few city routes would support competition the CAA considered the threat of substitution to be a more effective control over standards than direct competition.[31]

Clearly then any decision to replace any of BA's services with an independent operator would be capable of provoking political dispute and on European short-haul routes, problems at least as difficult as domestic issues would continue to arise— international considerations would further increase opportunities for political contention.

Nor does it appear that those in government believed political issues to be liable to decline. Mr Nott said in debate: 'There is inherent in a sound policy for awarding routes, a strong element of tension. I do not expect that tension to disappear'.[32] If, as Mr Tebbit indicated, the spheres of interest policy is to be abandoned and a more competitive approach encouraged, then the stream of contentious issues is more liable to rise to a flood than to dry up.

If such issues continue to thrust themselves before the CAA, then some sort of institutionalized system of governmental policy control seems to be unavoidable in civil aviation. Before considering the various devices that could be used for those purposes, however, the possibility should be examined of improving on the existing system of CAA 'self-administered guidance' as a supplement to statutory objectives.

The present regime was instituted by the Civil Aviation Act 1980 (see now section 69 of the consolidating Act of 1982) which imposed a duty on the CAA 'to publish from time to time a statement of the policies it intends to adopt' in licensing. Before publishing such statements, the CAA is obliged to consult such persons as appear to it to represent industry and users and, furthermore, the Secretary of State is empowered to require that statements of policy be made on any particular matter. Although the CAA's policy statement of April 1981 followed a period of intense consultation with the airlines and with users and involved the submission of a considerable volume of written representations to the CAA, the 1982 Act offers no detailed scheme of publication or hearings to correspond to the 'notice and comment' rule-making procedures of the Federal Administrative Procedure Act 1946 (APA). For a number of reasons, however, those procedures now adopted by the CAA seem hardly to be inferior. The APA does call for notices of rule-making to be published in the Federal Register and it does allow an opportunity for the submission of written arguments. It does not, however, provide for hearings, oral or otherwise, neither does it apply to an agency's 'general statements of policy'. Since, as now formulated, the CAA's statements of policy are set out as descriptions of 'regulatory philosophy' it is less than certain therefore whether they would be covered by section 4 of the APA. In any case, to give the CAA a broad discretion as to how it consults and publishes statements seems preferable to imposing a uniform notice and comment procedure. Under existing arrangements it is possible for the CAA to produce new policy statements and minor amendments in policy in a far more responsive manner than would be possible under more rigidly structured procedures.

In Canada, the Law Reform Commission has looked at more demanding proposals that, on one formulation, would provide for public hearings to be incorporated in the policy statement process. There would almost certainly be pressures to judicialize these hearings but to allow lawyers to have a prominent role in the formulation of the most general of agency polices would seem to be unwise: it would slow down the policy-making process, produce disputes as to which rules or policies were covered by the formal procedures, it would favour the regulatees with the largest resources and would undermine the people who are paid to develop policy—the specialist administrators in the agency. (It will be argued below that,for similar reasons, public hearings should not be used in the process of issuing government guidance.) Although a more formalized policy-making process would give CAA activity a higher political profile than the present discretionary system it is doubtful whether the agency would thereby derive either increased political legitimacy for its actions or would arrive at policies of a more astute nature.

To conclude on this point, it appears that if instead of governmental guidance there are to be CAA-issued policy statements there is little to be gained, in terms of the efficacy of consultation, in imposing more formal requirements on the CAA. It also seems plain, in looking at accountability, that even if more cumbersome procedures were adopted, these might involve policy-makers in more publicity but they would not be a substitute for the system of political control that ministers seem uniformly to demand in one form or another. We therefore return to the question of the various forms of governmental supervision that are available and whether policy guidance is the most feasible. The main options are: (a) no control; (b) statutory objectives; (c) appeal decisions; (d) traffic rights negotiations; (e) section 4 style powers of direction; (f) guidance.

(a) *No control.* As already stated, it is difficult to believe that, future governments will agree to every CAA decision on all contentious issues. If there is one fact of life in aviation regulation it is that governments, by one means or another, will seek to control general policy. Given recurrent calls to abolish quangos or make them 'responsible',[33] parliamentary demands for government control will be loud. To remove opportunities to debate policy guidance before it goes to the CAA is to increase the likelihood and strength of these demands. Even if the Thatcher government resists the pressures to interfere there is no guarantee that other governments will exercise similar restraint.

(b) *Objectives.* It should be clear from the chapters above, firstly, that statutory objectives, being composed of conflicting elements, have offered in themselves no clear guidance and, secondly, that they are incapable of precision. They are certainly incapable of giving such detailed guidance as would usefully rule out contention in their application to particular facts and they generally fail to anticipate regulatory issues.[34] Although CAA officials in mid-1979 favoured the incorporation of a codified guidance within the parent statute this may have been to overlook an important difference between guidance and objectives. Whereas guidance allows the exposition of a regulatory philosophy this is less easily done by objectives that are set out in mutual tension. Guidance may be changed without making demands of parliamentary time but any change in statutory objectives may pose greater problems: indeed one of the major reasons why the Labour government did not change the CAA's objectives in 1977 following the 'Skytrain' case was shortage of such time.

(c) *Appeal decisions.* The ATLB experience stands as a stark reminder of the confusion made possible by appeal decisions that are uncoordinated with the policies of the licensing agency. Mr Nott said in the Second Reading debate in 1979:

> There will continue to be a right of appeal to me against air transport licensing decisions. However, I intend to continue the practice of the previous administration in not interfering with the Authority's licensing decisions unless there are good reasons for

doing so; but the right of appeal is a safeguard against arbitrary decisions by the Authority.[35]

His use of the word 'arbitrary' was crucial. By January 1980 none of the 23 appeals against CAA decisions had been upheld, but removal of the guidance left Mr Nott's words as the only guarantee that CAA decisions would not be undermined.

Even during the debates on the 1980 Civil Aviation Bill, appeal decision-making evidenced a new approach. In the space of eight months Mr Nott overruled three CAA decisions on appeal in order to allow increased airline competition. On two of these occasions CAA findings were directly contradicted. In March 1980 the CAA allowed British Caledonian onto the London to Hong Kong route to compete with British Airways. Laker Airways and Cathay Pacific were refused licences as the CAA said that traffic would not support more than two carriers. Mr Nott granted licences to all three additional operators. In October of the same year, he ordered the licensing of Laker for Prestwick and Manchester to Miami routes after the CAA had refused these in order to protect London services.

The latter appeal decision provoked comment in the House of Lords on 23 October. Lord Boyd-Carpenter, the former CAA Chairman, spoke in favour of amending the Civil Aviation Bill at report stage to limit the Secretary of State's appeal power over the CAA. Unless this was done, he said, the CAA's status and the civil aviation industry's confidence in its licences would be 'seriously undermined'.[36]

By early 1983 some in the industry feared that the CAA was already being weakened by appeals: one major airline's lawyer commented: 'The appeals system is not much better than the ATLB now, it's virtually automatic to appeal. Real power is with the Secretary of State. The CAA acts as a quasi-judicial body—almost as a consultant to the Secretary of State'.[37]

Given governmental enthusiasm for a positive competition policy and the doubts expressed in debate concerning the CAA's spheres of interest approach, it seems likely that the CAA will continue to make decisions with which governments will disagree. Although it is Clearly a Minister's prerogative to overrule the CAA on political grounds (and Hong Kong together with Miami may come under this heading) the position would be dangerous if appeals were increasingly to be allowed in either a manner reflecting on the CAA's expertise or else for trivial reasons.

The ATLB experience stands as a warning. If the CAA is to fulfil its potential, airlines should not see it as a first hurdle *en route* to the Trade Secretary—otherwise resources and expertise to the tune of over £3 million per year will have been ill-used. In order to regulate appeals, one CAA staff member suggested to me that the Secretary of State might issue a statement of policy to govern the decision of appeals. Although likely to encourage greater consistency of appeals in themselves, such a system of policy guidance at the second remove would be unlikely to provide for detailed consultation and parliamentary approval as did the former system. One great virtue of that system was that it helped to make Parliament the forum for essentially political decisions instead of burying these beneath a guise of judiciality.

(d) *Traffic rights negotiations.* On international routes the greatest (but least open) threat to the licensing system lies in the necessity for governmental negotiation of traffic rights following licensing. Mr Nott put the case: 'In the last resort the decisions of the CAA are dictated by the facts of what my Department is able to negotiate in air service agreements.'[38]

In the 1960s many licenses granted by the ATLB were never operated because traffic rights were not obtained.[39] Since it is a governmental decision whether rights can be obtained on suitable terms, there must always exist a danger that such negotiations may turn into a second licensing tier. This is especially so where, as in the 1960s, governmental and agency policies differ and where there is no open guidance system available. As was argued in Chapter 9, there seems little prospect of the judges exercising effective control over governmental negotiation of traffic rights. The relationship of the DoT and CAA must here depend on good faith. Mr Nott has said that ASA negotiations involve 'national prestige, national aggrandizement, national ambition and just plain nationalism, sometimes regardless of any financial reality . . .',[40] it is unrealistic, therefore, to expect any court to fetter the executive in an effective manner in such an essentially political arena. (The 'Skytrain' case was distinguishable as involving designation under an *existing* ASA and not the procedure of *negotiating* a new ASA.) The real possibility here is to relieve the pressure to pre-empt by preserving other more open channels of policy control. This again points towards written guidance.

(e) *Section 4 style powers of direction.* The Court of Appeal suggested that the Secretary of State might have used directions under section 4 of the 1971 Act to stop 'Skytrain'. The potential of wider powers of direction was also discussed by CAA and DoT officials at meetings in the summer of 1979. Section 4(3) of the Act allowed their use only in the interests of national security or in connection with foreign relations, international obligations or such matters as noise, vibration and pollution. It would be necessary to give a broadened power of either general or specific direction to overcome legal difficulties: furthermore, the direction power would not be subject to the prior parliamentary constraints that apply to either written policy guidance or to statutory objectives. Direction powers were used to control the ATLB on certain contentious matters in the 1960s.[41] Their use did not rescue that agency from its lack of overall policy direction. There is little reason for thinking that the device would prove more successful if applied to the CAA.

(f) *Guidance.* Rejection of the above options lends weight to the arguments for written policy guidance. It should be emphasized that, although the Court of Appeal invalidated guidance of a peremptory nature, the option still remains of statements that do not constitute 'directions'. When, in May 1979, DoT officials met CAA staff to discuss the guidance system, the Department's lawyers advised that they had little confidence in their ability to draft guidance that would withstand challenge in court. In legal terms, this seems to have been unduly pessimistic: liberal prefacing of advice with phrases such as 'the CAA shall consider', or 'shall take into account', would have kept to the path of 'guidance' without straying into 'direction'. Departmental reluctance to persevere with the guidance is best explained by a contradiction: the administrators wanted a stronger form of control than mere 'taking into account' and the lawyers were afraid to draft anything to satisfy such demands. As a result of this bureaucratic conflict, the guidance had to be abolished, but guidance as such was not shown to be unworkable at law. Providing that an element of discretion is left to the CAA, guidance of suitable detail would still be possible. This would offer the advantage over 'objectives' of setting out a coherent policy as opposed to a jumble of 'considerations to be taken into account'.

There are further general arguments against abandoning guidance, especially on the issue of accountability. The freeing of this quango while others are abolished may be taken as confidence in its philosophy of enterprise but a forum for parliamentary and wider debate of civil aviation policy has been lost. Such public debate would be worthwhile even on the assumption that the CAA and not the DoT was the real fountain of the policies set out in the guidance. Without the guidance there remains little restraint of the largely self-financing CAA other than by legislative action or by way of the Secretary of State's powers of appointment to the CAA board. Unless the CAA is chosen for scrutiny by one of the departmental Select Committees of the Commons,[42] neither Parliament nor the Ombudsman will exercise any real control over the Authority. Although staff of the CAA welcomed the freedom that came with the ending of guidance this freedom might increasingly be bought at a price in terms of other methods of control.

The necessity for the CAA to justify its general policies to the DoT also brought with it elements of healthy self-appraisal. Thus the 'Shore review' of 1976 involved the CAA in a wholesale reassessment of its policies. Such forces might be expected to aid the resistance of an agency to that apathy against which the American literature cautions us.[43] Similarly, the use of guidance that has been tempered in the heat of parliamentary debate and which has received governmental sanction might arguably reinforce the independent agency against the undue pragmatism and excessive orientation towards industrial interests that has also been criticized in the United States.[44]

It may thus have been a mistake to have abandoned the device that gave the government a new way of hiving-off a regulatory function. To have done so may be to have made at least one of a number of errors: to have assumed that political problems have disappeared: to have placed undue faith in the indefinite concurrence of agency and governmental policies; to have hoped to replace guidance with another less open form of control or to have abandoned department control completely.

14
Regulation by Agency: Unaccountable or Efficient Government?

Bodies resembling the CAA are likely to play an increasing role in government as, more and more, it is deemed necessary to regulate the private and public sectors in specialist economic or technical areas. It is important therefore to learn from the experience of Britain's first multi-powered agency. The problems of operating a powerful discretion under a variety of constraints have been looked at but there are two further questions that need attention: What is the role of such bodies in democratically accountable government? How can governments best go about designing agencies that are suitable for particular regulatory tasks?

(i) Accountability and Control.

There is little doubt about the utility of the commission type of agency. The development of expertise does mean that a coherent system of control can be established in a highly complex, rapidly changing and politically contentious sector of industrial activity. Private companies and public corporations can be controlled in the public interest in a manner that could not be achieved by a tribunal or a court and in areas where the need for independent determination rules out departmental control. Where trial-type procedures have to be used in the interests of fairness and openness, then, as we have seen, the 'layering' of discretion that is possible with the commission provides a way of rendering decisions more coherent than would be the case with a tribunal. As for policy-making, there seems no reason why combining functions in one body should not allow as flexible and informed a system as is possible under departmental regulation.

There are, however, a number of general objections to the

agency device, some of which are contained in the quotation from Otto Newman set out in Chapter 1 (*supra*, pp. 5–6). It could could be said that the agency is guilty of: illegitimately mixing governmental funtions; of 'debasing the majesty of the law' (Newman); of making policy in an unaccountable fashion; of favouring industrial rather than public interests and of creating a system of control that is closed to participation by those beyond a small group.

Those reservations concerning the mixture of functions and the majesty of the law rest, however, upon the old-fashioned assumption discussed in Chapter 1 — that decisions must be either 'political' and for Ministers or else 'judicial' and for courts. It is said, accordingly, that to mix, say, policy-making with adjudication by trial-type procedure is to 'debase' the law. Although the dangers of losing legitimacy by incoherent decision-making have to be acknowledged, this line of argument is exaggerated and fails to consider alternatives. We have seen how a division of regulatory functions between the ATLB and Minister led to a lack of coherence. There are good grounds for asserting both that it is the very *mixing* of judicial, policy-making and political functions in a body like the CAA that fosters coherence and that, without such coherence, notions such as accountability via Ministers and the 'majesty of the law' are undermined. In regulation, as was argued in Chapter 11, the first need is that the bases for decisions be open and intelligible—evaluation of the merits of those decisions can only come after that point.

As for the closed nature of CAA regulation, it is true that a system of regulation by licensing can involve a very small group of participants. The same faces appear at most CAA hearings and nearly everyone knows everyone else. In spite of the work of the AUC, the CAA's regional advisory bodies and various consumer organizations, it could be said that the average citizen has little opportunity to put his or her case to the CAA at a weekday afternoon hearing. On the other hand, the CAA has a discretion to hear evidence, which it uses, and private individuals have over the years enjoyed considerable input into the system. Departmental regulation without the hearings system would afford less access of this kind and the development of consultative procedures by specialist agencies does lead to further opportunities of participation.

It is on the matter of accountability that graver difficulties are encountered. Why, it could be said, should a body as free from judicial and parliamentary controls as the CAA, be allowed to make policies of importance to the national economy and security? The simple answer here is that Parliament has chosen to set up a body that is independent and specialist so as to reap the benefits of an expertise that is seen to be exercised fairly between parties. In the end, though, such notions of independence are illusory and agencies are inevitably subject to a variety of ministerial controls. Those controls provide the thread that connects Parliament and agency and it is, therefore, important to provide channels that maximize openness and accountability.

We have seen in this book how written policy guidance emerged in response to the problems of agency accountability. The device has been abandoned in aviation but I have argued that this has been the result of its mistaken application and departmental uncertainties rather than the product of its illegality or inutility. It should, therefore, be asked now whether a policy guidance system of some sort has wider potential as a way of both having the benefits of agency regulation and of satisfying democratic requirements of accountability. In doing so it is helpful to bear in mind those trends towards increased executive control over agencies that exist here and across the Atlantic.

As noted in Chapter 12, critics of the independent agencies in both the United States and Canada have long suggested that such problems as capture and lack of policies, standards, leadership or co-ordination derive from the political isolation of agencies and might be remedied by some form of external policy control.[1] In 1941 R. E. Cushman[2] proposed the use of separate planning agencies to direct regulatory commission in the United States and in 1956 Louis L. Jaffe[3] advocated political direction by the President, the executive departments or Congress and its committees. More specific proposals came in 1960 from James M. Landis[4] who was principally concerned with the co-ordination of agency policies and favoured a White House 'Czar', to oversee the agencies and to regulate policy development in transportation, communications and energy.

Other commentators have looked to other methods of increasing executive control. In 1960 also, Emmette S. Redford proposed the creation of an 'executive centre' within government to develop 'policy guides' which the commissions could apply in day to day decisions;[5] Louis J. Hector proposed that the agencies' functions be split up, that policy-making be transferred to an executive agency of government, that judicial functions go to an administrative court and that investigations be given to the Department of Justice.[6] Lon Fuller later agreed that if there was to be policy planning at all, it had to be separated from the agencies and given to a separate body that was free from any obsession with adjudication.[7] (In contrast Henry Friendly said that he found it 'hard to think of anything worse'[8] than the proposal to separate adjudication from policy-making.)

More recently, studies by lawyers,[9] political scientists[10] and governmental committees[11] have emphasized the need for clearer policy guidelines for agencies, and proposals for increased presidential control over agencies have gained popularity. Of the latter, the most influential has been the Cutler-Johnson scheme[12] which would authorize the President, subject to strict limitations, to modify or reverse an agency decision, or direct an agency to take up and decide a regulatory issue within a specified time. The American Bar Association adopted this approach in 1979 in its report on regulatory reform[13] and, by its 'Resolution A', it recommended, not only an increased power of direction on the Cutler-Johnson lines, but also the use of an Executive Order to direct agencies contemplating regulatory action to prepare regulatory analyses for public comment and to allow the President to order and supervize an inter-agency impact review. More fuel was added to demands for executive control when Harold H. Bruff argued the same year[14] that the President should be involved, by means of a direction power, in agency rule-making. This, he said, would increase accountability, political effectiveness, attention to the legality of rule-making and co-ordination between agency and wider policies.[15] He reasoned that, because of Congress' poor position to co-ordinate policies and because of the courts' limited powers of review, the power of control must rest with the chief executive.

For his part, President Reagan took a major step in February 1981 and increased presidential controls over agency rule-making by passing Executive Order 12291 which demanded that all new major rules promulgated by agencies should be submitted to a cost-benefit test.[16] This test was made subject to review by the Office of Management and Budget's Office of Information and Regulatory Affairs (OIRA) and thus provided, not so much for a power of Presidential direction over agencies, as for more effective Presidential input into agency policy-making.

Canadian commentators have, in spite of constitutional differences, moved in a similar direction. Largely influenced by the work of Hudson N. Janisch[17] and the Lambert Commission,[18] the Law Reform Commission of Canada has recently attempted to devise a system of administrative policy direction that would match the degree of openness provided by the imposition of statutory objectives. It proposed that there should be a governmental power to direct agencies in writing at a general policy level but that:

> . . . prior to the issuance of a policy direction to an independent agency, the Government should refer the matter to the agency, which may request public submissions thereon and shall make a public report within ninety days or such longer period as the Government may specify, and further, such direction should be published in the Canada Gazette and tabled in the House of Commons.[19]

In order to provide for democratic control, it was suggested that Parliament should retain a power to pass a negative resolution within seven days of a direction being issued. As for governmental control, the Governor in Council would have the power to issue a 'stop-order' halting agency proceedings for up to 90 days in order that a general direction might be made. Agencies seeking clarification of directions would be able to refer them back to the issuing authority for interpretation. As a general conclusion the Commission said: 'the directive power is particularly suitable for guiding the policies of independent regulatory agencies'.[20]

In contrast to the amount of thought that has been given to the problem of controlling regulatory bodies in North America little attention has been paid to this issue in Britain. This is largely due to the haphazard approach to agencies mentioned at the start of this book and detailed below. Only in the case of the nationalized industries has there been sustained discussion of ministerial powers of control over public corporations: a range of relationships has either been tested, proposed or effected— including White Paper objectives,[21] and new oversight Ministries,[22] Policy Councils[23] and a new corporate approach[24] but the problems of operational and regulatory bodies are of different kinds. Indeed the difference between operation and regulation has implications for the kind of control devices appropriately used.

A principal factor in *regulation* is the obligation to choose between competing interests, public, private or both. From the onus to choose between parties flow expectations that the agency should act fairly, should be seen to act fairly and should act on the basis of open principles. Such an expectation is typically discharged (as in aviation and road transport) by the adoption of trial-type hearings systems. Where judicialized functions of any kind are involved, the problem of political control becomes more acute than where issues are principally *operational* as in the nationalized industries. Because agency decisions are accompanied by reasons in order to maximize their acceptability to regulated interests, the forms of political control seen as appropriate will tend to be more formal than in the case of operational bodies. The terms of such control must provide the foundations of that reasoning and private parties will demand that there be open disclosure in advance of the rules and principles governing choices.

In cases where governments prefer agency regulation to departmental control, there may be strong reasons why the controlling body should be set up at a remove from government. Thus, in broadcasting licensing, libertarian considerations rule out any departmental interference other than on an open basis and, in a mixed industry like aviation, private interests will demand that the government, as 'owners' of nationalized industries, should be distanced from the regulatory body. Such factors again favour arms-length control rather than the concerted or corporate approach to the nationalized industries that was advocated by the National Economic Development Office (NEDO) in 1976 and the Labour Government's 1978 White Paper.[25]

A further distinction between regulation and operation lies in the involvement of the private sector in the former. NEDO argued that a major reason why governments could not resist interfering with nationalized industries and why the latter could not adhere to targets was the extent to which the economic and social policies of those industries impinged on wider governmental strategy. In the case of regulation, competitive forces exist and, to some extent, keep a check on regulatees in a manner missing with monopolistic nationalized industries, furthermore, regulation, though often involving issues of a politically contentious nature, tends not to bear the same close relationship to overall governmental policy. Such factors indicate the greater chances of successfully using a guidance system in regulation than in relation to large scale public enterprises. One message that may clearly be taken both from the nationalized industries and civil aviation licensing is that Ministers will always exert control by some means and that, if undue restrictions are placed on open forms of control, then covert methods will be resorted to[26]—indeed the elected official may well prefer low visibility control so as to avoid responsibility for unpopular decisions.

When put next to the alternatives, the advantages of the CAA's kind of guidance system are apparent. Informal corporate plans could be developed by agencies and governments as is provided for in the case of many statutes dealing with nationalization—such as the 1977 Aircraft and Shipbuilding Industries Act, which provided in section 7(1) that British Aerospace and British Shipbuilders should formulate corporate plans and 'conduct operations within lines settled from time to time with the approval of the Minister'. As already noted, however, such a system of concerted control based on financial plans that are phrased in general terms and not backed by force of law is deficient for the purposes of regulation. Informality would fail to provide the basis for decisions made between parties. It would prove lacking in terms of agency needs for legitimacy, planning and openness.

Another option — to rely on statutory objectives, as is now the case in aviation licensing — would bring certain advantages insofar as the basis for decision-making is openly stated and clearly backed by legal sanction. More than offsetting those advantages, however, are the drawbacks noted in the last chapter. In addition, statutory provisions have to withstand judicial interpretation. Thus, if the courts are not to intrude as regulators of the regulators then any agency would have to be given powers incorporating wide safety margins.[27] Expression of wide powers in statutory form would result in vague statements of 'matters to be taken into consideration', many of which would stand in opposition to each other, and this would not cater for layering of discretion in the manner allowed by guidance. Parties affected by such provisions would find it difficult to come to any conclusions worthy of use as foundations for planning. As guidance such a statute would be so lacking that its role would soon be superseded by less formal material such as rules issued by the agency itself. Demands for political control over such an agency would soon follow and the problem returned to square one.

In controlling the policies adopted by an agency, a major factor in other areas as much as in aviation is the facility with which changes in strategy may be communicated openly to that body. If a new Act of Parliament was required each time a change in governmental approach took place then too great an obstacle would be placed in the Minister's way. Instead of inhibiting governmental interference, such a system would drive Ministers to use less formal and open methods of control and would then prejudice the reputation for impartiality that is necessary to a regulatory body.

There is another general point. To ask an agency merely to apply statutory objectives to particular cases on the 'transmission belt' model creates problems of legitimacy — as Richard Stewart has stated:

> Broad legislative directives will rarely dispose of particular cases once the relevant factors have been accurately ascertained. More frequently the application of legislative directives requires the agency to reweigh and reconcile the often nebulous or conflicting policies behind the directives in the context of a particular factual situation with a particular constellation of affected interests. The required balancing of policies is an inherently discretionary, ultimately political procedure.[28]

In this respect, policy guidance offers a statement of standards and policies that is more full than is usual in statutory form[29] but, in being composed by the Minister's staff, it pays heed to its political basis. In addition, departmental guidance that is implemented by parliamentary resolution allows a depth of supervision of which the elected body is incapable — Stewart again:

> Detailed legislative specification of policy would require intensive and continuous investigation, decision, and revision of specialized and complex issues. Such a task would require resources that Congress has in most instances been unable or unwilling to master.[30]

A final alternative to written guidance would be reliance on administrative controls. As the NEDO report pointed out,[31] certain statutes after 1974 have innovated by making provision for greater government involvement in corporation policy-making without countervailing the arms-length approach. Thus, the Petroleum and Submarine Pipe-lines Act 1975 set up the British National Oil Corporation (BNOC) as the first public corporation subject to a statutory requirement that a specified number of civil servants should be appointed to the board. Extended requirements that public corporations consult with governments or seek approval for their proposals were provided for in the Railway Act 1974, the Petroleum and Submarine Pipelines Act 1975 and the Aircraft and Shipbuilding Industries Act 1977. Such arrangements, however, would be less appropriate in the case of regulatory bodies for, as with other informal methods of control, there would be losses in terms of ability to justify decisions, acceptability to parties, planning and openness. Reliance on staff appointments to increase control would similarly result in diminished confidence in the decisions of the agency and would bring with it losses in continuity as changes were made.

Such reasoning favours a system of control over regulatory agencies in which written policy emerges after wide consultation, in which there is open publication backed by force of law, which offers a blend of precision and flexibility yet which is not so awkward or weak a system of control that Ministers are driven to use less desirable methods. These considerations point in the direction of the kind of statutory policy guidance system that was used in civil aviation licensing in the 1970s and which has been advocated by the Canadian Law Reform Commission.[32] Assuming that Ministerial powers of direction can be redrafted in broad terms, the issues of *vires* that arose in the 'Skytrain' case can be avoided. It seems to matter little whether the terminology of 'guidance' or 'general or specific directions' is used: what is important in the individual case is the level of generality chosen by the Minister. Guidance must have a sustainable life without being all things to everyone. It may be argued that all such guidance is unworkable since it will be out of date once it has undergone every element of the consultative process but this is a problem to be lived with: to re-legislate and create new statutory objectives would take longer and any faster method would operate below the surface of administrative life.

If the statutory guidance scheme, as varied in accordance with the particular circumstances of each regulatory task, is accepted as a useful device on its face, it remains to consider those areas of regulation in which it might appropriately be used. Where there are strong reasons for having freedom from political control, as in broadcasting there are clearly good arguments against guidance and in favour of setting down statutory objectives for a body such as the Independent Broadcasting Authority (IBA). Guidance would appear appropriate, however, in a number of instances of licensing, for example in civil aviation, data protection, discrimination, telecommunications, road transport and gaming. Privatization of public utilities such as gas and electricity might properly involve agencies operating under guidance. Wherever an agency is used to share a social resource between parties the device could be used, as for example in supplementary benefits. Agencies such as the pre-privatization BNOC that act in a quasi-regulatory manner and whose activities need to be co-ordinated with governmental strategies might also be subjected to written control. This was the case with the National Enterprise Board (NEB): section 7(1) of the Industry Act 1975 empowered the Secretary of State for Industry to give the NEB 'directions of a general or specific charter as to the exercise of their functions'. Such directions were issued (for example in 1980)[33] in the form of 'guidelines' and were subject to presentation before Parliament. A vote of parliamentary approval was not, however, made a precondition of the guidelines' legal validity.

Conclusions

It should not be assumed on the basis of the abolition of policy guidance in civil aviation licensing that the device has been discredited. From developments in other countries, and from experience with bodies such as the NEB and BNOC, a movement may be perceived in the direction of 'hybrid' control by expanded powers of direction or government involvement in agency policy-making and by publication of policies that have been negotiated between different arms of government. The requirement that guidance be approved by both Houses of Parliament offers a balance: it avoids the rigidity and delay of legislation but allows debate of major policy issues.[34] Since Ministerial control cannot be avoided, it may be seen from a wide range of political viewpoints as wise to channel this into a form that is agreed, open and subject to parliamentary scrutiny.

As far as institutions are concerned, NEDO's Policy Council's idea[35] is less appropriate to regulation than to the nationalized industries where, rightly or wrongly, it has been forgotten: there would be no need for an extra bureaucratic buffer between Minister and agency if statutory guidance was provided for. The requirement that such guidance should be subjected to the consultative and parliamentary processes would provide sufficient restraint on Ministerial action without further delegation of that function. To demand that guidance should take the form of a statutory instrument would be to run the risk of indulging in excessive detail and so of restricting the ability of an agency to exercise any expertise. On the other hand, a less formal system of guidance (for example one lacking a requirement of parliamentary approval) would be the poorer for having avoided debate and the agency would be deprived of the authority given by Parliament's approving its policy guidance.

The Canadian proposals mentioned above have attempted to produce a scheme of direction that involves both parliamentary control and improved participation.[36] The system suggested in that country resembles the CAA's guidance procedure but goes further in making formal provision for public involvement in the direction-making process. (The British Civil Aviation Act 1971 (section 3(2)) merely demanded that the Secretary of State should *consult* the CAA before issuing guidance.) The Law Reform Commission of Canada (LRCC) envisaged that the agency be notified of proposed directions and that it should be able to request 'public submissions' on them. Professor Hudson N. Janisch has written of public hearings being held to discuss proposed directions.[37] Following such public debate, both the LRCC and Janisch advocate that the agency should publish a report on the proposals so that any subsequent direction might be publicly assessed in the light of that report.

What would be the losses and gains of a statutorily open process? CAA experience implies, in the first instance, that there would be clear gains in terms of public accountability. Instead of the process adopted in British aviation in which a committee of civil servants consulted privately with the CAA and the airlines before drafting proposed guidance, one might envisage a hearings procedure in which the arguments would be made publicly, the agency would report and then civil servants and minister would deliberate on the directions appropriate. Both agency and

Minister would be rendered more accountable to the public and to Parliament by the airing of views. MPs would be in a position to argue the merits of changes in policy direction in a more intelligent manner than formerly. Against these gains, however, there stand a number of difficulties. First, it has to be asked whether public debate of policy directions is feasible.[38] In the 1970s the CAA demonstrated a willingness to conduct public hearings to discuss policy matters (for example its 'public consultation' on European air fares in 1977); it also used its licensing hearings to discuss policy issues at length. Debates on overall *policy guidance* as opposed to *policy* present more severe problems. Whereas the CAA has consulted openly on issues within its area of expertise, it has not used public hearings to discuss the most politically contentious issues. It has looked at problems of air fares but no 'public consultation' was held, for example, on the *politics* of allowing 'Skytrain'. Since changes in general policy direction tend to be based on party political grounds and tend to follow a change in government (as did Mr Shore's guidance of 1976), it is arguable that the public hearing is an inappropriate means of debating such issues. If Ministers were to favour changes in policy on philosophical grounds they would not welcome any requirement that they should refer their new guidance for public assessment by an independent agency. Not only that, they would strongly be tempted to by-pass the process and resort to covert techniques. On the agency's part, it might be felt both that consultation on the technical merits of any change would be less than fully relevant to a decision made on a political basis and also that the agency was placed in an embarrassing position in being compelled to take a stand on matters that might be decided against it on grounds that it was not free to consider. Where a Minister was to overrule an agency this would diminish that agency's authority in the regulatees' eyes, weaken its position in relation to them and open up the possibility of a clear division of policies between agency and department. Although public accountability would improve, there is a danger that the agency and Minister would compete for constituencies before the public eye. It is questionable whether any gains would compensate for the increased risk that, instead of working towards harmony of policies between government and agency, the proposed procedure might drive a wedge between them.

A second difficulty with more formal discussion of policy

direction stems from the process of formalization. Parties to hearings or consultations would quickly realise both the economic importance of the decisions being taken, and the opportunities for influencing governmental opinion. Counsel would be employed: they would argue in terms not only of law but also of administrative precedent and political policy. A wide ranging debate that might more properly belong in Parliament would be conducted in lengthy hearings and at prohibitive expense. There would be pressures to judicialize the consultation process and to use more formal hearings and in the end only the lawyers would profit from this. These two difficulties alone cast doubts on the feasibility of proposals aimed at formally opening out any direction-making process. At some point in policy control it has to be admitted that an issue has become political and is a matter for debate in Parliament rather than within the administration. There is a limit to the extent that an 'expert' body can take matters out of politics.[39]

(ii) Arms-Length Government and the Choice of Agency

Present failings
The regulatory agency is criticizable from very different viewpoints: to some it is a corporatist device used to shore up capitalism, to others it constitutes creeping socialism.[40] Between these two political positions, however, it may be viewed as almost unavoidable. Thus, for example, in Labour Party terms it allows increased control of the private sector in the public interest and for Conservatives it provides a means of public control that may be substituted for nationalization. Given such utility, it is therefore surprising that administrators, researchers and governments have not taken a closer look at how such bodies can be fitted as a group into the British system of government.

When designing and setting up regulatory agencies, the British way has been to muddle through in an *ad hoc* fashion without a great deal of regard for the suitability of the agency to the task set or the appropriateness of the system of accountability created.[41] Parliament is not perhaps renowned for dealing with subtleties of detail but a review of parliamentary debates on those agencies that were set up in the seventies shows the remarkable extent to which *ad hoc*cery was substituted for a considered approach. Typically ministers setting up regulatory bodies have stressed their promotion of an innovatory structure. Thus when the CAA was set up in 1971 the Minister for Trade, Mr Michael Noble, emphasized its novelty and, when proposals for a Director-General of Fair Trading emerged at the end of 1972, the post was heralded again as 'an institutional innovation'.[42] When the National Enterprise Board (NEB) was debated in 1975 Mr Meacher, the Under-Secretary of State, urged that in the NEB structure of accountability he too was 'making an innovation'.[43] His colleague, Mr Varley, shortly afterwards made a matching comment on the British National Oil Corporation (BNOC).[44]

Similar claims were made of the Welsh Development Agency[45] but in none of these instances was any rigorous attempt made to substantiate the claim of innovation or the need for innovation. Discussion of the manner in which proposed agencies were to differ in type from those already in existence was conspicuously absent. It was as if governments, in setting up *ad hoc* agencies, were glad to emphasize the uniqueness of the problems faced. There was a sense in which they were relieved of the responsibility to analyse and learn from experience in other areas.

Perhaps somewhat exceptionally, in the case of the CAA, there was some consideration in the Edwards Committee's Report[46] and in the ensuing White Paper[47] of the type of agency to be used, of the balances to be effected between flexibility and judiciality and the system of ministerial supervision appropriate in this area. What was lacking in those documents and in the parliamentary debates was any real attempt to draw on the experience of regulatory agencies (other than the ATLB) in either Britain or elsewhere. Analysis of the American Civil Aeronautics Board was not undertaken: oft-repeated criticisms of the American regulatory commissions were not debated, nor were regulatory schemes in other areas of British industry. Again, when the 1972 Sound Broadcasting Act created the Independent Broadcasting Authority (IBA), the Independent Television Authority (ITA) had been in existence for 16 years but little attention was given to the experience gained in that time.[48] No review of ITA regulatory activity in television was undertaken, nor was any discussion devoted to the regulatory powers that, given experience with television, would be appropriate to radio.

The National Enterprise Board was set up also with low priority being given to the machinery yoking it to the governmental system. The policy guidance given to the CAA in 1972 was perhaps the form of general guidance closest approximating that envisaged for the NEB, but there was no discussion of the success or failure of controls in that area.

Only, it seems, where an unavoidable parallel existed was prior experience considered. Thus, the Equal Opportunities Commission (EOC) emerged from a comparative perspective. The White Paper *Equality for Women*, of September 1974 argued that 'two possible approaches to the machinery'[49] presented themselves—the Equal Pay Act model or the Race Relations Act model. Although in the end neither prototype was relied upon exclusively, at least an attempt was made to apply lessons learned in related fields.

Ministers have often been guilty of speculative legislation. Perhaps the classic admission came from Mr Bruce Millan, Minister of State at the Scottish Office, in debating the Secretary of State's powers to direct the Scottish Development Agency. He was asked how the powers would be exercised and replied:

> We may, however, find it necessary to give a general or specific direction. It is difficult in advance to enumerate what we might wish to do and what matters we might wish to have covered and the occasions on which we might wish to give a direction. I am sorry to be so vague, but I honestly do not believe that I can give a definite answer.[50]

Whereas ministers have relied on a hoped-for evolution or emphasized *ad hoc* considerations, ordinary Members of Parliament have given little information concerning the machinery that they have been asked to vote for. When the Fair Trading Bill was being debated in 1972 and the 'institutional innovation', the Director-General of Fair Trading, was being considered, members were ill-informed as to the regulatory strategy involved: no White Paper had been published before the Bill in order to explain governmental reasoning and the Opposition claimed that there had been no opportunity for consultation on the proposals.[51] Similarly with the Price Commission and the Pay Board: MPs protested that they knew nothing about the code of 'practical guidance' that was provided for in the 1973 Counter Inflation Bill.[52] When BNOC was being debated in committee, it was again clear that few MPs knew how the agency's structure would operate.[53] Ministers have repeatedly taken general and specific powers but have failed to indicate whether (as in the case of the CAA and NEB) these would be used as substantial methods of broad policy direction or whether (as in the case of the Health and Safety Executive (HSE) or the nationalized industries) the powers would merely serve as a measure of a last-resort or as back-up to the informal ('lunch-table') directive.

It could well be argued that Ministers might, quite properly, be ignorant of a new agency's operations—the necessity to develop expertise might have been a main reason for creating an agency. The point is, however, that such arguments can be taken too far so that Ministers fail to give attention to all those problems of accountability, procedure and mix of functions that should be dealt with if the agency is to be anything other than an ill-designed, unaccountable and inefficient depository for problems that governments would like to get rid of.

Not only have issues relating to ministerial powers been neglected, little attention has been given to the basic question of whether an independent agency (rather than, for example, a department) should have been used for a particular task at all. In the case of some bodies, such as the CAA, a committee had considered the options and favoured the agency, on other occasions, however, the agency system was almost assumed without argument. Thus, following the Robens Committee on *Safety and Health at Work*,[54] the Health and Safety Commission and Executive were set up largely for managerial reasons. The Government elected for a semi-departmental body (staffed by civil servants) but (beyond the war that went on in Whitehall concerning the hiving-off) little debate occurred on the merits of making the body fully independent. Even in Robens such questions were answered by a brief reference to 'constitutional issues'.[55] The departmental system was favoured in order to provide accountability, but the pressing need for such accountability was not publicly examined.

There have been failures in respect of agency regulation on a number of levels: the *ad hoc* approach has been extolled as a virtue; relevant experience in other agencies and countries has not been drawn upon; MPs have been ill-informed and have voted for structures that they knew little about and they have been concerned with issues of political immediacy to the neglect of issues of machinery. Governments have set up bodies to regulate difficult areas and then *hoped* that (by a mysterious process of evolution?) appropriate methods both of regulating and of keying a body into the governmental machine would emerge.

So much for Parliament. It may, however, be said that in the above comments too much is expected of an assembly dealing with what are often experimental bodies, that Parliament should not be expected to concern itself with anything other than rhetoric and that we must look to other places for a more intelligent assessment of agency potential. The proposition that adequate extra-parliamentary consideration is given to issues of regulatory machinery is, however, questionable. It may be argued that in Whitehall the science of agency selection operates on a high plane,[56] but there are a number of limiting factors. A major difficulty is the departmental system and its resistance to the cross-flow of ideas. If the proposal for a new agency emerges within one department, there may be little consideration of similar agencies simply because these happen to be sponsored by another department. (One CAA member commented on proposals for a CAA-style telecommunications agency: 'They keep re-inventing the wheel: no-one comes and asks us how we work it' (Interview, March 1983)). If the personnel in one department have experience in other fields, then some breadth of perspective may be gained, but this rests on a fortuitous basis.

At the time of writing, co-ordinating functions rest with the Machinery of Government Division (MGD) that was formerly part of the Civil Service Department (CSD) but was transferred in 1980 to the Management and Organization Division of the Management and Personnel Office. In theory, the MGD should be able to engage in comparative studies, but practical considerations limit its opportunities for the broad evaluation of agencies. A first pressure is the 'in-tray'. At present, one Under-Secretary and one Principal in the MGD deal with new agencies. Neither does so on a full-time basis. Civil servants in this position simply do not have the time to conduct research into the operation of agencies nor are they able to read and keep up to date on the relevant literature—in this country, never mind others.

If civil servants working on a daily basis hold few hopes of taking a broader look at the use of agencies, then recourse must be taken to committees or other institutions. These, however, have not, in parliamentary or other form, effectively reviewed agency government. In the case of the nationalized industries, there have been reports from Select Committees,[57] from the National Economic Development Office (NEDO)[58] and in White Papers,[59] but such studies have neither taken in the wider issue of agencies in general nor have they been referred to in debates on agencies. Committees on the civil service have similarly failed to guide legislative activity in this area. The Haldane Committee on the *Machinery of Government* in 1918 gave non-departmental bodies scant attention, believing that 'there should be no omission in the case of any particular service, of those safeguards that ministerial responsibility to Parliament alone provides'. Similarly, apart from recommendations of broad implication, such as the creation of a new Civil Service Department and the 'hiving-off' of certain types of function, the Fulton Committee of 1967 hardly touched upon the role of non-departmental bodies.

When the Thatcher Government came to power in May 1979, a limited review of agencies was undertaken when Sir Leo Pliatzky was commissioned to report on *Non-Departmental Public Bodies*[60] as part of an exercise in cutting expenditure on quangos. The review asked whether a function was essential, whether the money spent was justified, whether the task might best be carried out by another means, and whether there would be a substantial loss if the body were wound up. The Pliatzky report, with its emphasis on trimming, may, however, be seen not so much as a review of the theoretical and practical bases for various kinds of agency but more as an economic appraisal of costs. Announcing the publication of that report, the Prime Minister, Mrs Thatcher, said, on 16 January 1980, that she would look critically at proposals for new bodies and would be opposed to the further hiving-off of functions to non-departmental public bodies.[61] In 1981 the Civil Service Department (CSD) published its Machinery of Government Division's guide for departments on non- departmental bodies and sought to build on Pliatzky in the light of Mrs Thatcher's announced policy.[62] Although much of the CSD guide comprised only general comments and an expanded checklist of matters to be taken into account in dealing with any non-departmental body, its advice on new bodies (section 8) was of interest. The CSD emphasized, *inter alia*, that, before creating new bodies, departments should have established clear policy objectives, be satisfied that the costs to be incurred were justified and that the task could not be undertaken equally well by departments, local government or the private sector. A particular question to be addressed, it was said, should be the relationship between any new body and the minister. In the case of new executive, administrative, regulatory, commercial or judicial bodies, the CSD emphasized the binding requirement on departments to consult central departments concerning their proposals.

These and the other points for consideration set down by the CSD offer only the most general advice and apply to a huge range of bodies, nevertheless they do move towards a more coordinated approach to the establishment of all agencies of government. Whether or not it is possible to produce more substantive guidance on the role of regulatory bodies in government is our final issue.

Towards More Rational Use of the Regulatory Agency

Regulatory agencies are engaged in many different tasks. In making use of present experience, therefore, a first need is for sufficient information to be collected to apply the lessons of one sphere to others. Here a relevant research background is necessary, and British academics can follow the North Americans in broader analysis of the administrative process in its political and legal contexts.[63] Developments need also to be encouraged in institutionalized research. Work on regulatory laws and strategies could (and should) be undertaken by standing bodies such as the Law Commissions but, unfortunately, the past has seen British Law Commissions being forced to concentrate on issues of a legally technical nature rather than taking a wider view of the potential of particular legal and political institutions. This has been due partly to limitations on resources but has also stemmed from a traditional treatment of law as a technical issue somehow divorceable from political or social considerations. We have, as a consequence, failed to match the detailed studies conducted in the USA on agencies and in the papers of, for example, the Law Reform Commission of Canada.[64]

A revised research background would inform those involved in politics of the issues raised when decisions to regulate are taken, it would also help to concentrate the minds of politicians on these topics. As well as raising political consciousness concerning agencies there is also a need to improve the process whereby the machinery of regulation is given consideration. Mr Nevil Johnson has argued[65] that there should be a 'Standing Advisory Commission on Administrative Organization' placed outside the Civil Service Department and free to analyse and report on the administrative structure of government. Such a body—or one devoted to fringe bodies alone—would allow more detailed consideration to be given to the potential of various regulatory devices. (At present the Council on Tribunals covers a limited number of bodies — including the CAA — but it does not cover, for example, the Gaming Board beause of the restrictive notions of 'tribunal' prevalent in government.) A new commission on the lines suggested could take both a more independent and a more broadly-based view than a department of government. The commission might, for example, deal with the role to be played by Ministers, departments or Parliament in reviewing such matters as agency powers, duties and performance, and whether imported procedures (such as legislative approval of agency rule-making) should be adopted. The Commission would thus seek ways by which agencies can be harnessed to the system of ministerial government.

Substantively, stress might be placed (both inside and outside Parliament) on three questions:

(1) Why regulate by agency in the first place and, if so, why use this particular form of body?
(2) What is the appropriate regulatory strategy?
(3) What are the appropriate forms of ministerial, parliamentary and judicial control?

Not merely should agencies' structures be created in the light of experience in different fields, but steps should be taken to produce a more rational model of regulatory agency: a prototype to replace the hotch-potch of characteristics now making up our agencies. In addition, our public law and parliamentary systems should attune themselves to cater for the control of agencies. To do this is to accord to the regulatory body a place within the political system.

To give a more precise example: on the issue of accountability work should be done to regularize relationships between Ministers and regulatory bodies and to open out both the policy-making process and the division of responsibility. The following kinds of proposal, for instance, might be considered: regulatory agencies should employ their own staff; they should be subject to statutory objectives and ministerial policy guidance which should be written and approved by Parliament in advance. The agency should be under a duty to issue periodic statements of its own policies and such statements should include all major rules to which it adheres in decision-making. Such periodic policy statements should be issued after a period of notice and comment so as to allow the widest interests, including the regulatees, a chance to participate in rule-making. Major decisions between parties should be heard in public except where disclosure of information might prejudice the parties or the agency's attainment of its statutory objectives.

To propose a rationalized model of agency is by no means to assert that the same legal framework will work in widely differing regulatory contexts. Variations on the model should be allowed. To endorse the model is, however, to impose some order on the chaos of regulatory bodies so as to allow public discussion of their role and to move towards the defined organizational categories as are encountered in continental Europe.[66] At present, the nationalized industries boards, their procedures and political status, can be debated publicly and they have been subject to a special Commons Select Committee. In the United States and Canada the regulatory agencies are similarly talked of as bodies with peculiar functions, capabilities and difficulties. As things stand in Britain, our present confusion of fringe bodies does not allow talk of 'the regulatory agencies' and, as a result, the performance and structure of bodies like the IBA, CAA, CRE, EOC, Gaming Board, Health and Safety Commission/Executive, Monopolies and Mergers Commission and BNOC are dealt with individually rather than collectively or comparatively.[67] The departmental Select Committees deal with regulatory bodies only in an *ad hoc* manner and many of the latter are excluded from the Ombudsman's jurisdiction.

Even in the United States the need to look yet more closely at the institutional capabilities of agencies has been urged. Richard Stewart said in his paper 'The Reformation of American Administrative Law':[68]

> . . . a classification of agency functions and institutional contexts might be paralleled by a similar classification of the various techniques for directing and controlling administrative power, including judicial review, procedural requirements, political controls and partial abolition of agency functions. The two systems of classification might then be meshed to determine the most harmonious fit between the purposes and characteristics of particular agencies and various control techniques. Any design quite so grandiose is of course unlikely to be achieved in full, but it marks out a potentially rewarding line of inquiry that may represent our best hope of realistic future progress in administrative law.

On parliamentary as opposed to governmental scrutiny of regulatory agencies, there is a case to be made for a House of Commons Select Committee on Regulated Industries on the lines of the nationalized industries' equivalent. As well as paralleling the work of the hypothetical Standing Advisory Commission on Administrative Organization (SACAO) on developing procedural standards for regulatory bodies, such a body would be able to investigate in depth the strategies pursued by the regulators and it would, for instance, be able to review the effects of regulatory activity on industry and affected consumers.

Arguments *against* review by Select Committee have recently been made by Richard Wilding of the Civil Service Department[69] and by Nevil Johnson[70] who state, *inter alia*, that insofar as quasi-independent bodies are made accountable to Parliament directly, this increases the pressure on Ministers to assert control over such bodies as they sponsor and that this process rapidly undermines any independence these bodies enjoy. According to this argument, there is more promise in improved 'public law regulation'[71] of agency activity than in increased accountability to Parliament.

It is difficult to know whether increased ministerial bullying of agencies will result from, or indeed, is too high a price to pay for, greater accountability. Though acting sporadically, Select Committees have investigated the activities of regulatory bodies in some detail in the past—to no apparent ill-effect.[72] Furthermore, the Select Committee on Procedure proposed, in 1978, that the new Select Committees set up to shadow individual departments should also look at fringe bodies sponsored by those departments, and other Select Committees have argued that the jurisdiction of the Exchequer and Audit Department should cover all public bodies receiving money voted by Parliament.[73] A Select Committee on Regulated Industries would increase the accountability of regulators and would lend further political legitimacy to regulatory activity. As for the effect this would have on Ministers, this may be less dramatic than has been predicted since they have never been short of reasons for interfering with fringe bodies and there is little evidence that the considerable amount of parliamentary scrutiny that has been conducted randomly in the past has led to drastic ministerial action. In any case, more rigorous opening out of the processes of accountability and policy-making may do much to counteract any such tendency to interfere.

From the lawyer's point of view, a final point should be considered: increased use of the regulatory agency, and especially the use of trial-type procedures by bodies of special expertise, will inevitably involve greater pressure on judges to review agency actions. Serious thought has to be given on the lawyer's part to the manner in which control powers over agencies (and agency powers themselves) are both defined in statute and interpreted by the courts. On the one hand, clearly defined powers may lead to less ministerial interference, but, on the other, there may be disadvantages in very detailed definitions of powers because of delays resulting from challenges in courts and through appeals systems. There are other difficulties: if an agency fears challenge to its powers, this may lead to 'capture' by vested interests in terms of safe or 'defensive' decision-making:[74] if a statute gives an agency an autonomy that is too protected in law there may be pressure to re-legislate or for ministers to by-pass their legally defined control powers. Whatever constitutes the governmentally desired balance of legal discretion and duties, the first need is for lawyers, politicians and administrators to work towards mutually understood strategies on regulatory bodies. If they do not, they will continue to obstruct one another and to hinder the agency's development as a tool of accountable and efficient government rather than a means of sweeping problems under the carpet.

Notes

Chapter 1: Introduction: A History of Neglect

1. Throughout this book the phrase 'trial-type procedure' is used to refer to the process of adjudication in which pre-existing rules, principles or policies are applied to sets of facts on the basis of oral or written arguments and evidence presented adversarily in public. 'Trial-type procedure' is preferred to 'adjudication' or 'judicial procedure' as the latter terms cover too broad a range of informal and formal procedures to be helpful: see K.C. Davis, *Administrative Law Treatise*, 2nd ed., San Diego (1979), pp. 311–12.

2. See e.g. the White Paper *The Development of Cable Systems and Services* Cmnd. 8866 (1983), *Report of the Committee on Restrictions against Disabled People*, DHSS (May 1982) (proposing a body like the CRE and EOC) and the *Report of the Committee on Data Protection* (Chairman Sir Norman Lindop) Cmnd. 7341 (December 1978) (recommendations on the creation of a Data Protection Authority).

3. See e.g. M.H. Bernstein, *Regulating Business by Independent Commission*, Princeton University Press (1955); R.E. Cushman, *The Independent Regulatory Commissions*, Oxford University Press, New York (1941); J.M. Landis, *The Administrative Process*, Yale University Press (1938); T.J. Lowi, *The End of Liberalism*, Norton, New York (1969); P.W. MacAvoy (ed.), *The Crisis of the Regulatory Commissions*, Norton, New York (1970); R.G. Noll, *Reforming Regulation: An Evaluation of the Ash Council Proposals*, Brookings Institute (1971); E.S. Redford, *The Regulatory Process*, University of Texas Press (1969); J.O. Freedman, *Crisis and Legitimacy*, Cambridge University Press (1978).

4. See Anthony Barker, *Quangos in Britain*, Macmillan, London (1982); D.C. Hague, W.J.M. Mackenzie and A. Barker, *Public Policy and Private Interests: The Institutions of Compromise*, Macmillan, London (1975).

5. See G. Bowen, *Survey of Fringe Bodies*, Civil Service Department (1978).

6. See Sir Leo Pliatsky, *Report on Non-Departmental Bodies* Cmnd. 7797 (1980).

7. See J.F. Garner, 'New Public Corporations' [1966] *P.L.* 324 and *Administrative Law*, 5th ed., Chapter 10.

8. Civil Service Department, *Non Departmental Public Bodies: A Guide For Departments* (1981). This book follows the CSD report in attempting to avoid the term 'quango' as too vague a concept to be a useful tool of analysis (see para. 12). On this, see also Barker, op.cit., Chapter 1 and Appendix.

9. See also Richard Wilding, 'A triangular affair: quangos, ministers, and MPs', in Barker, op.cit., esp. pp. 36–7.

10. J.F. Garner, 'New Public Corporations' [1966] *P.L.* 324. See also Bowen, op.cit. Useful details are contained in, *A Directory of Paid Public Appointments Made by Ministers,* HMSO (1978).

11. C.C. Hood and W.J.M. Mackenzie, 'The Problem of Classifying Institutions' in Hague, Mackenzie and Barker, op.cit. See Hood in Barker, op.cit., p. 56.

12. P. Holland and M. Fallon, *The Quango Explosion,* Conservative Political Centre, London (1978). See also Otto Newman, *The Challenge of Corporatism,* Macmillan, London (1981), Chapter 8.

13. See D. Coombes, *Representative Government and Economic Power,* Heinemann, London (1982), Chapter 6.

14. On the general issue of tripartism see e.g. Coombes, op.cit., Chapter 8; Newman, op.cit., Chapter 5; T. Smith, *The Politics of the Corporate Economy,* Martin Robertson (1979), Chapters 5 and 8.

15. On the difficulties of attempting to categorize agency types see: W.A. Robson, *Politics and Government At Home and Abroad* (1967), p. 110 ('a no-man's land full of nebulous forms'); Sir Norman Chester, 'Public Corporations and the Classification of Administrative Bodies' (1953) *Political Studies* 34, and 'Fringe Bodies, Quangos and All That' (1979) *Public Administration* 51; Christopher Hood, 'Keeping the Centre Small: Explanations of Agency Type' (1978) 26 *Political Studies* 30, and *The World of Quasi-Government,* University of York Institute of Social and Economic Research (1979); Hague, Mackenzie and Baker, op.cit.; Nevil Johnson, 'The Public Corporation: An Ambiguous Species' in *Policy and Politics* (Butler and Halsey, eds., 1979); Grant Jordan, 'Hiving-Off and Departmental Agencies' (1976) 21 *Public Administration Bulletin*; Bowen, op.cit.; Pliatzky, op.cit.; *The Outer Circle Policy Unit, What's Wrong with Quangos?,* OCPU (1979); P. Holland and M. Fallon, op.cit.; Barker, op.cit., Chapters 1, 3 (by C. Hood) and Appendix.

16. See Roger G. Noll, 'What is Regulation?' (June 1980) *California Institute of Technology: Social Science Working Paper* 324.

17. R.A. Kagan, *Regulatory Justice,* Russell Sage (1978), p.

18. See Abel-Smith and Stevens' distinction between 'court-substitute' and 'policy-oriented' tribunals in, *In Search of Justice* (1968), pp. 220–1, discussed in J.A. Farmer, *Tribunals and Government,* Wiedenfeld and Nicholson, London (1978), p. 183.

19. In terms of the classifications cited these regulatory bodies would come in Pliatsky's group iv(a); Garner's (iii); Hood and Mackenzie's (iii); Holland and Fallon's (vi); and Coombes' (iii).

20. On tribunals and regulatory agencies, see Farmer, op.cit., pp. 53, 182–5; also B. Schwartz and H.W.R. Wade, *Legal Control of Government,* Clarendon Press, Oxford (1972), p. 148.

21. See Hood, loc.cit. (1978).

22. Frans F. Slatter, *Parliament and Administrative Agencies,* Law Reform Commission of Canada, Ottawa (1982); see also H.N. Janisch, 'The Role of the Independent Regulatory Agency in Canada' (1978) *U.N.B.L.J.* 27 at 83.

23. See Newman, op.cit., p. 157.
24. Ibid., p. 149.
25. See Mr M. Noble introducing the second reading of the 1971 Civil Aviation Bill, H.C.Deb. Vol. 814, col. 1173 (29 March 1971).
26. See H. Parris, *Constitutional Bureaucracy* (1969); D. Roberts, *Victorian Origins of the British Welfare State* (1960); F.M.G. Willson, 'Ministers and Boards: Some Aspects of Administrative Development Since 1832' (1954) 32 Public Administration 43.
27. See Roberts, op.cit., p. 38.
28. Ibid., p. 126.
29. O. MacDonagh, *Early Victorian Government* (1977), pp. 107–8.
30. See Willson, loc.cit., p. 46.
31. Ibid., pp. 52–3. See also F.G.M. Willson, unpublished Ph.D. thesis, 'A Consideration of the experience in Britain of Administrative Commissions represented in Parliament by non-ministerial commissioners, with special reference to the Ecclesiastical Commission, the Charity Commission and the Forestry Commission', Oxford (1953).
32. Ibid., p. 48.
33. See H. Parris, *Government and the Railways in Nineteenth Century Britain* (1965), pp. 84–6.
34. M.E. Dimock, *British Public Utilities and National Development*, London (1933).
35. H.J. Laski, W.I. Jennings and W.A. Robson, *A Century of Municipal Progress*, London (1935), p. 301.
36. See P.W.J. Bartrip, 'State Intervention in Mid-Nineteenth Century Britain—Fact or Fiction' (1983) *Journal of British Studies 63.*
37. W.A. Robson, *Nationalised Industry and Public Ownership*, London (1960), p. 28.
38. Cd. 9230 (1918).
39. See H. Morrison, *Socialisation and Transport*, London (1933).
40. See also the hiving-off of Department of Employment functions to the Manpower Services Commission (1973), the Health and Safety Commission (1974), and the Advisory, Conciliation and Arbitration Service (1975), Jordan, loc.cit. (1976).
41. Cmnd. 3638 (1967), Vol. 1, paras. 188–190. See Jordan, loc.cit., p. 48.
42. See A.V. Dicey, *Introduction to the Study of the Law of the Constitution*, 10th edn. (1959).
43. Robson, op.cit., p. 25. See also Schwartz and Wade, op.cit., p. 38.
44. See *Report of the Royal Commission on Transport* Cmd. 3365, 3416, 3751 HMSO (1929–30).
45. See *Report of the Committee on the Licensing of Road Passenger Services* HMSO (1953) (The Thesiger Report).
46. *Report of the Committee on Carriers' Licensing* (1965) (The Geddes Report), para. 2.55.
47. The Thesiger Report, para. 16.
48. Evidence to the Franks Committee: Memoranda of Departments, Vol. III, p. 65.
49. For details see infra, Chapter 2.

50. For a more recent analysis see N. Lewis 'IBA Programme Contract Awards' [1975] *P.L.* 137.

51. On independent agencies and investment see Gabrielle Ganz, *Government and Industry* (1977).

52. See Hood, loc.cit. (1978) and J.T. Winkler, 'Law, State and Economy: The Industry Act 1975 in Context' (1975) *British Jounral of Law and Society 103*. For a Northern Irish example see J.C. McCrudden, 'Law Enforcement by Regulatory Agency: The Case of Employment Discrimination in Northern Ireland' (1982) 45 *Modern Law Review* 617.

53. See, for example, the Coal Industry Nationalization Act 1945, s. 3.

54. See Report of the Select Committee on Nationalized Industries: Ministerial Control of Nationalized Industries (HC 1967–8, 371-i) paras. 650–1; Q 339 where Treasury witnesses stated that the Law Officers had been reluctant to pronounce on the legality of 'general directions'.

Chapter 2: Civil Aviation Regulation to 1960

1. See H.J. Dyos and D.H. Aldcroft, *British Transport*, Leicester University Press (1969), Chapter 13. On the development of British aviation see R. Higham, *Britain's Imperial Air Routes 1918–39* London (1960); E. Birkhead, 'The Financial Failure of British Air Transport Companies 1919–24' (November 1958) *Journal of Transport History*..

2. See the *Report of the Advisory Committee on Civil Aviation* (Chairman Lord Weir) Cmd. 449 (1919).

3. *The Times*, 11 December 1919. See the similar views of General Brancker in the lecture reported in *The Times*, 8 October 1921.

4. *The Times*, 17 January 1921 (Leader).

5. *Government Financial Assistance to Civil Air Transport Companies*, Cmd. 1811 (1923).

6. D. Corbett, *Politics and the Airlines*, London (1965), pp. 26–32; Dyos and Aldcroft, op.cit., Chapter 13. In 1927 the Government took a decision to subsidize Imperial Airways' empire routes in preference to others (see *Report of the Committee of Inquiry into Civil Aviation*, Cmd. 5685 (1938) (The Cadman Report), p. 41).

7. Dyos and Aldcroft, op.cit., p. 414. See also D.H. Aldcroft, 'Britain's Internal Airways: The Pioneer Stage of the 1930s' in *Studies in British Transport History 1870–1970*, David and Charles, London (1974).

8. *Development of Civil Aviation in the United Kingdom*, Cmd. 5351 (1937), (The Maybury Report).

9. Ibid., para. 104.

10. *Report of the Royal Commission on Transport*, Cmd. 3365 (1929); Cmd. 3416 (1929); Cmd. 3751 (1939).

11. The Maybury Report, paras. 106, 125, 126.

12. The Air Navigation Act 1936, gave the Secretary of State for Air power to subsidize air transport services (s. 1). S. 5 stated that provision could be made (by Order in Council) for the prohibition of any persons carrying for hire and reward by air, or anyone flying for the purposes of trade, 'except under the authority of and in accordance with a licence granted to the said persons by the licensing authority specified in the Order'.

13. The Maybury Report, paras. 133–5.
14. *Report of the Committee of Inquiry into Civil Aviation*, Cmd. 5685 (1938), (The Cadman Report) 123 (xxvi) para. 72.
15. Ibid., para. 22.
16. Ibid., para. 21.
17. Ibid., para. 46.
18. Ibid.
19. Ibid., para. 48.
20. Ibid., para. 36.
21. See Air Navigation (Licensing of Public Transport) Order 1938 (S.R. & O. 1938, No. 613) and Regulations thereunder (S.R. & O., 1938, No. 1106). The subsidy scheme is set out in *Civil Air Transport Services: Internal Air Lines*, Cmd. 5894 (1938).
22. (S.R. & O., 1939, No. 1558).
23. Dyos and Aldcroft, op.cit., p. 425.
24. See Higham, op.cit., Chapter 15.
25. British Overseas Airways Act 1939. See Corbett, op.cit., pp. 98–102.
26. See H.C.Deb., Vol. 349, col. 1831, Dyos and Aldcroft, op.cit., p. 417.
27. See e.g. Coal Industry Nationalization Act 1945, s. 3.
28. D.N. Chester and F.M.G. Willson, *The Organisation of British Central Government 1914–64*, London (1968), pp. 106–7.
29. Ministry of Civil Aviation Act 1945 (consolidated under Civil Aviation Act|1949, Pt. 1).
30. Ministerial power to regulate air navigation so as to give effect to the Chicago Convention was given in the Air Navigation Act 1947.
31. See *International Air Transport*, Cmd. 6561 (1944), 'The Swinton Plan'.
32. *The Times*, 14 March 1945.
33. See H. Morrison, *Socialization and Transport*, London (1933).
34. Civil Aviation Act 1946, s. 23; repeated as s. 24 of the Air Corporations Act 1949.
35. Corbett, op.cit., p. 103; H.C.Deb., Vol. 422, cols. 596–8 (6 May 1946).
36. H.C.Deb., Vol. 422, col. 662 (6 May 1946).
37. H.C.Deb. Vol. 422, col. 623 (6 May 1946).
38. Civil Aviation (Air Transport Advisory Council), Order 1947 (S.R. & O. 1947, No. 1224).
39. Article 12 of the 1947 Order gave the ATAC the discretion to hold a public or private meeting.
40. As provided for in s. 14(4) of the Civil Aviation Act 1946, and s. 15(3) of the Air Corporations Act 1949. This avoided the corporation monopoly as set out in s. 24 of the Air Corporations Act 1949.
41. ATAC Annual Report (1949–50), para. 10.
42. H.C.Deb., Vol. 505, col. 2181.
43. Ibid., col. 2179.
44. See ATAC Annual Report (1952–3), Appendix E.
45. In accordance with article 15 of the Civil Aviation (ATAC), Order 1947 it was the Minister's decision rather than the ATAC's recommendation that was publicly disclosed.
46. ATAC Annual Report (1952–3), para. 25.

47. *The Times,* 7 May 1958.
48. On 28 February 1958, Mr Stewart argued in the House of Commons that there was an urgent need to re-think the place of the private operators since they were robbed of stability and tenure.
49. *The Times,* 13 November 1958.
50. After the October 1959 General Election, the Civil Aviation responsibilities of the Minister of Transport and Civil Aviation were transferred to the Minister of Aviation (from 21 October 1959).
51. H.C.Deb., Vol. 598, col. 198.
52. (1958–59; H.C. 213).
53. H.C.Deb. Vol. 612, col. 64 (27 October 1959).
54. See Wheatcroft, op.cit., Chapters 2 and 7.
55. See the Paymaster General, Lord Mills H.L.Deb., Vol. 223, col. 595.

Chapter 3: A Hopeless Compromise? The Air Transport Licensing Board is Created

1. B. Abel-Smith and R. Stevens, *In Search of Justice,* London (1968), p. 228, discussed by J.A. Farmer in *Tribunals and Government,* London (1974), p. 186. See also P. Weiler, 'Two Models of Judicial Decision-Making' (1968) 46 *Can. Bar. Rev.* 406.
2. See *Committee on Administrative Tribunals and Enquiries* (Franks), Cmnd. 218 (1975), p. 9.
3. On British conservatism on the model of the tribunal, see Farmer, op.cit., p. 185
4. H.C.Deb., Vol. 618, col. 1228.
5. *Committee on Administrative Tribunals and Enquiries,* Cmnd. 218 (1957), para. 105. The Council on Tribunals (Annual Report 1960–1, para. 18) was to note that the Bill's allowing an appeal from an independent body to a Minister contravened the Franks' advice.
6. H.C.Deb., Vol. 618, col. 1228.
7. H.L.Deb., Vol. 223, col. 594.
8. H.C.Deb., Vol. 618, col. 1231. Lord Mills hoped that a case law as found in road passenger transport licensing would emerge: H.L.Deb., Vol. 232, col. 595.
9. H.C.Deb., Vol. 618, col. 1235.
10. Ibid., col. 1236.
11. Ibid., col. 1237.
12. London (1953). He did not note the Franks (op.cit., para. 105) recommendation against ministerial appeals from independent bodies, nor did he mention that road *goods* appeals went to the Transport Tribunal, not the Minister. The Geddes Committee of 1965 did not suggest ministerial appeals in goods cases: *Report of the Committee on Carriers Licensing,* London (1965), paras. 13.15–13.17.
13. Standing Committee B (1959–60), col. 109.
14. Ibid.
15. *Flight,* 13 May 1960, p. 662.

16. See e.g. Sir Gilmour Jenkins, *The Ministry of Transport and Civil Aviation*, Allen and Unwin, London (1959).

17. In 1967 the Board of Trade handed over to the ARB the function of issuing certificates of airworthiness (Civil Aviation (Air Registration Board) Order 1967 (S.I. 1967 No. 1060), of 1 August 1967). These related to the aircraft themselves and the operators' standards of technical maintenance.

18. S. 4(1). The ATLB considered only a small number of complaints annually (e.g. 4 in 1967–68; 6 in 1968–69; 6 in 1970–71—see Annual Reports).

19. Two main sets of regulations governed ATLB procedure in the 1960s: the 1960 Civil Aviation (Licensing) Regulations (S.I. 1960, No. 125), and the revised 1964 Regulations (S.I. 1964, No. 2137).

Chapter 4: The ATLB and Governmental Control

1. *Flight* magazine recorded that 24 ATLB staff joined the CAA's licensing division: 'Enter the CAA', 30 March 1972. The ATLB's annual expenditure given in the civil appropriation accounts for 1965–66 was £65,580 (in 1974–75 the CAA spent £1.6 million on Economic Regulation—Annual Report, p. 79).

2. In 1960 the parent department was the Ministry of Aviation; in 1966 the Board of Trade took over Ministry of Aviation functions under the 1960 Act (S.I. 1966, Nos. 741 and 1015). The Department of Trade and Industry succeeded in 1971.

3. Sir Daniel Jack was a political economist and David Dale Professor of Economics, at Durham University from 1935–61; Mr James Lawrie was a banker and financier.

4. See e.g. M.H. Bernstein, *Regulating Business by Independent Commission*, Princeton University Press (1955), pp. 89–90.

5. Interview. Mr H. West, July 1975.

6. Applications for services within the United Kingdom, Channel Islands, Isle of Man and between the United Kingdom and Europe, 23 November 1961. (The '1961 European Case'.)

7. Para. 8(d).

8. S. Wheatcroft, *Air Transport Policy*, London (1964), p. 165.

9. ATLB Annual Report (1963–4), para. 6.

10. Ibid., para. 7.

11. H.C.Deb., Vol. 706, col. 1186.

12. Thus complying with the demands of e.g. *British Oxygen Co.* v. *Minister of Technology* [1970] 3 All ER 165; *Merchandise Transport Ltd.* v. *British Transport Commission* [1962] 2 Q.B. 173.

13. ATLB Fifth Annual Report (1964–5), para. 7.

14. Ibid., para. 8.

15. H.C.Deb., Vol. 707, cols. 935–1058.

16. Ibid., col. 1048–9.

17. Ibid., col. 949.

18. Ibid., col. 1037.

19. Report of the House of Commons Select Committee on Nationalised Industries: British European Airways (The 1967 Select Committee), (1966–67; H.C., 673), XVIII Minutes, Q. 586.
20. BEA Annual Report (1965–6), p. 134.
21. 1967 Select Committee, Q. 1234.
22. Ibid., Q. 590–1.
23. Ibid., Appendix 14, para. 50.
24. ATLB Seventh Annual Report (1966–7), para. 5.
25. Decision A4560 of 25 July 1965.
26. ATLB Seventh Annual Report (1966–7), para. 11.
27. Ninth Annual Report (1968–9), paras. 44–6.
28. *British Air Transport in the Seventies*, Cmnd 4018 (1969) (Edwards).
29. Decision A12325 of 23 January 1972, paras. 24–5.
30. See *supra* p. 33.
31. 1967 Select Committee, Q. 615.
32. Application A7468/1.
33. Application A12825, 25 January 1972.
34. Ibid., para. 20.
35. Application A7147 of 22 May 1968.
36. 1967 Select Committee Appendix 14, para. 5.
37. H.C.Deb., Vol. 677, col. 965.
38. Edwards, Appendix 22, p. 326.
39. See *Flight*, 23 April 1970.
40. Which required the ATLB to consider representations and to report with any recommendations to the Minister.
41. In its 'Civil Aviation Licensing Notices', No. 256, Pt. viii (CALN 256).
42. CALN 287.
43. ATLB Ninth Annual Report (1968–9), para. 46.
44. Evidence to the 1967 Select Committee, Q. 1203.
45. See Wheatcroft, op.cit., Chapter 8; Edwards, paras. 629–53.
46. All references to routes are from London unless otherwise stated.
47. Decision and Reasons A1000, 1961.
48. CALN, 474.
49. Applications A1116, A1117, A1119 (Chester to Jersey, Belfast, Dublin).
50. Commissioner's Report A1116, 1 September 1962, para. 15.
51. ATLB letter A1116, 13 June 1962, para. 6.
52. See also applications A380/11 and A5189, September 1966.
53. Licence A2243, 25 February 1963.
54. Application T. 56.
55. Commissioner's Report on Appeal, T. 56, 8 January 1968, para. 16.
56. CALN, 474.
57. Applications B10153–61 etc., of 5 March 1971.
58. Appeal Commissioner's Report B10153, 5 March 1971, para. 18.
59. Ibid., para. 21.
60. Ibid., para. 63.
61. See K.C. Davis, *Discretionary Justice*, Baton Rouge (1969), Chapter 4.
62. London to Glasgow, Edinburgh and Belfast (Licences A361/2, A362/3, A365/2).
63. Commissioner's Report A361/2, 8 March 1962.

64. Appeal B7165, 24 July 1968. Appeal Commissioner's Report, 15 May 1968, para. 20.
65. Applications A4643, A4638, and A300/3.
66. Appeal Commissioner's Report, 3 November 1965, para. 16. See also case A1007/1 (April 1967).
67. Applications A5253 and A5278.
68. Application A10040, 1 December 1971.
69. Appeal Commissioner's Report A10040, 1 December 1971.
70. Ibid., para. 34.
71. Ibid., para. 43.
72. For similar discrepancies between hearing commissioners, see Jeffrey L. Jowell, *Law and Bureaucracy,* Port Washington, N.Y., Dunellan Publishing Co. (1975), Chapter 6, on the Commissioners of the Massachusetts Commission Against Discrimination.
73. Application E6411, E6422, E7029, E6439; see Appeal Commissioner's Report, 24 May 1968, para. 4 (Mr R.M. Forrest).
74. Ibid., para. 33 (Mr D. Beety).
75. Applications A4532, A4533, 25 June 1965.
76. Ibid., Appeal Commissioners' Report, 10 January 1966, para. 55, see also Appeal A2350/6, A4180, 28 January 1966.
77. Appeal decision A3545, 26 April 1965.
78. ATLB Eleventh Annual Report (1970–71), para. 19.
79. See M.H. Bernstein, *Administrative Regulation Law and Contemporary Problems,* Duke University (Spring 1961), p. 330 (quoted Andrew Shonfield, *Modern Capitalism,* Oxford (1965), p. 321).
80. Standing Committee A (1970–1), Vol. 1, col. 422.
81. See the arguments against ministerial appeals of the (Franks) Committee on *Administrative Tribunals and Enquiries,* Cmnd. 218 (1957), para. 105, and of the Law Reform Commission of Canada's Working Paper 25: *Independent Administrative Agencies,* Ottawa (1980), p. 88.

Chapter 5: Case Law, Rule-making and Justiciability in the ATLB System

1. *Report of the Committee on Administrative Tribunals and Enquiries* (Franks), Cmnd. 218 (1957), p. 9.
2. See G. Marshall, 'Justiciability' in A.G. Guest (ed.), *Oxford Essays in Jurisprudence,* Oxford (1961), esp. pp. 265–69; and R.S. Summers, 'Justiciability' (1963) 26 *M.L.R.,* 530. For a contrast between the traditional concept of adjudication and the 'public law model', see Abram Chayes, 'The Role of the Judge in Public Law Litigation' (1976) 89 *Harv. L. Rev.,* 1281.
3. See R.B. Stevens and B.S. Yamey, *The Restrictive Practices Court,* Weidenfeld and Nicholson, London (1965), p. 41.
4. On rules, principles and policies, see R. Dworkin, *Taking Rights Seriously,* Duckworth (1977), pp. 22–8.
5. Stevens and Yamey, op.cit., p. 140.
6. See *Merchandise Transport Ltd* v. *British Transport Commission* [1961] 3 All

E.R. 495, esp. p. 507, and the *Report of the Committee on Carriers Licensing* (Geddes) (1965).

7. See H.C.Deb., Vol. 618, col. 1231 (Mr Sandys). For a comparison of air and road transport licensing, see Noel W. Ingram, 'The Control of Discretion within a Licensing System: A Case Study of Air Transport Licensing and Road Haulage Licensing in the United Kingdom', Cambridge University Ph.D. Thesis (May 1979).
8. ATLB Annual Report (1961–2), para. 6.
9. On polycentricity, see infra Chapter 10.
10. See Civil Aviation Licensing Regulations 1960 (S.I. 1960 No. 4137), Regs. 10 and 11.
11. ATLB Annual Report (1961–62), para. 8(h).
12. Ibid., para. 8(i).
13. S. Wheatcroft, *Air Transport Policy* (1964), p. 114.
14. ATLB Annual Report (1966–67), para. 8.
15. Cf. Application A4560/3, 22 May 1968.
16. Application A4460, 11 November 1970.
17. Application A4560, 25 August 1965, para. 22.
18. Ibid., para. 22.
19. Ibid., para. 24.
20. Applications A3552/4 and A2430.
21. K.M. Gwilliam, 'The Regulation of Air Transport', *Yorkshire Bulletin of Economic and Social Research* (May 1966), pp. 20–33.
22. S. 2(2)f.
23. See the case of *Robinson* v. *Secretary of State for the Environment* [1973] 3 All E.R. 1045, which held that the Road Traffic Act 1960 did not give licensing authorities power to punish operators.
24. D.J. Gifford, 'Decisions, Decisional Referents and Administrative Justice' (1972) 37 *Law & Cont.* Probs 3.
25. Application A4560, etc., August 1965, paras. 21–2.
26. Ibid., para. 23.
27. Ibid., para. 30 (d).
28. Ibid., para. 34.
29. Ibid., para. 30 (b).
30. Decision A5253, para. 11.
31. Appeals A5253, 4 November.
32. ATLB Annual Report (1962–63); for a similar decision see BAF's application A2341/4, 15 July 1970 (Southend to Rotterdam).
33. See e.g. application A12825, 17 February 1972 (para. 15 (iii)).
34. K.M. Gwilliam, loc.cit., p. 31.
35. Application T. 56, 1967.
36. Commissioner's Report on Appeal T. 56, 8 January 1968, para. 16.
37. Applications T. 171–184, 1971.
38. Appeals T. 171–184, 26 March 1971.
39. Application A4423, 18 November 1964.
40. Application A12612, 9 November 1971.
41. Applications A7147, A7148, etc., 22 April 1968.
42. See Wheatcroft, op.cit., p. 174.
43. Applications B7700, B7666, etc., 5 November 1968.

44. Commissioner's Report on Appeals B7700, etc., 27 March 1969, para. 33.
45. Ibid., para. 55.
46. Commissioner's Report on Appeals B7700, etc., 27 March 1969, para. 65.
47. Appeal Decision letter B7700, etc., 29 April 1969, para. 3.
48. ATLB Annual Report (1968–69), para. 46.
49. Appeal B10092, 19 October 1970.
50. ATLB Annual Report (1970–71), para. 13.
51. Stevens and Yamey, op.cit., p. 140.
52. Summers, loc.cit., pp. 535–7.
53. See ATLB Annual Report (1960–61), para. 6.
54. Application A1048, 9 October 1963, also application E9767, 20 March 1970.
55. Application C8461, 15 September 1971.
56. See e.g. Application B9360, 11 November 1969.
57. E.g. Applications C6492, 2 September 1970; B10143, 22 July 1970; C6770, 28 October 1970. See also ATLB Annual Report (1970–71), para. 14.
58. E.g. Application B9770, etc., 11 March 1970.
59. Appeal decision A300/4, 24 January 1968, para. 10.
60. See Report of the House of Commons Select Committee on the *Nationalized Industries: British European Airways* (1966–7; H.C. 673), Appendix 14(BEA), Q1859 (BUA).
61. See Civil Aviation (Licensing) Regulations 1964 (S.I. 1964, No. 1116), Reg. 10(8).
62. See J.L. Jowell, *Law and Bureaucracy*, Port Washington (1975), Chapter 5; and Marshall, loc.cit., esp., p. 278.
63. Appeal B10153, etc., February 1971.
64. Appeal Commissioner's Report B10153, 5 March 1971.
65. On fairness and consistency in administrative action, see *HTV* v *Price Commission* [1976] I.C.R. 170.
66. See K.C. Davis, *Discretionary Justice*, Baton Rouge (1969).
67. Annual Report (1961–62), para. 8(a).
68. See *supra* Chapter 2, 2.3(d).
69. ATLB 8th Annual Report (1967–68), para. 18.
70. Ibid., para. 20.

Chapter 6: Conclusions: Regulation by Tribunal

1. Regulation 9 dealt with the provision of information relevant to a particular application or objection. Regulation 18 concerned the supply of data relating to the use of those licences or air operator's certificates already held.
2. See ATLB Third Annual Report (1962–63), para. 89.
3. ATLB Second Annual Report (1961–62), para. 21.
4. ATLB Eighth Annual Report (1967–68), para. 89.
5. Ibid., para. 85.

6. ATLB Ninth Annual Report (1968–69), para. 50.
7. ATLB Twelfth Annual Report (1971–72), para. 11.
8. ATLB Fourth Annual Report (1963–64), para. 58.
9. Barry. B. Boyer, 'Alternatives to Administrative Trial-Type Hearings for Resolving Complex Scientific, Economic and Social Issues' (1972) 71 *Mich.L.Rev.* 111. On polycentricity see Chapter 10, infra, and L.L. Fuller, 'The Forms and Limits of Adjudication' (1978–9) 92 *Harv.L.Rev.* 353; J.L. Jowell, 'The Limits of the Public Hearing as a Tool of Public Planning' (1969) 21 *Ad.L.Rev.* 123; D.L. Shapiro, 'The Choice of Rulemaking or Adjudication in the Development of Agency Policy' (1965) 78 *Harv.L.Rev.* 921. G.O. Robinson, 'The Making of Administrative Policy, Another look at Rulemaking and Adjudication and Administrative Procedure Reform' (1970) 118 *U. Pa.L.Rev.* 535–9.

Chapter 7: From Tribunal to Regulatory Agency

1. (1966–67; H.C. 673) (The 1967 Select Committee).
2. 1967 Select Committee, Appendix 14.
3. Ibid., para. 46.
4. Ibid., para. 47.
5. Ibid., Minutes, Q. 1859.
6. Ibid., Q. 1838.
7. Ibid., Q. 1899.
8. Ibid., IV, para. 46.
9. Ibid., para. 23.
10. Ibid., para. 46.
11. Cmnd. 4018 (May 1969), the Edwards Report.
12. Ibid., para. 627.
13. Ibid., para. 629.
14. Ibid., para. 630.
15. Ibid., para. 631.
16. Ibid., para. 639.
17. Ibid., para. 640.
18. Ibid., para. 646.
19. Ibid., para. 648.
20. Ibid., para. 649.
21. Ibid., para. 651.
22. Ibid.
23. Ibid., para. 748.
24. Ibid., para. 654.
25. Ibid., para. 654.
26. The ATLB and the Air Registration Board (ARB) were both independent. In the USA the independent CAB is responsible for economic matters but the departmental Federal Aviation Authority (FAA) is responsible for safety regulation.
27. Edwards, para. 280.
28. Ibid., para. 1002.
29. Ibid., paras. 1020–1.

30. Ibid., para. 1031.
31. See *Report of the Committee on the Civil Service*, Cmnd. 3638 (1966–68), para. 190.
32. Ibid., para. 1034.
33. Ibid.
34. The Committee (para. 1045) did not make a recommendation on whether the Board of Trade or the Ministry of Technology should be the parent department.
35. Ibid., para. 495.
36. Ibid., para. 495.
37. Ibid., para. 403.
38. Ibid., para. 423.
39. Ibid., para. 455.
40. Ibid., para. 613.
41. Ibid., paras. 566–595.
42. Ibid., para. 716.
43. *Civil Aviation Policy*, Cmnd. 4213 (1969).
44. Ibid., para. 8.
45. Ibid., para. 104.
46. ATLB Tenth Annual Report (1969–70), para. 15.
47. Cmnd. 4213 (1969), para. 110.
48. Ibid., para. 120.
49. Ibid., para. 121.
50. Ibid.

Chapter 8: A New Way to Regulate: The CAA is Created

1. See *British Air Transport in the Seventies, Report of the Committee of Inquiry into Civil Air Transport* (Edwards), Cmnd. 4018 (1969) Chapter 8.
2. *Civil Aviation Policy*, Cmnd. 4213 (1969).
3. H.C.Deb., Vol. 798, col. 440 (18 March 1970).
4. H.C.Deb., Vol. 807, col. 257 (25 November 1970).
5. The British Overseas Airways Corporation Order 1971 (S.I. 1971 No. 426).
6. H.C.Deb., Vol. 814, col. 1173 (29 March 1971).
7. Ibid., col. 1174.
8. Ibid. The Council on Tribunals was consulted on this matter, reporting: 'The Department also accepted our view that there should be a general right of appeal to the Secretary of State from decisions of the Authority in air transport licensing applications, and not one strictly limited to the ground that the Authority had failed to comply with the objectives prescribed under section 3'. (Annual Report (1970–71), para. 28).
9. H.C.Deb., Vol. 814, col. 1189.
10. Ibid., col. 1191.
11. Ibid., col. 1190.
12. Ibid., col. 1235.
13. Standing Committee A, 1970–1 (following references will give column number only).

14. Ibid., col. 420.
15. Ibid.
16. Ibid., col. 423.
17. Ibid.
18. Ibid., col. 424.
19. Ibid., col. 430.
20. Ibid., col. 433.
21. Mr Colegate became a full-time member of the Authority in 1974–75.
22. See Select Committee on Nationalized Industries (Sub-Committee A), (1974–5; H.C. 389—iii) ('The 1975 Select Committee'), Q. 127.
23. J. Boyd-Carpenter, *Way of Life,* Sidgwick & Jackson, London (1980), p. 223.
24. Cmnd. 4213 (1972), para. 118.
25. See Civil Aviation (Air Travel Organizers Licensing), Regulation 1972 (No. 223).
26. Largely due to the efforts of Lady Burton of Coventry (see e.g. H.L.Deb., Vol. 344, col. 377, 1820 (5 July 1973; 25 July 1973).
27. See the Counter Inflation (Modification of the Civil Aviation Act 1971) Order 1973 (S.I. 1973 No. 810).
28. S. 24(2) empowered the Secretary of State to order the CAA to delay acting on a matter pending his or her reconsideration of the policy guidance.

Chapter 9: Regulating Under Government Constraint

1. D. Coombes, *Representative Government and Economic Power,* Heinemann (1982), p. 65.
2. Quoted *supra* p. 96
3. Interview, 29 October 1980.
4. *Civil Aviation Policy Guidance,* Cmnd. 4899 (1972) (The first guidance).
5. H.C.Deb., Vol. 833, col. 120.
6. Decision 12825, 17 February 1972.
7. H.C.Deb., Vol. 833, col. 166.
8. Ibid., col. 125.
9. Ibid., col. 146.
10. Ibid., col. 180.
11. First Report of the Select Committee on Nationalized Industries, Session 1975–76, *British Airways: The Merger of BEA and BOAC* (1975; H.C. 56). Minutes para. 128.
12. *Flight International,* April 1972.
13. See CAA Annual Report (1973–4), p. 20.
14. The 'Cannonball' routes. Decision A15250, etc., 17 August 1973.
15. Decisions A15922 and 15923.
16. Lloyds List, 7 April 1975.
17. 'The Statutory Role of the CAA', *Financial Times,* 4 September 1975, in *Aerospace* Suppt. VIII.
18. H.C.Deb., Vol. 271, col. 61.
19. H.C.Deb., Vol. 882, col. 572.

20. 21 March 1975. This was disclosed in response to a Parliamentary Question.
21. Michael Donne, 'Clear Skies after an Aviation Storm', *Financial Times*, 16 February 1976, p. 15.
22. *Financial Times*, 8 July 1975, p. 16; also *Flight International*, 7 August 1975, p. 174. On opening out the guidance process, see Chapter 14, *infra*.
23. H.C.Deb., Vol. 894, cols 7–10 (23 June 1975).
24. H.C.Deb., Vol. 896, col. 1502.
25. H.C.Deb., Vol. 896, col. 1505 (Mr Warren).
26. Ibid., col. 1509. (Mr Tebbit) See also *Flight International*, 7 February 1976, p. 261.
27. See 'Too many direction changes in the air', *Financial Times*, 27 October 1975.
28. See *Flight International*, 7 February 1976, p. 261.
29. B.Cal. was to keep its 'Cannonball' route to Atlanta and Houston (then without traffic rights).
30. I.e., the provision in an air services agreement allowing two operators from a state to operate on a route.
31. H.C.Deb., Vol. 905/6, col. 107 (23 February 1976).
32. J. Boyd-Carpenter, *Way of Life* (1980), p. 239.
33. H.C.Deb., Vol. 906, col. 643.
34. *Laker Airways Skytrain: The Balance of Payments Effects*, Department of Trade (1976)
35. Ibid., para. 11.
36. Application A12449, December 1971 (CALN 553).
37. Decision IB/24214/R, 5 February 1975.
38. Roger Eglin and Berry Ritchie, *Fly Me, I'm Freddie*, Futura (1981), p. 173.
39. H.C.Deb., Vol. 896, col. 504. Mr Shore's policy was based on the confidential policy review document of May 1975. The DoT did produce a public document entitled 'Future Civil Aviation Policy Supplement Material', to accompany the 29 July statement. This booklet was phrased in general terms and did not disclose detailed calculations.
40. *Sunday Times Business News*, 3 August 1975.
41. [1976] 3 W.L.R. p. 561.
42. *Laker Airways* v. *Department of Trade* [1977] 2 WLR 234. For a detailed discussion of the case see G.R. Baldwin, 'A British Independent Regulatory Agency and the 'Skytrain' Decision [1978] *P.L.* 57.
43. Ibid., p. 245.
44. Ibid., p. 248; see Roskill L.J., p. 259.
45. Ibid., p. 260.
46. [1977] 2 WLR 251.
47. Ibid., p. 271.
48. See e.g. Roskill L.J., p. 260 (quoted supra).
49. In this they followed Mr Justice Mocatta's approach. See Hugo Young, 'The Judges begin to fight back', *Sunday Times*, 1 August 1976, p. 12 (on the 'Skytrain' and Tameside decisions) cf. J.A.G. Griffith, 'Power of Judges: Dangerous Tameside precedent', *Sunday Times*, 8 August 1976.
50. H.C.Deb., Vol. 916, col. 1208 (2 August 1976) (Mr Dell).

51. H.C.Deb., Vol. 926, col. 29.
52. H.C.Deb., Vol. 942, col. 70.
53. Decision 1B/24367, etc. (March 1976), para. 4.
54. Decision 1B/24159 etc. (June 1978).
55. Ibid., para. 58.
56. Appeal Decision 1B/24045/2, CAA Official Record (ATLN) 350, part iv.
57. Decision 1B/24412, para. 23.
58. Cmnd. 4899 (1972), para. 17; cmnd. 6400 (1976), para 17.
59. 1972 Regulations, reg. 16(b).
60. ATLB Eleventh Report (1970–71), para. 19.
61. Civil Aviation Authority Regulations 1972 (S.I. 1972 No. 178), reg. 16(7).
62. This did not occur in the period to June 1982 in relation to any appeal.
63. Reproduced in *CAA Official Record* Series 2, No. 467, part 4.2.
64. Appeal letter A6272, 8 December 1972.
65. Appeal 1B/24214—ATLN 40.
66. Appeal 1B/24367—ATLN 328.
67. Appeal A429/1B—ATLN 76.
68. Decision A15250, 17 August 1973.
69. Appeal A15250, 31 December 1973.
70. Appeal 1B/24252—ATLN 161.
71. Appeal 1A/200 14/12—ATLN 202.
72. Appeal 3A/40010—6 April 1976.
73. Appeal 1B/24296—ATLN 267.
74. Appeal 1A/20136—ATLN 279.
75. Appeal 1B/24214/6—ATLN 308.
76. Appeal 4G/67317—ATLN 341.
77. Appeal A6272/4—ATLN 39.
78. Appeals 1B/24323; 1B/24329 etc.—ATLN 322.
79. Appeal 1B/24252—ATLN 161.
80. Appeals 1A/21022, 1A/20123—ATLN 165.
81. Application 1A/20122, 23 September 1975.
82. Appeal 3B/45518—ATLN 258.
83. Between 8 April 1980 and 15 October 1982, 27 appeals were decided, of which 6 resulted in amendment or reversal of a CAA decision.
84. The new s. 23A(1)(a) of the 1971 Act contained in the Civil Aviation Act 1980, replaced the CAA's instructions in paras. 5 and 18 of the respective guidances (to consider traffic rights implications in licensing) with a statutory duty to consider the Secretary of State's advice on this (see now Civil Aviation Act 1982, s. 68(1)(a)). The CAA will not license services that are likely to be inoperable—see applications 3B/45530, 21 December 1971; 1B/24323 etc., 26 October 1977, para. 125.
85. See *Official Record* Series 2, No. 467, part 4.2.
86. J. Boyd-Carpenter, *Way of Life* (1980), p. 240.
87. Application 1B/24367, 5 May 1978.
88. Ibid., para. 36.
89. Ibid.
90. Ibid.

91. Applications 1B/24340 etc., 26 October 1977.
92. Applications 1B/24340 etc., 23 March 1979, para. 45.
93. Ibid.
94. Ibid., para. 50.
95. Interview with Director of Office of International Policy and Programs, Department of Transportation, Washington D.C., 5 October 1982. This view was also expressed to the author by a former General Counsel to the CAB on 6 October 1982.
96. Boyd-Carpenter, op.cit., p. 247. See Edwards, para. 1012.
97. See Christopher McCrudden, 'Anti-Discrimination Goals and the Legal Process' in K. Young and N. Glazer (eds.), *Ethnic Pluralism and Public Policy*, Heinemann (1983).
98. B. Schwartz and H.W.R. Wade, *Legal Control of Government* (1977), pp. 207, 314–23.
99. See *R* v. *Electricity Commissioners* [1924] I K.B. 171; *R* v. *Leg. Committee of the Church Assembly* [1928] I K.B. 411.
100. *Nakkuda Ali* v. *Jayaratne* [1951] A.C. 66.
101. See *Ridge* v. *Baldwin* [1964] A.C. 40, 77–79, 133; *Re H.K. (An Infant)* [1967] 2 Q.B. 617; *R* v. *Gaming Board*, Ex.p. Benaim and Khaida [1970] 2 Q.B. 417.
102. *R* v. *Gaming Board*, Ex.p. Benaim and Khaida [1970] 2 Q.B. 417, 430.
103. [1978] 1 W.L.R. 1521.
104. See the references to *R* v. *Gaming Board*, Ex.p. Benaim and Khaida and to *Re H.K. (An Infant)* in *McInnes* v. *Onslow-Fane* [1978] 1 W.L.R. at 1531–2.
105. For a review, see de Smith's *Judicial Review of Administrative Action*, 4th Edn. by J.M. Evans (1980), pp. 221–5.
106. *R* v. *Gaming Board*, Ex.p. Benaim and Khaida [1970] 2 Q.B. 417; *McInnes* v. *Onslow-Fane* [1978] 1 W.L.R. 1531–2; *R* v. *Liverpool Corporation*, Ex.p. Liverpool Taxi Fleet Operators Association [1972] 2 Q.B. 299; *R* v. *Barnsley M.B.C.*, Ex.p. Hook [1976] 1 W.L.R. 1052; *Laker Airways Ltd.* v. *DoT* [1977] 2 All E.R. 182.
107. See de Smith, op.cit., p. 222.
108. See *infra*, Chapter 10.
109. [1971] A.C. 297.
110. Ibid., p. 308.
111. See de Smith, op.cit., pp. 166–170.
112. *Bushell* v. *Secretary of State for the Environment* [1980] 2 All E.R. 608.
113. See e.g. *Rogers* v. *Secretary of State for the Home Department* [1972] 2 All E.R. 1057; [1973] A.C. 388.
114. *R* v. *Gaming Board*, Ex.p. Benaim and Khaida [1970] 2 Q.B., p. 431.
115. The Civil Aviation Authority Regulations 1972 (No. 178), Reg. 12.
116. See D.J. Galligan, 'The Nature and Function of Policies Within Discretionary Power' [1976], *P.L.* 332.
117. See the judgment of Roskill L.J. in *Laker Airways* v. *DoT* [1977] 2 All E.R. 182 at pp. 195–206.
118. See *Sagnata Investments Ltd.* v. *Norwich Corporation* [1971] 2 Q.B. 614.
119. *British Oxygen Co.* v. *Board of Trade* [1971] A.C. 610.
120. Ibid., also *Merchandise Transport* v. *BTC* [1962] 2 Q.B. 173, *Sagnata*

Investments Ltd. v. *Norwich Corporation* [1971] 2 Q.B. 614; *R.* v. *Rotherham Licensing Justices* [1949] 2 K.B. 710.
121. de Smith, op.cit., p. 182, n. 92.
122. *British Oxygen Co.* v. *Board of Trade* [1971] A.C. p.625.
123. [1972] 2 W.L.R. 1262.
124. Ibid., p. 1268.
125. [1976] I.C.R. 170.
126. Ibid., p. 185.
127. For operation of the policy committees, see *infra*, Chapter 10.
128. *Darlassis* v. *Min. of Education* [1954] 118 J.P. 452, 466; *Denby (William) & Sons Ltd* v. *Min. of Health* [1936] 1 K.B. 337.
129. *R* v. *Stepney Corporation* [1902] 1 K.B. 317; *Lavender (H) Sons* v. *M.H.L.G.* [1970] 1 W.L.R. 1231.
130. See cases cited supra, n. 120.
131. See W. O'Connor, *An Introduction to Airline Economics*, Praeger, New York (1978) for a short account of CAB procedures.
132. See Paul J. Quirk, *Industry Influence in Federal Regulatory Agencies*, Princeton University Press (1981).
133. Interview with author, 1 March 1982.
134. A senior member of the CAA who had served both Labour and Conservative governments opined to the author that both administrations were equally trusting or distrusting of the CAA.
135. Interview with author, 1 March 1982.
136. Cmnd. 4899 (1972), para. 29; Cmnd. 6400 (1976), para. 25.
137. The CAA employs its own auditor as well as reports to the Comptroller and Auditor General.
138. Interview with author, 1 March 1982.
139. Cmnd. 4899 (1972), para. 23; Cmnd. 6400 (1976), para. 18.
140. Interview with author, 1 March 1982.
141. See H.L.Deb., Vol. 369, col. 90 (15 March 1976).
142. H.C.Deb., Vol. 845, col. 131–3.
143. H.C.Deb., Vol. 897, col. 238.
144. *British Airways: The Merger of BEA and BOAC* (1975–6; H.C. 56).
145. (1978–9; H.C. 160–1).
146. (1979; H.L. 235).

Chapter 10: Regulatory Issues and CAA Procedures

1. L.J. Hector 'Problems of the CAB and the Independent Regulatory Commissions'(1960) 69 *Yale L.J.* 931.
2. L.L. Fuller, *The Morality of Law* (1964), p. 33; see also J.L. Jowell, *Law and Bureaucracy*, Port Washington (1975), pp. 151–5; M. Polanyi, *The Logic of Liberty* (1951), pp. 174–84; P. Weiler, 'Two Models of Judicial Decision-making' (1968) *Can. Bar Rev.* 406.
3. L.L. Fuller, 'The Forms and Limits of Adjudication (1978) 92 *Harv. L.Rev.* 353 at p. 400.
4. Ibid., pp. 394–5.
5. K.C. Davis, *Administrative Law Treatise*, 2nd Ed., Vol. 2 (1979), para. 12.2–3.

6. Hector, loc.cit., p. 961.
7. Davis, op.cit., para. 3.15; see also *The President's Advisory Council on Executive Organisation, A New Regulatory Framework: Report on Selected Independent Regulatory Agencies* (1971) 38–39 (The Ash Council Report).
8. See Nathanson, Book Review (1961) 70 *Yale L.J.* 1210.
9. David L. Shapiro, 'The Choice of Rulemaking or Adjudication in the Development of Agency Policy' (1965) 78 *Harv. L.Rev.* 921; G.O. Robinson, 'The Making of Administrative Policy: Another Look at Rulemaking and Adjudication and Administrative Procedure Reform', (1970) 118 *U. of Pa. L.Rev. 485.*
10. Barry B. Boyer, 'Alternatives to Administrative Trial-Type Hearings for Resolving Complex Scientific, Economic and Social Issues' (1972) 71 *Mich. L.Rev.* 111; Clagett, 'Informal Action – Adjudication—Rulemaking: Some Recent Developments in Federal Administrative Law' (1971) *Duke L.J.* 51, 70.
11. Shapiro, loc.cit.
12. Shapiro, loc.cit.
13. Davis, op.cit.; *Discretionary Justice*, Baton Rouge (1969); on Davis's approach see R. Baldwin and K. Hawkins, 'Discretionary Justice: Davis Reconsidered' *P.L.* (forthcoming 1984).
14. Daniel J. Gifford, 'Discretionary Decision-making in the Regulatory Agencies: A Conceptual Framework' (1983) 57 *Southern California L.Rev.* 101; see also K.O. Hawkins and J.M. Thomas (eds.), *Policymaking in Regulation,* (forthcoming 1985) and D.J. Gifford, 'Decisions, Decisional Referents and Administrative Justice' (1972) 3, *Law & Cont. Prob.* 3.
15. Davis, op.cit.; H.J. Friendly, *The Federal Administrative Agencies: The Need for Better Definition of Standards,* Harvard (1962).
16. I.L. Sharfman, *The Interstate Commerce Commission* (1931).
17. Gifford, loc.cit., pp.117–21.
18. Compare Y. Dror, 'Muddling Through—Science or Inertia?' (1964) 24 *Pub. Admin. Rev.* 153 with C.E. Lindblom's defence of 'The Science of Muddling Through' (1959) 19 *Pub. Admin. Rev.* 79.
19. Lindblom, loc.cit., p. 80.
20. Gifford, loc.cit., p.120.
21. See J.M. Landis, 'Report on Regulatory Agencies to the President-Elect' (1960) pp. 41–5; also Fuller, loc.cit. (1978), p. 355.
22. See CAA Annual Report (1974–5), p. 25. On 1 January 1974 the CAA changed the classification of licences that had been used by the ATLB. It introduced seven basic classes of licence divided into sub groups and changed the standard definitions of licences, e.g. the Class 1 schedule licence allowed 50% part charter facility and the Class 3 charter licence allowed 'blanket' authorization, thus ruling out the need for separate applications on each charter route.
23. In pursuance of its powers under s. 21(1) of the 1971 Act.
24. Given in ATL forms 5, 28 and 29.
25. Reg. 7(3).
26. Reg. 4(6).
27. 14 days under Reg. 14(5) and 21 days in the case of unilateral action by the CAA (Reg. 8).

28. ATLN Series 2, No. 466, part 4.2., 6 May 1981.
29. 7(11), 14(5).
30. Edwards, paras. 641–3.
31. An example of the use of pre-hearings in a complex case was given in the 20 March 1974 hearing on the reallocation of 117 scheduled service licences allowing 50 per cent part-charter facility. Two pre-hearings were held to discuss the onus of proof in the case, the order or argument and the use of five 'test cases' to shorten debate.
32. Formal powers exist in s. 35 of the 1971 Act to serve notice on operators to require the submission of information but this section is seldom used.
33. Interview with author, March 1982.
34. Under Reg. 11 of the Civil Aviation Authority Regulations, 1972 (S.I. 1972 No. 178).
35. In complex cases, a month or six weeks is the normal lapse between hearing and decision.
36. Experienced advocates before the CAA and ATLB have told the author that they consider the CAA hearing to be a little more formal than that before the ATLB.
37. For an account of CAB procedures see e.g. W.E. O'Connor, *An Introduction to Airline Economics,* Praeger, New York (1978), Chapter 3.
38. Letter, 2 March 1981.
39. See CAA Official Record Series 2, No. 466, 6 May 1981, p. 10.
40. As required by Reg. 14(10).
41. The negotiation of traffic rights may take place in parallel with the CAA hearing and hearings have been adjourned on occasion to allow clarification of the Traffic Rights position.
42. 1973–4, Report, p. 34.
43. Ibid.
44. Ibid.
45. 1971 Act, s. 5(3).
46. 1972–3 Report, p. 31.
47. 1972–3 Report, p. 32.
48. See e.g. B. Schwartz and H.W.R. Wade, *Legal Control of Government,* Oxford, Clarendon Press (1972), p. 148.
49. These statistics include figures on aircraft used, aircraft hours, revenue loads, revenue passenger analyses and are used by the CAA to calculate the variable charge on licences (a charge per passenger or tonne/kilometer).
50. E.g. the CAA met Donaldson International Airlines in 1973 to discuss the company's fitness and gained an assurance that two aircraft would be sold in order to increase capitalization.
51. 1973–4 Report, p. 26.
52. The Authority receives an operator's annual reports and if dissatisfied with results will call the airline to a meeting.
53. 1974–5 Report, p. 23. Thus when Severn Airways Ltd. applied for a Bristol to Leeds/Bradford scheduled service (Application 1A/20107) the CAA delayed reaching a decision until the company had increased its capitalization. This was done and the licence granted.
54. Due to the fact that s. 22(1) specifies no time limit for the submission of

statistics before hearings, ECS staff often have to press operators to submit them in time. S. 35 could be used to order such information but seldom is, as it requires formal notice from the Authority as opposed to a staff member. As already noted, 25 days notice was demanded administratively in May 1981.

55. A £400 fine is provided by s. 36(3). See Arnold Kean, 'Confidentiality of Civil Aviation Information in the United Kingdom', McGill, *Annals of Air and Space Law* (1976) Vol. 1, 83–96.

56. The Civil Aviation Act 1980 took that decision-making function from the Department and gave it to the CAA.

57. A Secretary to the CAA panel told the author that problems of disclosure arise in about a third of cases going to hearing.

58. Often parts of Domestic Tariff hearings are held in camera when detailed costings are discussed; in other cases in camera hearings have been used where argument was heard on a matter relating to a bilateral agreement (the CAA may not want the foreign government to gain information on UK bilaterals policy).

59. 3A/40010/1; see also the 'Part Charter' case of 9 April 1974.

60. Decision letter, 6 May 1975.

61. See e.g. Tariff hearings of 7, 9 and 14 October 1975, 9 March 1976, 31 March 1976, 1 November 1975, 5 and 6 August 1975.

62. E.g. Tariff decisions of 1 August 1973, 11 March 1975.

63. A party to a case would usually receive another operator's costings in summarized rather than in detailed form.

64. 'B.Cal. expressed concern that few figures on BAED's Shuttle operating costs had been made available at the hearing so it was difficult for them to assess the viability of Shuttle', para. 21 of Decision of 24 March 1975.

65. Decision letter, 6 May 1975, para. 2.

66. Interview with author, February 1983.

67. See Shapiro, loc.cit. (1965).

68. See ATLB Tenth Report (1970; H.C.68, para. 10).

69. Edwards, para. 702.

70. *Flight* Magazine of 27 September 1973 questioned the policy in an article 'Secrecy and the CAA'.

71. See Abram Chayes, 'The Role of the Judge in Public Law Litigation', (1976) 89 *Harv.L.Rev.* 1281; P. Weiler, 'Two Models of Decision Making' (1968) 46 *Can. Bar. Rev.* 406; Jowell, op.cit. (1975), Chap. 5. On the 'transmission-belt' theory of agency discretion see R.B. Stewart, 'The Reformation of American Administrative Law', (1975) 88 *Harv. L.R.* 1667.

72. See Jeffrey L. Jowell, 'The Legal Control of Administrative Discretion' [1973], *P.L.* 178, esp. p. 216 on 'institutionalized access'.

Chapter 11: Discretionary Justice and the Development of Policy.

1. See H.J. Friendly, *The Federal Administrative Agencies: The Need for Better Definition of Standards*, Harvard (1962); also James O. Freedman, *Crisis and Legitimacy*, Cambridge University Press (1978).

2. See e.g. M.H. Bernstein, *Regulating Business by Independent Commission*, Princeton University Press (1955), pp. 74–102.

3. See e.g. R.M. Titmuss, 'Welfare "Rights", Law and Discretion' (1971) 42 *Pol.Q.* 113.

4. See e.g. G. Ganz, 'The Control of Industry by Administrative Process' [1967] *P.L.* 93; B.B. Boyer, 'Alternatives to Administrative Trial-Type Hearings for Resolving Scientific, Economic and Social Issues' (1972) 71, *Michigan L. Rev.* 111; S. Breyer, 'Analysing Regulatory Failure: Mismatches, Less Restrictive Alternatives and Reform' (1979) 92 *Harv. L. Rev.* 547.

5. Interview with author, 1 March 1982.

6. For an assessment of the limitations of administrative principles and standards in agency regulation, see C. Auerbach, 'Some Thoughts on the Hector Memorandum' (1960), *Wis. L.R.* 183 at p. 185. (Reprinted in R.L. Rabin, *Perspectives on the Administrative Process*, Boston, Little Brown (1979)).

7. J.L. Jowell, *Law and Bureaucracy*, Port Washington (1975) p. 134; see also L.L. Fuller, 'The Forms and Limits of Adjudication' (1978–9) 92 *Harv. L.R.* 353.

8. Decision 3B/45521, 2 February 1977.

9. On individuation as recognition of 'a context of continuity' see D.J. Galligan, 'The Nature and Function of Policies within Discretionary Power' [1976] *P.L.* 332, 335.

10. E.g., Decisions B14299, 3 January 1973; 4G/67035, 2 July 1974; 4AX/51307, 14 September 1978; 3B/45526, 8 July 1977; 49Y/68242, 24 August 1978.

11. Decision 3B/45547, 2 November 1978.

12. Decision 3B/45533, 2 February 1978.

13. Decision 3B/45554, 28 September 1978.

14. Decisions 3B/45524, 10 June 1977; 1B/24034/1, 25 November 1977; 4G/67263, 1 November 1977; 4G/67298, 27 January 1978; 3B/45547, 2 November 1978; 1B/24314, 7 March 1979.

15. Decision A4560/9, March 1979.

16. Decisions 5A/70098, 11 August 1978; 4B/53039, 27 January 1978.

17. Decisions 1A/20182/2, 10 October 1978; 1B/24367, 5 May 1978.

18. Decision 1B/24417, 8 August 1979.

19. Decision on Class 1B Applications to operate schedule services between Gatwick and various European destinations, 26 October 1977.

20. Civil Aviation Authority Statement on Air Transport Licensing Policies, 27 November 1979.

21. Decisions 1B/24340, etc., of 20 April 1979; 1A/20241, 7 August 1979.

22. Decision A15922, 4 December 1973.

23. Decision A429/18. See CAA Annual Report (1973–4), p. 20.

24. Application 2/30022.

25. Decision A12967/1, October 1972.

26. Decision A14011.

27. A14011, 26 September 1972.

28. Decision 1B/24214/R.

29. Decisions 1B/24367, 5 May 1978; 1B/24159/3, 11 August 1978;

1B/24412, 29 May 1979—for details see Chapter 9.

30. Decision 1B/24412, 29 May 1979, para. 23.

31. Decision 1B/24367, 5 May 1978, para. 34. See also Decision 1B/24429, 17 March 1980.

32. Ibid.

33. Decision 1B/24429.

34. Decision 1B/24240. See also decisions A14180, September 1972; A9643, 3 October 1972.

35. Decision A15922.

36. Decision 1A/20122, 8 August 1974 (and 23 September 1975 on re-hearing after appeal).

37. Decision 1B/24252, etc. See also CAA letter to the Secretary of State, 21 October 1974, para. 6.

38. Decision 1A/20107, 3 December 1974, para. 38. See also Derision A/15946, 10 October 1973.

39. Decision 1A/20114; 1A/20115, 10 July 1974.

40. Decision 1A/20114.

41. Decision 1A/20116, 7 November 1974.

42. Decisions C12884 and C12885.

43. Decision 49X/68066.

44. Decision 1A/20124, August 1974.

45. Decision 1A/20136.

46. Decision 1B/24084/1.

47. Decision 1B/24084.

48. On the gearing of adjudication to individual instances rather than planning, see Jowell, loc.cit., pp. 198–200; Shapiro, loc.cit.

49. ATLN, No. 207, pt. 4.

50. Ibid., para. 2.

51. A piece of rule-making likely to meet the approval of at least one commentator—see K.C. Davis, *Discretionary Justice*, Baton Rouge (1969), Chapter 4.

52. See ATLN, No. 316, 23 May 1978.

53. Decision 1A/20000/13.

54. Decision 1A/20161, 24 January 1977. See also decisions 1A/20180, 21 September 1977 and 1A/20260, 26 July 1978.

55. Decision 1A/20184.

56. Decision 1A/20164, etc., 10 April 1978.

57. Decision 1A/20197, etc., 9 October 1978, para. 37.

58. See e.g. Decisions 1A/20204, 10 October 1978; 1A/20182/2, 10 October 1978; 1B/24313/1, 23 November 1978; 1A/20223, 24 November 1978; 1B/24374, 7 March 1979; 1B/24409, 18 May 1979.

59. Decision 1B/24393.

60. Ibid., para. 23.

61. See e.g. Decision 1A/20212, 5 January 1979; 1B/24389, 6 June 1979.

62. See e.g. Decision 1B/24389, 6 June 1979. For a comparative view of CAA and IBA reasons for decision see Norman Lewis, 'IBA Programmed Contract Awards' [1975] P.L. 317.

63. CAP, 420 (1979).

64. Ibid., para. 1.4.

65. Ibid., para. 3.33.
66. Ibid., para. 5.1.
67. Ibid.
68. Ibid., para. 4.3.
69. See Decisions 1B/24340, 23 March 1979; 1A/20230, 13 June 1979; and 1A/20241, 7 August 1979.
70. Decision 3B/45557, 1 March 1979, para. 18.
71. Decision 3B/45560, 2 April 1979, para. 13.
72. Decisions 1A/20230, 13 June 1979; 1B/24409, 18 May 1979.
73. Decision 1A/20238, 29 July, 1979.
74. See second guidance, cmnd. 6400 (1976), para. 14. The Civil Aviation Act 1982, s. 68(1)(b) refers simply to 'the effective use of airports'.
75. See e.g. Decision A/15940, 18 September 1973.
76. E.g. 'The Development of the UK Airport System' (CAP 372); 'Airport Development in the Central England Area' (CAP 373); 'Airport Planning: an approach on a National Basis'.
77. See e.g. Decision 1B/24283, 14 January 1976.
78. H.C.Deb., Vol. 929, col. 392.
79. Decision on Class 1B Applications to Operate Scheduled Services between Gatwick and various European Destinations, 26 October 1977.
80. Ibid., para. 118.
81. See Decisions 1B/24340, etc., 20 April 1979; 1A/20241, 7 August 1979 and 1B/24417, 7 August 1979.
82. 'Airports Policy', Cmnd 7084.
83. Decision 1B/24340.
84. Ibid., para. 65.
85. Ibid.
86. Decision 1A/20241, 7 August 1979.
87. Ibid., para. 63.
88. Decision 1B/24417, etc., 8 August 1979.
89. Ibid., para. 82.
90. Decisions 1B/24340, 20 April 1979; 1A/20241, 7 August 1979.
91. CAA Annual Report (1972–3), p. 11.
92. Ibid.
93. CAA Annual Report (1972–3), p. 32.
94. Decisions 2/15228, and 3/15852.
95. E.g. Decision 2/30022, 22 May 1975.
96. Ibid.
97. Edwards, paras. 704–719, 750.
98. First guidance, para. 7, second guidance, para. 1.
99. See Decision C12382; see also Decisions C12884, 16 March 1973; C14299, 3 January 1973.
100. See Decision C10456, 18 July 1972.
101. Decisions B15107, 27 September 1972; and C13043, 14 April 1973.
102. See e.g. Decision 3B/45549, 16 February 1979.
103. Decision 3A/40010/1, 10 September 1975.
104. ATLN 209, pt. 4.4.
105. Decision on 117 Class 1B applications, 9 April 1974.
106. In accordance with Reg. 8(1)(c) and 9(1), 1972.

107. Decision on proposals by the Civil Aviation Authority to amend the Authority's official record series 1 in respect of the conditions governing the carriage of inclusive tour passengers, 2 December 1976, 10 January 1977.
108. CAA Annual Report (1975–6), p. 22.
109. 'European Air Fares' (CAP 409), p. 23.
110. Ibid.
111. See 'European Air Fares', CAP 409.
112. On the managerial as opposed to adjudicative method of licensing see L.J. Hector, 'Problems of the CAB and the Independent Regulatory Commissions' (1960) 69 *Yale L.J.* 931 esp. pp. 932–3, for comments see Boyer, loc.cit., pp. 150–70; and Auerbach, loc.cit.
113. Cmnd. 4018, paras. 742–3.
114. See e.g. Decisions E9486/1, 25 March 1970; E11022/4; and E12518, 30 November 1971.
115. Decision E12530/5, 24 October 1972.
116. Decision 6A/8006.
117. See also CAA Annual Report (1973–4), pp. 22, 32.
118. Under s. 36 of the Act.
119. Decision Class 6A licence, 12 March 1975, para. 2.
120. CAP 379.
121. Ibid., p. 16.
122. *Airtrade,* October 1975.
123. See ATLN No. 203, 24 February 1976, p. 15.
124. ATLN No. 255, pt. 4.2.
125. ATLN No. 270, pt. 4.2.
126. CAP, 405.
127. Decision on Applications for Class 6A (General) etc., licences, 30 December 1977.
128. Decision 5A/70096, etc., 4 July 1978.
129. Decision 5A/70098, etc., 11 August 1978; para. 20.
130. R.B. Stevens and B.S. Yamey, *The Restrictive Practices Court,* London (1965), e.g. p. 140; see also the Confederation of British Industry's criticisms of the RPC, in J.A. Farmer, *Tribunals and Government,* Weidenfeld and Nicholson (1974), pp. 31–2.
131. See D.J. Gifford, 'Decisions, Decisional Referents and Administrative Justice' (1972) 37 *Law and Cont. Prob.* 3.
132. Jowell, op.cit. (1975), p. 153.
133. Ibid., p. 154.
134. See P. Weiler, 'Two Models of Judicial Decisionmaking' (1968) *Can. Bar Rev.* 406 at 423–5.
135. Gifford, loc.cit.
136. Interview with author, February 1982.
137. For discussion of legally controlled discretions in relation to particular topics, see e.g. R. Titmuss, 'Welfare "Rights", Law and Discretion' (1971) 42 *Pol.Q.* 113; Stevens and Yamey, op.cit.; G. Ganz, 'The Control of Industry by Administrative Process' [1967], *P.L.* 93.
138. Interview with author, February 1982.
139. Interview with author, 1 March 1982.

140. Jeffrey L. Jowell, 'The Legal Control of Administrative Discretion' [1973], *P.L.* 178 at 183.

141. Davis, op.cit. (1969), p. 232.

142. Ibid., pp. 99–111, 226.

143. See E. Gellhorn, and Glen O. Robinson, 'Perspectives on Administrative Law' (1975) 75 *Col. L.R.* 771.

144. See M. Adler and A. Bradley (eds.), *Justice, Discretion and Poverty* (1976).

145. On processing by legal rules, see J. Bradshaw, 'From Discretion to Rules: The Experience of the Family Fund' in *Discretion and Welfare*, M. Adler and S. Asquith (1981), Heinemann. For an examination of reasons not to control discretion see R. Baldwin and K. Hawkins, 'Discretionary Justice: Davis Reconsidered' *P.L.* (forthcoming 1984).

146. See e.g. the treatment of tribunals as bodies with homogeneous needs in the Justice/All Souls Review of Administrative Law in the UK (1981); for comment, see R. Austin and D. Oliver (1981) *P.L.* at 441–52.

147. See G.O. Robinson, 'The Making of Administrative Policy: Another Look at Rulemaking and Adjudication and Administrative Procedure Reform' (1970) 118 *U. Pa. L. Rev.* 485, pp. 535–9; Baldwin and Hawkins loc.cit.

148. ABA 'Federal Regulation: Roads to Reform' (1979), p. 92.

149. Davis, op.cit. (1969), pp. 5–6.

150. Ibid., p. 216.

151. Ibid., p. 221.

152. See e.g. J.T. Winkler, 'The Political Economy of Administrative Discretion', in M. Adler and S. Asquith (eds.), op.cit.

153. D.J. Gifford, 'Decisions, Decisional Referents and Administrative Justice' (1972) 37 *Law and Cont. Prob.* 3.

154. Ibid., p. 12. But see: Colin S. Diver, 'The Optimal Precision of Administrative Rules' (1983) 93 *Yale L.J.* 65.

155. Ibid., p. 12.

156. On the problems of rapidly changing circumstances, see Jowell, op.cit. (1975), p. 135.

157. On principles as supportive of rules, see R. Dworkin, 'The Model of Rules' (1967) 35 *U. Ch. L.Rev.* 14; R. Hughes, 'Rules, Policy and Decisionmaking' (1968) 77 *Yale L.J.* 44; and Galligan, loc.cit.

158. Charles E. Lindblom, 'The Science of Muddling Through' (1959) 19 *Pub. Admin. Rev.* 79.

159. See Y. Dror, 'Muddling Through—Science or Inertia?' (1964) 24 *Pub. Admin. Rev.* 153. Dror argues that the Lindblom approach presupposes the generally satisfactory nature of present policies, the absence of a need for radical change and continuity in both problems and the available means for dealing with them.

Chapter 12: Regulatory Performance and the CAA

1. Civil Aviation Act 1971, s. 3(1); see now Civil Aviation Act 1982, s.4(1).

2. The Civil Aviation Act 1980 (s. 12), also imposed a duty to impose 'minimum restrictions' on the industry (see now Civil Aviation Act 1982, s.68).
3. (1980–1; H.C.4341), para. 13.
4. Airline Deregulation Act 1978, see Sub-Committee on Administrative Practice and Procedure, Committee on the Judiciary; US Senate, Civil Aeronautics Board Practices and Procedures, Report 1975. For an early view on airline deregulation, see Richard E. Caves, *Air Transport and its Regulators: An Industry Study,* Harvard (1962).
5. George Stigler, 'The Theory of Economic Regulation', *Bell Journal of Economics Management Science 2* (Spring 1971); Stigler, *The Citizen and the State: Essays on Regulation,* Chicago (1975); Milton Friedman, *There's no such thing as a Free Lunch,* Open Court Press (1975); M. Bruce Johnson (ed.) *The Attack on Corporate America,* New York, McGraw Hill (1978). See also Gabriel Kolko, *The Triumph of Conservatism,* Quadrangle (1963); G. Kolko, *Railroads and Regulation,* Princeton University Press (1965).
6. ABA Commission on Law and the Economy, *Federal Regulation: Roads to Reform* (1979).
7. Washington DC, Brookings Institute (1970).
8. See e.g. Report of the White House Task Force on Antitrust Policy; Congressional Record, Vol. 115, pt. 11, 91st Cong. 1st Sess. 1969; Report of the US Task Force on Productivity and Competition; Congressional Record, Vol. 115, pt. 12, 91st Cong. 1st Sess. 1969.
9. See e.g. Charles L. Schultz, *The Public Use of Private Interest* Washington DC, Brookings Institute (1977); S. Breyer, 'Analyzing Regulatory Failure; Mismatches, Less Restrictive Alternatives and Reform' (1979) 92, *Harv. L.Rev.* 547; S. Breyer, *Regulation and Its Reform,* Harvard (1982); T.B. Clark, M.H. Kosters and J.C. Miller III (eds) *Reforming Regulation,* American Enterprise Institute (1980); LeRoy Gramer and Frederick Thompson (eds.) *Reforming Social Regulation,* Sage, Beverly Hills (1982). *The American Enterprise Institute Journal,* 'Regulation', offers a regular supply of articles urging drastic deregulation.
10. See W.A. Jordan, *Airline Regulation in America,* Johns Hopkins (1970).
11. CAP 420; see pp. 6–10. See also Stephen Shaw, *Air Transport: A Marketing Perspective,* Pitman (1982), Chapter 4.
12. CAP 420, para. 3.33.
13. CAP 420, para. 4.3.
14. Ibid., para. 5.1.
15. See CAA Annual Report (1976–7), p. 3.
16. Interview with author, 1 March 1982.
17. CAP 420, para. 4.44.
18. 'European Air Fares', CAP 409, para. 5.7.
19. Ibid., para. 2.12.
20. (1979–80; H.L. 235) paras. 64–79; and (1980–1; H.C. 431).
21. CAP., para. 2.1.
22. See Final Report of the Attorney General's Committee on Administrative Procedure, Administrative Procedure in Government Agencies, Senate Doct. No. 8, 77th Cong., 1st Sess., 1941.
23. E.g., Breyer, loc.cit. op.cit.; R. B. Stewart, 'Regulation, Innovation

and Administrative Law: A Conceptual Framework' (1981) *Calif. L.Rev.* 1256, 1277–1311.

24. See Decision 1B/24252, 11 July 1974.
25. Decision 1A/20241, 7 August 1979; see also Decision 1A/20136, 29 January 1975.
26. See Decision 1B/24252, 11 July 1974 (Birmingham-Copenhagen); Decision 1A/20107, 3 December 1974; Decision 1A/15946, 10 October 1973.
27. CAP 409, February 1979; see especially Appendix 7.
28. Ibid., paras. 7 and 8.
29. See evidence to House of Lords European Communities Committee (1979–80, H.L. 235) p. 32.
30. E.g., Decision A16018, 7 November 1973.
31. See e.g. Decisions 1A/20135 and 1A/20137, January 1975.
32. E.g., in Decisions 1A/20147/1, 31 March 1976; 1A/20186 etc., 31 January 1978; 1B/24393, 21 February 1979. In August 1975 the CAA refused B.Cal's request to impose a premium fare on BA's London-Glasgow service but suggested that B.Cal. might seek a discount fare for themselves (Decision 1A/20014/12, 14 August 1975).
33. CAA Annual Report (1972–3), p. 25.
34. A scheduled equivalent to the ABC fare.
35. Allowed on the Glasgow route in 1975: licence 1A/20014.
36. L.J. Hector, 'Problems of the CAB and the Independent Regulatory Commissions' (1960) 69 *Yale L.J.* 931.
37. Edwards, para., 632.
38. H. Friendly, *The Federal Administrative Agencies, The Need for Better Definition of Standards,* Harvard (1962).
39. T.J. Lowi, *The End of Liberalism,* Norton (1969).
40. Friendly, op.cit., p. 6.
41. See J. Dickinson, *Administrative Justice and the Supremacy of Law in the United States,* Cambridge, Mass. (1927), pp. 215–16.
42. L.L. Fuller, *The Morality of Law,* Yale (1964), p. 46.
43. Ibid., p. 173; see Barry B. Boyer, 'Alternatives to Administrative Trial-Type Hearings for Resolving Complex Scientific, Economic and Social Issues' (1972) 71 *Mich. L.Rev.* 111; J.L. Jowell, 'The Limits of the Public Hearing as a Tool of Public Planning' (1969) 21 *Ad. L. Rev.* 123.
44. Friendly, op.cit., p. 145.
45. K.C. Davis, *Discretionary Justice,* Baton Rouge (1969), p.33; for the extravagant view see Franks (1957); Dickinson (1927); Dicey (1968); Hayek (1944).
46. Davis, op.cit., p. 59.
47. Ibid., p. 65.
48. Boyer, loc.cit., p. 124.
49. P. Nonet, *Administrative Justice,* New York, Russell Sage (1969), esp. Chapters 6 and 7; see also T. Lowi, op.cit.
50. Ibid., p. 170.
51. *Merchandise Transport Ltd* v. *BTC* [1961], 3 All E.R. 495 at 507. See Galligan, loc.cit.
52. On life cycles, see pp. 231–5. For a review of life cycle theories, see

Barry M. Mitnick, *The Political Economy of Regulation*, Columbia University Press (1980), pp. 34–78.

53. For a contrast in formal and informal rule-making, see the comparison of American and Swedish procedures in Kelman, *Regulating America Regulating Sweden*, Cambridge, Mass., MIT Press (1971).

54. See R. Noll, 'The Behaviour of Regulatory Agencies' (March 1971) Review of Social Economy 19, pp. 15–19; and *Reforming Regulation: An Evaluation of the Ash Council Proposals*, Washington DC, Brookings Institute (1971).

55. In the case of the Commission for Racial Equality it has been argued that judicial review already has considerable influence on agency regulation. See Christopher McCrudden, 'Anti-Discrimination Goals and the Legal Process' in K. Young and N. Glazer (Eds.) *Ethnic Pluralism and Public Policy*, Heinemann (1983).

56. See e.g. Paul J. Quirk, *Industry Influence in Federal Regulatory Agencies*, Princeton (1981); Stigler, loc.cit.; Kolko, op.cit.; Louis Kohlmeir, *The Regulators*, Harper and Row (1969); Marver H. Bernstein, *Regulating Business by Independent Commission*, Princeton (1955); Edward S. Greenberg, *Serving the Few: Corporate Capitalism and the Bias of Government Policy*, Wiley (1974); Jordan, op.cit.; Paul W. MacAvoy, (ed.) *The Crisis of the Regulatory Commissions*, Norton (1970); James Q. Wilson, 'The Dead Hand of Regulation' (1971) *Public Interest* No. 25, p. 39; US Senate, Committee on Governmental Affairs, *Study on Federal Regulation*, (1977–78), Vols. 1–6, 95th and 96th Cong.

57. For general reviews, see James Q. Wilson (ed.) *The Politics of Regulation*, Basic Books (1980); and Mitnick, op.cit.

58. Quirk, op.cit., p. 4.

59. See e.g. Murray L. Wiedenbaum, *The High Cost of Government Regulation*, Challenge (Nov./Dec. 1979), pp. 32–9.

60. Bernstein, op.cit.

61. Gabriel Kolko, op.cit. and *Railroads and Regulation*, Princeton University Press (1965); George Stigler, loc.cit. *The Citizen and the State: Essays on Regulation*, University of Chicago (1975); see also Alfred E. Kahn, 'The Political Feasibility of Regulatory Reform', in Grayner and Thompson (eds.), op.cit.

62. See e.g. Royal Commission on Transport 1929–30, Cmd. 3365, 3416, 3751.

63. Civil Aviation Act 1971, s. 3; now Civil Aviation Act 1982, s. 4.

64. Quirk, op.cit., Chapters 1 and 2.

65. AUC Annual Report (1973–4), p. 6.

66. AUC Annual Report (1974–5), p. 6.

67. AUC Annual Report (1973–4), p. 6.

68. AUC Annual Report (1977–8), p. 17; see also CAA Annual Report (1977–8), p. 4.

69. In the USA several agencies have established offices of 'public counsel' to increase consumer representation. See Quirk, op.cit., Chapter 1.

70. See CAA evidence to the H.C. Industry and Trade Committee (1980–1; H.C. 431–2), Q. 192.

71. (1979–80; H.L. 235) p.71. S. 36 of the 1971 Act demanded that no

information concerning particular persons and given to the CAA shall be disclosed by the CAA without permission (see now 1982 Act, s. 23).

72. For details, see Quirk, op.cit., Chapter 3; also Bernstein, op.cit., p. 82; Kohlmeir, op.cit., p. 484; US Senate, Committee on Governmental Affairs, *Study on Federal Regulation*, Vol. 1, *The Regulatory Appointment Process*, 95th and 96th Cong. (1977–8), p. 157.

73. J. Boyd-Carpenter, 'Where is UK Civil Aviation Going?', 32nd Brancker Memorial Lecture, London (1975).

74. S. 12 of the Civil Aviation Act 1980 instructed the CAA to impose 'minimum restrictions' on the industry (see 1982 Act, s. 68(4)).

75. *European Air Fares* (1979–80; H.L. 235).

76. Decision of 13 March 1980, on applications from British Caledonian, Laker, Britannia and Air UK; Decision 1B/24431, etc.

77. (1979–80; H.L. 235) p. xiv.

78. Ibid., p. 17.

79. Ibid., para. 69.

80. See 5th Report of the House of Commons Industry and Trade Committee, *European Air Fares* (1980–1; H.C. 431–41), Vol. II, Q. 16–30.

81. Ibid., Q. 160.

82. Ibid., Vol. I, para. 8.

83. Ibid., para. 13.

84. Ibid., Vol. II, Q. 159.

85. (1980–1; H.C. 431–1) p.34.

86. 1979–80; H.L. 235, Q. 97.

87. See e.g., Noll, op.cit.

88. H. Morrison, *Socialization and Transport*, London (1933).

89. See e.g. J.M. Landis, *The Administrative Process*, New Haven, Yale University Press (1938).

90. The President's Committee on Administrative Management, Report of the Committee with Studies of Administrative Management in the Federal Government, Washington DC, GPO (1937), ('The Brownlow Committee'). On 'crisis' in the agencies, see J.Q. Freedman, *Crisis and Legitimacy*, Cambridge University Press (1978), Chapter 1; Bernstein, op.cit.; see also Roger G. Noll, *et al*, *Economic Aspects of Television Regulation*, (Brookings) (1973). Cf. Freedman, op.cit., Chapter 5.

91. 'Politics, Personalities and the Federal Trade Commission', (1934) *American Political Science Rev.* 28, 1016.

92. 'The Independent Regulatory Agency—A New Scapegoat' (1956) 65 Yale L.J. 1068.

93. Bernstein, op.cit., pp. 284–5.

94. Ibid.

95. Ibid., pp. 74–91.

96. L. Brownlow's phrase—see Bernstein, op.cit., p. 92. For other concepts of agency senescence, see the 'arteriosclerosis' theory of L.L. Jaffe in 'The Effective Limits of the Administrative Process: A Re-evaluation' (1954) 67 *Harv. L.Rev.* 1105–35; W.L. Cary, *Politics and the Regulatory Agencies*, New York, McGraw Hill (1967), p. 67 ('hardening of the arteries'); Mitnick, op.cit., p. 45.

97. Interview, 30 October 1980.
98. Freedman, op.cit., p. 11.
99. Ibid., Chapter 2.
100. See e.g. P. Holland, *Quango, Quango, Quango*, London, Adam Smith Institute (1979), *Costing the Quangos,*, London, Adam Smith Institute (1980); and P. Holland and M. Fallon, *The Quango Explosion: Public Bodies and Ministerial Patronage*, London, Conservative Political Centre (1978).

Chapter 13: Freeing the Quango

1. H.C Deb., Vol. 814, col. 1173 (29 March 1971).
2. Decision 1B/24367 ('Skytrain' to Los Angeles), March 1978; 1B/24159, etc. (Dallas and Fort Worth), June 1978; 1B/24412 (Tradewinds Airways), April 1979.
3. E.g. para. 14 on airports policy.
4. Decision 1A/20230, 13 June 1979, para. 14; Decision 1B/24409, 18 May 1979, para. 25.
5. Decision 1A/20237, 29 July 1979, para. 84.
6. See *infra*. p. 244.
7. Decisions 1B/24340, etc., 20 April 1979, and 1A/20241, 7 August 1979.
8. On agency avoidance of judicial review, see Roger Noll, 'The Economics and Politics of Regulation' (1971) 57 *Va.L.Rev.* 1016.
9. H.C.Deb., Vol. 973, col. 45.
10. Ibid., col. 48.
11. Ibid.
12. Civil Aviation Bill, Clause 11(5); see now Civil Aviation Act 1982, s.68(i). Though the substance and priorities of the CAA's statutory objectives were changed, such provisions did not alter the nature of the objectives as devices of control. They remained a list of generally stated (and to some extent inconsistent) ends to be sought in licensing.
13. H.C.Deb., Vol. 973, col. 50.
14. Ibid., col. 61.
15. Ibid.
16. Ibid.
17. Ibid., col. 15.
18. Ibid., col. 51. No attempt was made to justify abolition of guidance in terms of economies in staffing the Department or CAA. The staffing implications of abolition appear negligible: see HC Standing Committee B. col. 684 (Mr Tebbit) 26 February 1980.
19. Ibid., col. 82.
20. Ibid., col. 156.
21. CAP 409 (1977).
22. See now, CAA Statement of Policies on Air Transport Licensing, CAP 444 (1981).
23. These terms are used per K.C. Davis, *Discretionary Justice*, Baton Rouge (1969).
24. In law the agency might structure its discretion but it must not fetter

this. There would be no objection to statements setting out criteria, principles and policies provided always that there is room for exceptions and the consideration of each case on its merits. See *Merchandise Transport Ltd* v. *B.T.C.* [1962] 2 Q.B. 173.

25. H.C.Deb., Vol. 973, col. 61 (Mr Smith).
26. Cmnd. 6400 (1976), Part 1, para. 3.
27. See CAA Annual Report (1976–77), p. 3.
28. 'Air Freight Policy', CAP 405 (1977), para. 79.
29. CAP 420 (1979).
30. Ibid., para. 3.33.
31. Ibid., para. 43.
32. H.C.Deb., Vol. 973, col. 45.
33. See e.g. P. Holland, *Costing the Quangos*, London, Adam Smith Institute (1980).
34. See K.C. Davis, op. cit., Chapter 2, p. 50: '. . . the emphasis should not be on legislative clarification of standards but on administrative clarification, because that is where the hope lies'.
35. H.C.Deb., Vol. 973, col. 47.
36. H.L.Deb., Vol. 413, col. 2068.
37. Interview with author, February 1983.
38. H.C.Deb., Vol. 973, col. 47.
39. See S.F. Wheatcroft, *Air Transport Policy* (1964), p. 165.
40. H.C.Deb., Vol. 973, col. 46.
41. The Conservative government issued four such directions to the CAA between April 1979 and June 1981. Only one direction had previously been issued in the CAA's lifetime. If the revived use of such directions indicated anything it might be that the DoT no longer saw direction or interference with the CAA as an extreme course of action.
42. For indirect discussions of CAA activities see the House of Commons Industry and Trade Committee Report, 'European Air Fares' (1980–1; H.C. 431–41; House of Lords Select Committee on the European Committees: 'European Air Fares' (1979–80; H.L. 235); and H.C. Select Committee on Nationalized Industries: British Airways (1974–75; H.C. 389).
43. See R.E. Cushman, The *Independent Regulatory Commissions,* Oxford University Press (1941); M.H. Bernstein, *Regulating Business by Independent Commissions,* Princeton University Press (1955), pp. 74–91.
44. See L.J. Hector, 'Problems of the CAB and the Independent Regulatory Commissions' (1960) *69 Yale L.J.* 931; Bernstein, op.cit., pp. 284–5; J.M. Landis, *The Administrative Process,* 2nd edn., Yale University Press (1966); Mitnick, op.cit., pp. 69–71.

Chapter 14: Regulation by Agency: Unaccountable or Efficient Government?

1. For a review see C. Byse, 'Comments on a Structural Reform proposal: Presidential Directives to Independent Agencies' (1977) 29 *Admin. L.Rev.* 157.

2. *The Independent Regulatory Commissions* (1941), p. 730.

3. 'The Independent Regulatory Agency—A New Scapegoat' (1956) 65 *Yale L.J.* 1068.

4. J.M. Landis, US Congress, Senate, Committee on the Judiciary 'Report on Regulatory Agencies to the President-Elect' (1960) (Committee Print), 86th Cong., 2nd sess.; but cf. L.L. Jaffe, 'James Landis and the Administrative Process' (1964) 78 *Harv. L.Rev.* 319–28.

5. E.S. Redford, 'The President and the Regulatory Commissions', Report to the President's Advisory Committee on Government Organization (1960); also (1965) 44 *Texas L.Rev.* 288.

6. L.J. Hector, 'Problems of the CAB and the Independent Regulatory Commission' (1960) 69 *Yale L.J.* 931.

7. L.L. Fuller, *The Morality of Law* (1966);

8. H. Friendly, *The Federal Administrative Agencies: The Need for Better Definition of Standards,* Harvard (1962), p. 153.

9. See e.g. K.C. Davis, *Administrative Law of the Seventies* (1976).

10. T.J. Lowi, *The End of Liberalism,* New York, Norton (1969).

11. The President's Advisory Council on Executive Reorganization, *A New Regulatory Framework: Report on Selected Independent Regulatory Agencies,* Washington D.C. (1971). For a review see Glen O. Robinson, 'On Reorganising the Independent Regulatory Agencies', (1971) 57 *Va. L.Rev.* 947.

12. Lloyd N. Cutler and David R. Johnson, 'Regulation and the Political Process' (1975) 84 *Yale L.J.* 1395. See also Glen O. Robinson, 'The Federal Communications Commission, An Essay on Regulatory Watchdogs' (1978) 64 *Va. L.Rev.* 169; Committee on Governmental Affairs, V.S. Senate, *Study on Federal Regulation* (January 1977) Vol. 1., 95th Congress, 1st sess. (The Ribicoff Report). On congressional veto as opposed to presidential direction or review see Harold H. Bruff and Ernest Gellhorn, 'Congressional Control of Administrative Regulation: A Study of Legislative Vetoes' (1977) 90 *Harv. L.Rev.* 1369.

13. American Bar Association. Commission on Law and the Economy, *Federal Regulation: Roads to Reform* (1979). But cf. Note: 'Delegation and Regulatory Reform: Letting the President Change the Rules' (1980) 89 *Yale L.J.* 561.

14. Harold H. Bruff, 'Presidential Power and Administrative Rulemaking' (1979) 88 *Yale L.J.* 451.

15. But on White House thwarting of regulation see Robert A. Katzmann, *Regulatory Bureaucracy,* M.I.T. Press (1980), pp. 196–7.

16. For details see George Eads, 'Harnessing Regulation', *Regulation,* May/June 1981, p. 19; G.R. Baldwin and C.G. Veljanovski, 'Regulation by Cost-Benefit Analysis' *Public Administration* 1984.

17. See H.N. Janisch, 'The Role of the Independent Regulatory Agency in Canada' (1978) *UNB L.J.* 27, 83 (1978); also 'Policy-Making in Regulation: Towards a New Definition of the Status of Independent Regulatory Agencies in Canada' (1979) *Osgoode Hall L.J.* 17, 46.

18. Royal Commission on Financial Management and Accountability Final Report (1979).

19. Law Reform Commission of Canada Working Paper 25, 'Independent

Administrative Agencies', Ontario (1980), p. 85. But cf. Lucinda Vandervort, 'Political Control of Independent Administrative Agencies', Law Reform Commission of Canada (1979), pp. 141–9.

20. Ibid., p. 85.
21. See e.g. 'Nationalised Industries. A Review of Economic and Financial Objectives' (1967) Cmnd. 3437.
22. See Report of the Select Committee on Nationalized Industries, Ministerial Control of the Nationalized Industries (1967–8; H.C. 371, i).
23. See National Economic Development Office, 'A Study of UK Nationalised Industries', NEDO, London (1976).
24. 'The Nationalised Industries', Cmnd. 7131 (1978).
25. Cf. Glen O. Robinson, loc.cit. (1978).
26. See N. Johnson, 'Accountability, control and complexity: moving beyond ministerial responsibility', in A. Barker (Ed.), *Quangos in Britain* (1982).
27. On 'hair-trigger unconstitutionality' see Antonin Scalia, 'The Legislative Veto: A False Remedy for System Overload', *Regulation*, (November/ December 1979), p. 19; James V. DeLong, 'Informal Rulemaking and the Integration of Law and Policy' (1979) 65 *Va. L.Rev.* 257. For powers insulating a commission from legal attack see C.C. Johnson, 'The Canadian Radio-Television and Telecommunications Commission', Law Reform Commission of Canada (1980), p. 21.
28. R.B. Stewart, 'The Reformation of American Administrative Law' (1975) 88 *Harv. L.R.* 1667, 1684.
29. On prohibiting broad legislative delegations to agencies, see Lowi, op.cit., pp. 297–8.
30. See Stewart, loc.cit., p. 1695.
31. Op.cit., Appendix Volume p. 92.
32. Law Reform Commission of Canada, Working Paper 25, *Independent Administrative Agencies*, Ottawa (1980).
33. See National Enterprise Board Guidelines, Department of Industry, London (1980).
34. Approval procedure involves one resolution of each House as opposed to the full legislative procedure involving three readings, committee and report stages plus royal assent.
35. NEDO argued that permanent Policy Councils representing participating interest groups should be created for each nationalized industry to set down corporate aims, objectives, strategies, etc.: NEDO: A Study of UK Nationalised Industries (1976), p. 46.
36. Law Reform Commission of Canada, op.cit., (1980).
37. Janisch, loc.cit. (1978).
38. On congressional oversight, see Robinson, loc.cit. (1978).
39. See D. Coombes, *Representative Government and Economic Power*, Heinemann (1982), p. 60.
40. See e.g. O. Newman, *The Challenge of Corporatism*, Macmillan (1981).
41. On *ad-hoccery* and quangos see N. Johnson, 'Editorial: Quangos and the Structure of British Government' (1979), *Pub. Admin.* 379, 384. See also G. Ganz, 'Allocation of Decision-Making Functions' [1972], *P.L.* 215,

299; A. Barker, op.cit., Chapters 1, 2 and 12.

42. H.C.Deb., Vol. 848, col. 454.
43. H.C.Standing Committee E Col. 770, (8 April 1975).
44. H.C.Deb., Vol. 891, col. 491.
45. H.C.Standing Committee E (23 July 1975).
46. 'British Air Transport in the Seventies', Cmnd. 4018 (1969).
47. 'Civil Aviation Policy', Cmnd. 4213 (1969).
48. See the White Paper, 'An Alternative Source of Radio Broadcasting' Cmnd. 4636 (1971).
49. See David J. Howells, 'The Manpower Services Commission' (1980), *Pub. Admin.* p. 305.
50. H.C.Scottish Standing Committee Col. 501, (22 July 1975). On delegating power where clear standards of implementation are lacking, see *A.L.A. Schechter Poultry Comp.* v. *United States* (1935) 295, US 495. On the British National Oil Corporation and the ad hoc approach to devising agency powers, see H.C.Deb., Vol. 857, col. 566 (Patrick Jenkin).
51. H.C.Deb., Vol. 848, cols 470, 493.
52. H.C.Deb., Vol. 849, col. 1024.
53. See e.g. Standing Committee D (15 May 1975).
54. Cmnd. 5034 (1971–2).
55. See also the vague references to 'links with the appropriate central and regional bodies' in the White Paper *Racial Discrimination* Cmnd. 6234 (1975), para. 110.
56. For an account of the civil service's approach to quangos see Richard Wilding, 'A Triangular Affair: Quangos, Ministers and MPs' in Barker, op.cit.
57. See e.g. the Select Committee on Nationalized Industries, 'Ministerial Control of the Nationalised Industries'.
58. 'A Study of UK Nationalised Industries', HMSO (1976).
59. See e.g. Cmnd. 7131 (1978).
60. Cmnd. 7797 (1980).
61. See Civil Service Department, 'Non-Departmental Public Bodies: A Guide for Departments' (1981).
62. Ibid.
63. On the comparative study of agencies, see e.g. R.L. Rabin, 'Administrative Law in Transition: A Discipline in Search of an Organising Principle' (1977) 72 *Nw. U.L.Rev.* 120, 138.
64. See especially, Law Reform Commission of Canada, op.cit., (1980) also H.N. Janishch, 'Policy Making in Regulation: Towards a New Definition of the Status of Independent Regulatory Agencies in Canada' (1979) *Osgoode Hall L.J.* 17, 46.
65. N. Johnson, 'Quangos and the Structure of Government' (editorial) (1979) *Pub. Admin.* 57; also Barker op.cit., Chapters 1, 2 and 12. Philip Holland MP argued in *Quango, Quango, Quango,* Adam Smith Institute (1979), for a Standing Committee of the House of Commons to scrutinize the accountability to Parliament of quangos.
66. See N. Johnson, loc.cit., pp. 209–10.
67. Lack of a comparative perspective in regulation is encountered in the case of departments as well as agencies: see W.G. Carson, *The Other Price*

of Britain's Oil, Martin Robertson (1982), p. 177.

68. (1975) 88, *Harv. L.Rev.* 1067. For an early attempt at the classification that he advocates Stewart instances, Ernst Freund's 'Administrative Powers over Persons and Property' (1928).

69. Wilding, loc.cit.

70. Johnson, loc.cit.

71. Barker, op.cit., pp. 32–3.

72. Thus, for example, the Civil Aviation Authority's regulatory functions have been reviewed by the Select Committee on Nationalized Industries in their 1975 report: British Airways: The Merger of BEA and BOAC (1975–6; H.C. 56); by the House of Lords Select Committee on the European Communities in 1980 (see European Air Fares (1979–80; H.L. 235), and the House of Commons Industry and Trade Committee in 1981 (see European Air Fares (1980–81; H.C. 431).

73. See Report of the Select Committee on Procedure (HC 588, 1977–78).

74. See R. Noll, 'The Economics and Politics of Regulation' (1971) 57 *Va. L.Rev.* 1016.

Index

Index